PRISON DIARY, ARGENTINA

Prison Diary, Argentina

Simon Winchester

CHATTO & WINDUS · THE HOGARTH PRESS

LONDON

Published in 1983 by
Chatto & Windus · The Hogarth Press
40 William IV Street
London WC2N 4DF

British Library Cataloguing in Publication Data
Winchester, Simon
Prison Diary, Argentina
1. Ushuaia Prison
I. Title
365'.6'0924   HV9585.U/
ISBN 0-7011-2748-1
ISBN 0-7011-2755-3 Pbk

Printed in Great Britain by
Redwood Burn Ltd
Trowbridge, Wiltshire

For Isabel Hilton and Cal McCrystal

Friends, indeed

Contents

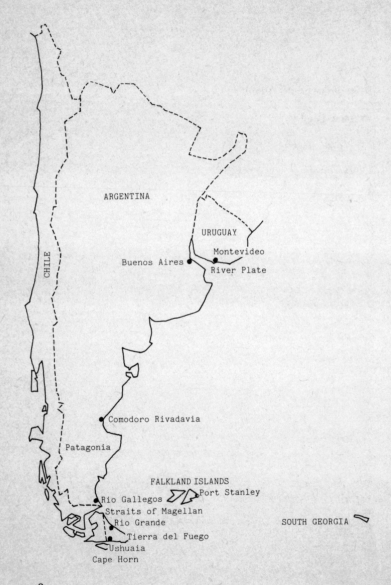

ARGENTINA

CHILE

URUGUAY

Montevideo

Buenos Aires

River Plate

Comodoro Rivadavia

Patagonia

FALKLAND ISLANDS

Port Stanley

Rio Gallegos

Straits of Magellan

Rio Grande

SOUTH GEORGIA

Tierra del Fuego

Ushuaia

Cape Horn

Preface......

People who have been kind enough to inquire about the unexpected way I spent my time during the Falklands war tend to ask three questions. What was it like? How did the Argentines treat you? What did you learn from the experience?

I hope that some of the answers to the first two questions will be found in the pages that follow. But as to the third – what did you learn? – I invariably find great difficulty in answering. I either try to be succinct, and end up sounding trite; or I attempt to explain, and become windy and pompous. But I clearly did learn; and two things in particular remain with me – two discoveries that I am sure I would never have made but for the good offices of the Argentine military police.

The first might sound rather obvious. It is that the British people are astonishingly kind, good-natured and generous. I must have had three hundred letters in prison – and Ian Mather and Tony Prime, my cell-mates, had as many. The fact that people – students, housewives, elderly ladies, civil servants, a dog breeder, several vicars, innkeepers, gardeners – took the time and trouble to sit down and, for page after page, write words of friendship and sympathy to three men quite unknown to them, struck me then, and still does today, as evidence of an essential goodness in our community. We are said to be a busy and intolerant people these days, uncaring and beset with wholly selfish concerns; and yet during that strange little war it seems that people behaved towards the three of us with the unity that some commentators insist has vanished long ago. They wrote to us; they telephoned and wrote to our families; they cared – when there was no need to do so, and no expectation that they might. I have reproduced in full or quoted from many of their letters in this book and I am most grateful to the writers concerned for allowing me to do so.

These people cared – so they said in their letters – not simply because we were three Britons, in trouble in the far away, southernmost town in the world. Their letters were not a mere extension of the patriotic mood that had taken hold in the country at large. The writers cared, many of them said, just because we were journalists – a breed supposedly held in relatively low esteem by most people. And that was the second discovery: that for all its faults and excesses, the British love their press, and care for its protection and survival. That three journalists managed to get themselves into trouble at the hands of those who, at the time, were judged to be our nation's enemies, seemed an outrage to many thousands of people back home who would, in ordinary circumstances, have little concern, and even less respect, for the people and the products of Fleet Street. Our arrest and detention seemed to remind people that such matters as freedom of speech and freedom of the press were, no matter how often abused, well worth having, and well worth preserving. And so they wrote and sent telegrams and formed committees and did anything that seemed suitable to win our freedom – and of course, eventually, they triumphed.

I am, naturally, eternally grateful to the then Editor of the *Sunday Times*, Frank Giles, for the sterling work he performed on our behalf, at a time when his journalistic concerns were rightly directed towards the paper's coverage of the war itself. I am grateful to many others besides: Magnus Linklater and Don Berry, Anthony Whitaker, Peter Wilsher, Rosemary Righter, James Adams, Parin Janmohamed, Brian Macarthur and a host of others on the *Sunday Times*; Donald Trelford and Anthony Howard of the *Observer*; many colleagues at the BBC and ITN; the distinguished editors and writers who joined the committee established to work for our release, and the then Irish Opposition Leader, Garret Fitzgerald, who agreed to be its chairman. In New York, the Committee for the Protection of Journalists was tireless in its work on our behalf, and it may be a useful legacy of our imprisonment that machinery now exists in Britain, modelled on that committee in New York, in case another such problem arises – as inevitably it will.

To all of these, my grateful thanks. But my deepest gratitude goes to all those Britons who wrote to us, thought about us and prayed for us – and who were reminded by our brief sojourn in a dictator's prison that the canons of our democracy are priceless, and must be guarded jealously. I may not have thought quite this way while I waited in the cell for my socks to dry – other things seemed then of greater moment. But today – well, I suppose it is easiest to say, in answer to that third question, that this is what I really learned in prison, and I doubt I'll ever forget it.

Simon Winchester
Iffley, Oxford. July 1983

Prologue.....

When the phone call came I was halfway down the garden, trying to control a huge bonfire which I had rather unwisely started with half a gallon of petrol. I had just embarked on a massive programme of clearing up the garden: a long tour of India was just behind me, and I was hoping for an untroubled fortnight, or even a week, so that I could get my Oxford jungle under some sort of control before spring. It was just after lunch on a warm Saturday, 27 March, and according to my wife, yelling down at me from the bedroom window, the call was very urgent indeed.

Cal McCrystal, the *Sunday Times* assistant foreign editor, was on the line. 'Sorry to bother you at home,' he said, with his unfailing politeness, 'but we think you should stand by to go to the Falkland Islands.'

I gulped, not sure if I had heard him properly. The Falkland Islands? I asked. You want me to go to the Falklands? 'We're not sure at the moment,' Cal replied. 'But we think there's a case for going; we've just got to persuade the powers that be that it's worth spending the money. Anyway – just stand by, and I'll let you know.'

My first reaction, I must confess, was of rather less than unbridled enthusiasm. It seemed a terribly long way – we pulled out *The Times Atlas*, and my God! it really did look a long way – for a story that, involving as it did merely a group of thirty Argentine scrap metal dealers behaving rather poorly on one of the Falklands Dependencies, seemed pretty small beer. Of course, I would love to go to the Falkland Islands – but was this the right moment?

Whatever my feelings, my marching orders came an hour or so later. Cal rang back. He had won approval for the trip from a rather sceptical editor – as sceptical as I was, it seems – and would I thus make my way, with all speed, to Port Stanley (which, I was told, was the name of the Falklands capital).

And so, as on so many similar occasions in the past, I moved into high gear. I rang the duty man at the travel agency, booked myself on a plane from Gatwick to Madrid the next lunchtime, checked my passport and visas, my jabs and the next week's appointments, 'cleared my desk', and then set about the wearying process of packing. I called the British Antarctic Survey in Cambridge to get some names and numbers of people down in the Falklands; I tried to get through to the various British consuls in Patagonia on the phone (I failed). I made lists of people to see, and got hold of some reference books and papers about these faraway islands. It all seemed quite an adventure in the making, though I wasn't sure for what ultimate journalistic purpose, or worth. Still, that was no longer my concern. I just had to get there.

The next morning, shortly before lunch – and just as a Sunday lunch party was assembling at home – a taxi turned up to take me off to Gatwick. I made the apologies which are part of the stock in trade of travelling journalists – having to disappoint one's friends and relations by having to cancel appointments and treats and dates is a constant factor of this sort of life – and set off. The driver wasn't sure of the way, and the trip took a good deal longer than usual. But shortly before five I was on a British Airways flight to Barjela Airport, Madrid, and had settled down, with a comforting whisky, to review just why I was bound for the South Atlantic at such short notice.

Juliet Walker, a friend who had arrived for lunch, had gone to the *Sunday Times* office the night before to photocopy all the available files on the Falkland Islands. There was a pile two inches thick – every time a British minister had paid a call on the islanders in the previous decade or two, a star colour writer had gone along as well, with the result that the spartan lives of the Falklanders – and their total opposition to any change in their status as colonials – was chronicled in loving detail. By the time the Boeing touched down in Madrid I felt I knew a fair bit about this sturdy breed of sheep farmers and mullet fishermen who kept the Union Jack flying all those thousands of miles from home. Perhaps it was the whisky, or perhaps it was reading about these curious and distant innocents, but I was feeling a lot better now, and looking forward, just a bit, anyway, to getting down South.

The specific reasons for this trip were clear enough. Ten days previously a small party of Argentine scrap metal dealers had landed, without permission, on the Falkland Islands Dependency of South Georgia. They had a contract to dismantle an old British-owned whaling station near the Georgian capital of Grytviken, and, had they checked with the local British Antarctic Survey official there before they hauled up their flag and started their work, all would have been well. But the fact that they had not gone through 'the proper channels' put the British backs up. The Falklands Governor, Rex Hunt, and the British Ambassador in Buenos Aires, Anthony Williams, had complained. The Foreign office in London had authorised the sole remaining Royal Naval vessel in South Atlantic waters, HMS *Endurance*, to sail for South Georgia to hurl the bounders off. The Argentine Navy had, in response, sent two frigates, the ARA *Granville* and the ARA *Drummond*, to protect their nationals. It all looked very dangerous, faintly ridiculous, rather romantic and very much a storm in a teacup. It would, I reflected as we pulled in to the Barjela terminal, make a jolly little tale.

Richard Wigg, the *Times* correspondent in Spain and an old friend from our days in New Delhi, met me at the gate: we hadn't seen each other for four years or so, and we went to dinner to catch up on each other's lives. He had been correspondent in Argentina in the early seventies, and, like so many journalists who had worked in South America, had a fascinated loathing for the place. He gave me names and telephone numbers of people to whom I should offer his greetings and who might, he supposed, be of some help to me.

My onward connection, an Iberia flight via Rio de Janeiro, was due to leave at midnight. Richard and I dined amiably until ten or so, and then I let him go home; I wandered around the rapidly emptying airport for a while, and then plunged through departures and to the gate. There was a small crowd waiting for the flight to be called. I looked around to see if there were any familiar faces and, inevitably – for newspaper foreign desks tend to think in very similar ways – there were. One was familiar: Ken Clarke of the *Daily Telegraph*, a delightful, wry man who I had last seen in, well, Belfast, I think it must have been. The other, a cheerful and amusing reporter from the *Sun*, was David Graves – if I didn't know him then, I was to come to know him very well indeed in the days to come.

By now the depression had lifted completely. I was back in my element – on a plane bound for exotic foreign parts, with good friends, a bottle of champagne to share, and the certain knowledge that we were going to have, if nothing else, good fun over the coming week or two. We settled back in our seats to watch the chosen film for the flight, *The French Lieutenant's Woman*, and drifted off to sleep.

We woke at six as we came in to a wet and foggy Rio. The hour's wait enabled Ken and David to call their offices – if only to check that communications from so far away were possible, and to find out if the story had advanced overnight. The lines were excellent of course; and no, the story had not changed. The ships were circling each other, governments were making menacing noises, editorial opinion was suggesting there might be a brief cannonade. We rejoined the waiting jumbo, and took off for Ezeiza Airport, Buenos Aires.

From five thousand feet, Argentina's capital looked the very model of twentieth century prosperity. I think I had expected more evidence of the Third World – acres of festering tarpaper houses, nightmare traffic jams, thick clouds of pollution. From the air at least the city appeared like another Madrid: wide boulevards, skyscrapers, parks, gardens, swimming pools glinting in the morning sun as we banked for landing. I knew I was going to enjoy this place.

It was much the same when we landed. The airport was shiny and clean. Customs and immigration took seconds – compare it to Bombay, say, where you can land at 2 a.m. and still be waiting before a harassed customs official at 8 a.m.! The others started to make phone calls: how, we all wanted to know, did one get to the Falkland Islands. The Falkland Islands? everyone said. The Malvinas, you mean. There's a flight every Tuesday afternoon. There should be one this week. You should make it.

This was Monday morning. We had a day to kill, before embarking for Patagonia, and what was to be – though we didn't know it at the time – the very last civilian flight into Port Stanley.

Buenos Aires lived up to most of my mile-high expectations. True, I found one of the military road checks a little sinister: our taxi slowed to walking pace as we went past rows of extraordinarily menacing looking soldiers, each armed with a machine pistol, and who peered into the car, checked papers and passports with what seemed more suspicion than was strictly necessary. I asked the driver if he minded. Not at all, he said; the city had been a terrible place a few years before, shootings, bombings, kidnaps. It was necessary for the soldiers to keep an eye on things. It was good for the people to have to behave. And anyway, he said, look at how clean and peaceful the city was these days.

No doubt about it. On the surface it was a fine and elegant city. It was a brilliantly sunny morning, warm with the underlying crispness of Indian summer – for this was autumn here, in the Southern hemisphere. The skyscrapers glittered. Small boats on the River Plate heeled over in the breeze, leaving trails of white foam against the brilliant blue of the water. In the parks Argentines – elegantly and expensively dressed, with women of stunning beauty and all a good deal taller than, for some reason, I had expected – strolled and sunned themselves. People sat drinking coffee at kerbside cafes. There were all the recognisable shops of the West: Gucci, Cartier, Ralph Lauren. There was, I knew, a Harrods somewhere in the depths of the souk.

Only one thing struck me as peculiar. I had been to northern Latin America many times, and in all the cities there – Caracas, Managua, Tegucigalpa, Quito – there were Indians, often poor, always small of stature, usually sitting at street corner stalls peddling their wares. Here there seemed to be none: this was a European city, Madrid-on-the-Plate, with all vestige of South America subsumed by the imported Latin culture. I knew nothing of the genocidal policies of the Argentine leaders of a century before. To me, at that moment, this looked simply like a civilised city, a good place for the three of us to lay our heads for the night before trundling down to Patagonia the next morning, bound for our tiny island colony. That a European colony could give so much apparent offence to these obviously European people here seemed to me, as I drifted off to my first siesta, something of a nonsense.

The siesta was all too brief. I had one or two contact names in Buenos Aires, two of them British military officers who might be expected to know what was going on. I telephoned one, and we arranged to have a talk – immediately, as it happened – and then lunch. He told me that it would be 'a very good idea' if I made my way to Port Stanley as quickly as possible, but would not explain why. Was it journalistically worthwhile? I kept asking him. 'Most definitely. You'll be able to write a good piece.'

Lunch provided my first opportunity to try Argentine beef, and it was, in truth, like no other I had ever had before. Until then I suppose my conventional ideal from the cattle world was that served in one famous little restaurant in Kansas City, or another, less well known, near Waco, in Texas – both places written about at length in the good food section of *The New Yorker*. But they couldn't hold a candle to this: together with a bottle of red Argentine wine and a loaf of freshly-baked bread, this seemed the world's ideal meal, plain and good and masculine. I looked forward to my next few days' dining, even though my friend said that he had tired of beef after a few months, and longed for more delicate flavours. 'That's one thing you notice about Argentina. It's all very direct and obvious. There's nothing fine and subtle here. Strong flavoured food, robust wine. All very *macho*.'

Later that night I went off to see the Ambassador, Anthony Williams, in the enormous mansion behind the British embassy that was said to be the finest ambassadorial residence in the country. The embassy itself, all bullet-proof glass and steel Department of the Environment standard Highly Secure Embassy Mark One, was guarded by four policemen. There had been a small demonstration the day before, demanding the end of British rule in the Malvinas; the embassy – and the Argentine Foreign Ministry – was taking no chances.

I took to Anthony Williams instantly. He was a tall, balding man, coming up to sixty, with all the elegance and charm one finds in an ambassador of the old school. He had paid his dues in the service of the Crown – Montevideo, Cairo, New York, Moscow, Washington; Ambassador in Phnom Penh and later in Tripoli, and now in the most sensitive posting in Latin America. He could expect to retire after this job, with his KCMG, and the grateful thanks of an Office which admires a man who plays the game well and loyally, as Williams appeared to have done. He was aware that he was having to deal with the latest crisis with immense delicacy; not only were the relations of two sovereign powers uneasily strained by the scrap merchants' antics, and the gathering shoals of warships in southern waters, but his own career, at the very moment of culmination, was being tried like never before in his life. He knew this, I fancied, when we met, and he looked drawn and weary. He had just returned from seeing the Argentine Foreign Minister, the Oxford-educated Nicanor Costa Méndez, and the tidings were not good. 'God, it's a difficult one, this,' he sighed, as he poured me a whisky, 'It's damned exasperating, no doubt about it.'

And then there was a power cut, and the lights went out, in the Residency, and in all the streets beyond. A servant padded up the marble stairs with a Tilley lamp, and we sat in the fizzing glow, drinking our whiskies and talking idly around the gathering storm. I became terribly tired: it was ten at night, I had been travelling and talking shop more or less continuously since dawn the day before, and I was exhausted. I said my farewells and left, travelling back to my hotel with the local Reuters correspondent. We compared notes. Did he think the Ambassador looked particularly worried? Yes, this did seem a peculiarly intractable situation, no one giving way, the Reuters man replied. It was hard to see how it would be resolved. 'Bit of an omen, the lights going out like that,' he said. It was no more than a poor joke. I waved goodbye, and went upstairs to bed.

Next morning, Tuesday 30 March, Ken Clarke, David Graves and I set off for Patagonia and, we hoped, Port Stanley. The local military airline, LADE, said it planned to fly that afternoon from the nearest point on the mainland, the Patagonian oil town of Comodoro Rivadavia. We drove over to the Buenos Aires domestic airport – on the banks of the Plate, in the very centre of the city – and boarded our blue-and-white Boeing for the South. The journey took two hours and when we arrived, in mid-morning, it was blowing a half gale, it was very dusty, and cold. Patagonia – especially this dirty little oil town – is not a pleasant spot in the gathering chill of the southern autumn.

The BBC Correspondent had been broadcasting saying that no journalists were being permitted on the Falkland Islands. It seemed doubtful that we would make the flight, after all.

It was late morning when, after a brief trip into town, we turned up back at the airfield – a hazardous journey over gravel roads, the way marked only with forty-gallon oil drums, and the banks littered with the wreckage of cars that hadn't made it – to see whether the flight was likely to go, and whether we were likely to be allowed on. There seemed to be no problem. It would be an exaggeration to say that the staff at the field were falling over themselves with delight at our decision to fly with them, but they indicated that they would take off at 2.15 p.m., and yes, we could fly. There was one other man from London, too – a Mr Langley, over there.

Bill Langley from the *Daily Mail*'s New York office. None of us knew him, and, like all journalists who had formed a guardian clique over an apparently uncharted territory of a new story, we were a little wary of this newcomer. He had flown down the night before, he said; the *Mail* reckoned this was about to be a big story. Well, it was good to have confirmation that others in Fleet Street had the same news judgement as our editors; we sat down and had a beer, and waited for the plane.

Given the BBC report about journalists being forbidden from travelling to the Falklands we were a little concerned about our being turned back at the last minute. My passport had the suitably anodyne description 'Representative', so I planned to describe myself as a sheep farmer, if asked. But no one asked anything: at 2.15 the fifteen or so of us who were due to fly boarded the old Lockheed Electra and a few moments later were thrumming our way eastwards, bound for British crown territory

Three of our fellow-passengers fell into conversation. One was a young man from Cairo – he was a Scot – who had had a lifelong ambition to own a farm in the Falklands. The Government had now said he could buy a small one, and he had made the extraordinarily complicated journey from Cairo to Comodoro Rivadavia to set eyes on it. Then there was a minor Spanish count from Amersham, in Buckinghamshire, who was thinking about buying a much larger spread, and was off to see it, too. And finally there was a stern, erect man named Edmund Carlisle – brother, as it turned out, of a junior Minister in Mrs Thatcher's government back home – who was likewise off to see some sheep farm in which he had an interest. All three could fairly be described as optimistic and unworried. Did they think that the Falklands would always be British – were they confident their investments would be protected? Oh yes, they chorussed, no doubt about it. We wouldn't be investing otherwise, would we?

And then we began our descent. It was cloudy, and very bumpy. There was nothing to see until the very last few seconds of flight – and then suddenly, beneath the wheels, came the landscape we had been expecting. Rain-sodden, windswept, bleak – all green and black and grey, scrubby grassland dotted with sheep, curling clouds of gulls wheeling over the low cliffs. It looked for all the world like Shetland, a group of islands in almost exactly the same latitude north. And as I was besotted with Scottish islands, and had been for years, I knew from the very start that I would love these islands, too. The journey from London had, I knew in an instant, all been worthwhile.

Rain hurled itself horizontally at us as we clambered down from the plane and beat our way over to the tiny aerodrome buildings. A gaggle of islanders, all in sou'westers and thick sweaters, were waiting to see what and who the weekly flight had brought with it. The customs and immigration man – I later came to know him well; his name was Les Halliday – took us through the formalities which were, I was surprised to find, carried out with great earnestness. I think I had imagined we would show our passports and be waved airily through. Not a bit of it: great passport stamps were laboriously affixed, our cases were examined, the length of time we were due to remain was determined. It was considerably more formal an arrival than at Ezeiza airport two days before. I kept wanting to say 'Wait a minute – we're British. We've come from home.' But on the other hand everyone was so very friendly – and a faded portrait of the Queen and Prince Philip above Mr Halliday's head confirmed, if we had any doubts, that we were on British soil again. There seemed no point in making a fuss.

Three ancient landrovers waited outside, and, without ceremony, we bundled ourselves in and were driven, without asking, to Port Stanley, and the island's only hotel, the Upland Goose on Ross Road. Everything was so Scottish! The sweet smell of peat smoke hung in the gusty air. Gulls mewed and swooped at the sea. The little streets were filled with shabby houses and miserable, ill-stocked shops. The islanders, red-cheeked and bent down against the wind, walked purposefully between one and the other. I had once lived for some weeks on a remote island off Skye called Raasay; East Falkland was identical, I mused, from the appearance of the town and the houses, to the cut of the people's jib. There was a mite more liberal use of red corrugated iron, maybe; but otherwise, identical.

Des King, the owner of the Upland Goose, welcomed us with little ceremony – yes, he had rooms, but only just. We might have to double up in a day or two, some people were coming in from Bluff Cove. There was one journalist there already, a photographer from Buenos Aires, an Argentine. We introduced ourselves: his name was Raphael Wollmann; he had been there a week, doing some general feature work for a French agency, and planned to go back on the next flight.

We sat down to tea and cakes, and looked out at the rain. A green landrover sped past: two Royal Marines, part of the Falklands defence force. We were jerked out of our Scottish reverie. There was a crisis on, for heaven's sake; we must go down and see those marines, and the Governor, too, and everyone who was anyone on the islands. And, most of all, I mused, I must work out some way to get out to where this crisis was centred – the island of South Georgia, eight hundred miles further east, over the ugly, rain-swept sea.

We rang Government House – ancient, hand-cranked telephones that must have weighed twenty pounds each, and a cheery operator on the other end. Our number was '25 two rings', and Government House '35 three rings', or somesuch. It all seemed delightfully eccentric. Government House said yes, His Excellency would be delighted to see you, come on over. So we strapped on our parkas and I polished my brogues, and set out for the half mile walk along the Front, and to the Victorian manse with its Union Jack snapping in the gale, from which Britain ruled this tiny colony.

The first surprise was to find an old acquaintance there already: Steve Hiscock, who I had once met in Islamabad, had somehow ended up in the Governor's private office down here – a posting that reinforced the notion that the Foreign Office likes to give its men the widest possible range of experience (he had worked in Malaysia and Zambia, too, and yet was only thirty-six). So it was an affable introduction, one reinforced by an enthusiastic welcome from Rex Hunt, the cheery Spitfire pilot who was the latest in a century and a half's worth of Falklands Governors to take the ostrich feathers, the sword and the grand imperial uniform to this remote speck of land.

Rex Hunt gave us a long and generally sanguine account of the week's developments. We were the first reporters he had seen for a long while; he was keen to know how the crisis was being regarded back home, and was prepared to accept that Britons saw it as all a rather small storm in a very big teacup. He was a bit perplexed as to why Señor Wollmann, the Argentine photographer had come over – did he know something we didn't? he mused. The chat lasted over coffee, then beer, then retired into his sitting room where Mavis, the island's First Lady, poured us all stiff brandies. It was all a pleasant fantasia – listening to Beethoven, idly staring into the smouldering peat fire, hearing the rain drum against the window panes, talking about the prospects for Wimbledon and the coming Test match. Tony, the Hunt's seventeen-year-old, a sixth former at Radley, came in from a wild ride on his motorcycle; Diana, about to become engaged to a Royal Marine, was already back home in England. The scene was one of unalloyed domestic bliss, and if scrap metal men were causing the Foreign Office a headache eight thousand miles away, it was easy to ignore it, for a while. Anyway, the governor said, as we were driven away by his faithful chauffeur, Don Bonner, in the equally faithful maroon London taxi that was the Official Car, there would be an opportunity for a chat with HMS *Endurance* the next morning, and we would see if anything new was going on in the Georgias.

There were others to see. The Royal Marines, with both their outgoing commander, Gary Noott, and the Major who had just come in from London, via Montevideo, in the research vessel *Bransfield*, Mike Norman. They gave us tea at their concrete barrack compound at Moody Brook, a couple of miles west of town; it was as elegant as the distance from home allowed, and I do remember a silver teapot, and sugar tongs. They, I remembered, were concerned at the possibility of some dust-up with the Argentines – and at their inability to deal with it. They showed us their guns – a few rifles, a couple of mortars, half a dozen boxes of ammunition. 'We're on alert now', Mike Norman remarked, adding wrily 'but if there's an invasion by some of the 78,000 they've got over there, we've only limited chances of success.'

Thursday morning dawned gloomily, lowering clouds and scudding squalls. There was a telegram for me at the Cable and Wireless shack, an office which we had sniffed out within minutes of our arrival (the first duty of any foreign correspondent is to establish communications links with the outside – the C&W crew here seemed able and willing to help. Their usual traffic tended to consist of the odd birthday telegram from, or to, one of the 40 marines. News stories, especially about them, were a welcome change). The cable was from *The Times* Foreign Editor – would I file a piece for *The Times*, please, in addition to whatever I planned to file for the Sunday paper. I signalled a terse acknowledgement, wrote 900 words about the 'heightened tension' and the 'increased state of readiness', and quoted Mike Norman's laconic judgement on the likely outcome of a confrontation. As I wrote it I felt as though I was recounting a rather lengthy joke, nothing of great moment which deserved space on Page One.

In fact, however preposterous the story, it was actually rather good to be able to write a real news story again, and for a real daily newspaper. It was only a year since I had left the routines of daily journalism, and I missed them rather acutely. Listening to Ken Clarke hammering out his evening file for the *Telegraph* on the telex reminded me of the excitement and the romance of meeting the nightly deadline, getting the next-morning playback, hearing your story read out on the BBC the following dawn. With a paper that only published once weekly, the journalism became rather like magazine writing. You saw history being made and – if ill-fortune determined that it was made on a Monday, there was nothing you could do about writing it – not until Friday, or Saturday, at least. And if you did manage to find an exclusive angle on a story you worried all week lest an eager 'daily' chap should find it too, and ruin your chances of getting something original in the paper. No, I thought as I finished my *Times* piece – I wasn't unhappy at all at having to write for the sister paper; the only question was – what exclusive angle might I get for my own masters, back at the Sunday?

And then I hit on an idea. Waiting around here in Port Stanley suddenly seemed an idiotic way to waste time. All I was getting here was colour, that universally loathed coinage of the journalist who has not really got a tale to tell. The story, such as it was, was over on South Georgia. The best scheme – and, moreover, one which daily newspapermen like my colleagues could not afford to emulate – was to take myself off there, and file an exclusive from the epicentre of the crisis. How to get there? I wondered. And there, bobbing in front of me as I gazed out from the breakfast room of the Upland Goose, was the answer. A yacht – a solo round-the-world mariner who had just arrived the day before. He would take me, surely. I rushed down to the little dock.

Yes, the man said, delighted to have company. He was a Czech, a great, red-bearded man who had been on the move from the Baltic since Christmas. No, he had no radio, no electronic aids. But he had made it this far, and since he was off to South Africa he could quite easily give me a lift. Tomorrow morning we set off? And this afternoon we sail around the harbour to align the compass? It should be simple. Four days, if we have a good storm.

I was overjoyed. I dashed back to the cable office, sent a breathless telegram to Cal McCrystal in London. 'Chance to go to South Georgia tomorrow with round-the-world sailor. Request you okay journey immediately.' It says something for my impetuous mood that nowhere in the planning had I thought of how, once I was on South Georgia, I intended to get back. I ran down to the quayside again, where our intrepid mariner was uncoiling ropes, and jumped aboard. Raphael, the Argentine photographer, came along for the ride, as did a Polish fisherman who, along with six of his friends, had jumped ship from a factory vessel, and was waiting in somewhat informal police custody to know if the British government would grant him political asylum.

We made an odd crew – a Czech, a Pole, an Argentine and an Englishman, hurling ourselves around Stanley harbour in the stiff wind, tacking back and forth endlessly through the afternoon so that the compass would be perfectly accurate for the next day's marathon crossing. The captain offered what appeared to be his staple diet – chunks of dried bread, which he kept in great plastic rubbish bags. I looked below. He seemed to have fifty of them, nothing else. The trip did not have the look of a gastronomic holiday about it.

We were making our last few turns when I noticed something rather odd – unexpected, at least. Two Royal Marines, men I had had tea with the day before, suddenly swished ahead of us in a rubber speedboat. They landed, hurriedly, at one of the rocky points at the harbour's natural entrance – The Narrows, it was called – and with what I fancied was unusual urgency, went about the business of setting up a mortar, and a machine gun. It must be a practice, I said to myself as we turned for home, the lights of Stanley twinkling in the gloaming.

As we coasted in to dock, Ken Clarke was holding up a slip of paper. 'Your office says no', he cried. 'You mustn't go to South Georgia'. I tore the message from him. 'THANKS YOUR MSG GREAT IDEA BUT REGRET YOU SHOULD REMAIN STANLEY', Cal had cabled. 'FEELING HERE IS THAT STORY CENTRES AROUND SOUTH GEORGIA NOT ON SOUTH GEORGIA. KEEP WELL, REGARDS, CAL'. I was furious, and stumped back to the hotel, dying for a drink. Of course it was a sensible decision, but it meant that I had to hang around in what was rapidly becoming a somewhat tedious little town. Tedious so far as stories were concerned, I meant – if I had to hang on there would be nothing to do but write colour, and that was a pretty dire fate to anticipate.

'Never mind', said Ken. 'I had a lousy day, too. Had an appointment with the Chief Secretary. He cancelled it at five minutes' notice. Urgent meeting, he said. Silly sod.'

Urgent meeting, I thought. Mortars on The Narrows. Marines racing about in the sound. Messages from London telling me to stay put. Was something in the air?

Confirmation came at eight, just as we were settling down to one of Mrs King's Ten Thousand Ways with Mutton. The telephone rang. It was the Governor. Could we come down to Government House, in fifteen minutes? He was going to make an emergency broadcast, and wanted to talk to the British press immediately afterwards. I hung up the phone, and we turned up the radio, always on in every Falklander's house. The hotel fell silent, and we heard Patrick Watts, the young manager of the station, announce 'His Excellency the Governor'.

The events that followed have been well enough chronicled not to bear repeating here at length. The Governor's announcement was far more serious than anything we feared: there was an imminent threat of invasion, a State of Emergency was about to be declared, the local defence force was being called up, the Royal Marines were being deployed.

We rushed over to Government House, while startled islanders, who had heard the same news, gazed open-mouthed from their windows.

While I went in to see Mr Hunt, the others went to open telex lines to London, to tell them of the apparently grave developments. Hunt was clearly shaken. Never before in his long diplomatic career – Kuching, Jesselton, Brunei, Djakarta, Saigon, Kuala Lumpur – had anything so extraordinary happened to him. He showed me the cables from London. An invasion force was fifty miles off our western bow, and steaming towards us at battle speed. We could expect them here by three in the morning, expect to be invaded by dawn, expect to be Argentine territory by breakfast time.

He shook his head. 'D'you think we should intern all the Argentine citizens on the island?' he asked me. (There were a dozen Argentine workers staying in our hotel, all laying pipe for a new gasworks.) I wasn't sure I was hearing him properly. Invasion? Battle speed? Intern Argentines? It all seemed insane, like a curious dream. 'No', I said, without thinking. 'If you intern them and we report it – or if they have a radio link to the mainland – that'll be just the excuse they need to invade. I'd hold off until you have to.' 'Perhaps you're right', he said. 'But I still think I was right to wonder about that blessed photographer of yours.'

Raphael Wollmann. Of course. Why was he there? What tip had he been given that would allow him to make what would, in essence, be the official photographic record of the coming events?

The night passed quickly, the adrenalin pumping relentlessly. We opened a telephone line to London, sending out as much news as we could possibly think of for the front page of that morning's papers. *The Times* had struck lucky, I remember thinking. They have a man on the spot without ever having sent one. There was a charming young woman on the Night Desk, a North American, who took copy expertly and enthusiastically: she was as fascinated by events as we were, and her parting words, as we closed down the line, were 'take care!'

As the British troops and their hastily trained reservists were deployed from one end of Stanley to the other, we dashed hither and thither, looking for odd items that we knew, in a few hours' time, would be written into history. I remember going to see the hapless Argentine who was the representative of the state airline on whose flight we had arrived. He was there with his former boss, an impressive Admiral named Hector Gilobert; no, they said, they had no idea of what was happening, or what was about to happen; no, they were not in radio contact with Buenos Aires, or even with Comodoro Rivadavia, let alone the invasion fleet. Invasion? What invasion? Would we perhaps like some whisky? And since the phone lines were down, and the magic hours of deadline were long past, we said what the hell and set about the casual wounding of a new bottle of Johnny Walker. Señor Gilobert and his colleague knew, all right, as we knew, and they knew we knew. The attempts at polite conversation over drinks were part of a charade, on all our parts.

At about three the Governor was on the radio, declaring a full-scale State of Emergency; movements were going to be severely restricted, we were told, so we half ran towards Government House where, we supposed, we would hide for the duration. We were stopped by a menacing-looking reserve soldier who lunged from a hedge and demanded to know who we were. Press, we said; like hell, he returned, you're Argentines. We insisted, but it took a good three minutes before we were allowed to move on. They were that nervous.

At Government House, surrounded by the Marine elite, we were told, politely, to get lost. We might be able to use the house next door, a two storey frame house belonging to a junior Foreign Office official, but it would hardly be secure. Secure or not, it was a vantage point, and we scurried to it, keeping upstairs, as the marines suggested, and well away from the windows. There were six of us – the four reporters, Raphael Wollmann, and Don Bonner, the Governor's chauffeur, an ebullient man who seemed not to worry in the slightest that his island home was about to be invaded.

The Argentine troops stormed ashore at first light. My notebook recorded the first shots at 6.08 a.m., the first armoured cars at 7.45 a.m., the white flag at 8.35 a.m., the surrender at nine. We spent most of the time lying flat on the floor, though during one of the lulls I got up and made some scrambled eggs for breakfast. When the shooting was over we peered out, and then wandered into the chill morning. The invading forces were in total control, and were happy for me to record their triumph on film. One of the best and most poignant pictures was of the little red-headed girl from the Cable and Wireless office who had been so helpful to us in getting our copy over the nights before; she had been manning the office all night, and was being searched by the Argentines. The Royal Marines were being forced to lie face down on the ground. She refused, and stood there, looking sullenly contemptuous of those who had dared smash their way onto her homeland.

Later I found Rex Hunt, unshaven, a sardonic smile playing across his face, writing his official notes amid the ruins of the communications and encoding equipment his assistants had wrecked – essential emergency drill laid down in *The Diplomatic Handbook*. I thought he had handled the whole unseemly affair with the grace and sangfroid one would expect of a graduate of King Charles Street. It was sad to see him turned out of his house later in the day, Mavis clutching a Dick Francis novel in her hand and saying over and over 'How will the people get on without us? How will they manage?', and the Governor, splendidly comic in full Imperial fig, being forced to change into a sober suit by his unsmiling Argentine masters.

It was sad, too, to see the defeated Royal Marines lying face down in the mud, being roughly searched by the invaders; or later, to see these same men with whom the four of us had taken tea, being bundled without ceremony onto a departing Hercules. It was terrible to see the old taxi driver, Don Bonner – with whom I had lain under a bed during those dawn hours, as bullets crackled and spat through the air above us – it was terrible to see him, tears in his eyes, waving farewell to what he said he fully expected to be the very last Crown representatives on the islands. The Falklanders themselves were stunned and angered by what had happened; most of them remained at home, watching with awed disbelief at the invading army that was growing before their eyes, as ship after ship disgorged fresh troops for what Buenos Aires intended to be permanent residence.

The four of us, and Raphael, were allowed to remain on the island for another full day. We were allowed to make one phone call

– monitored, by an Argentine infantryman who spoke good English – to our relations back home. We all, of course, remembered we had 'brothers' or 'wives' who worked on our various papers' Foreign Desks. I had a long and somewhat mystifying conversation with a man on my Foreign Desk who took – understandably – some seconds to realise that it wasn't exactly his brother who was calling from Port Stanley. Once he had, he fell into the game with gusto. 'Lots of tourists there? How many came on the cruise ships, would you say? Bring their cars, did they? How long are they planning to stay?' The guard knew something fishy was going on, but his English wasn't good enough to be certain.

I had a brief and unpleasant talk shortly before we left with the Argentine army commander, a small, dapper man named General Oswaldo Garcia. How long, I asked him, was he planning to stay? 'For ever', Garcia snorted back. 'These are our islands now. Las Malvinas. We stay for ever.' I told him that I had just heard on the BBC that Mrs Thatcher was sending a Royal Navy Task Force; it was leaving on Monday; it would take a fortnight to get to Stanley harbour. 'If I were you', I said, 'I wouldn't even bother to unpack your kit. You're going to be thrown off.'

'Go away please now', he said, turning his back on me. 'I am very busy. We stay here for ever.' And he guffawed towards his brother officers, dismissing me with a peremptory gesture. I was, I must say, furious. Bloody spic, I said to myself. We'll toss you off by midsummer, you'll see. It was not a sentiment of which I felt particularly proud a few hours later; I was to wonder for many weeks following whether sentiments like mine had steered the course of the war that was to follow.

The last few hours on the islands were melancholy. Ken Clarke and I drove over to Moody Brook barracks, now half destroyed by fire and by the explosion of a couple of howitzer shells dropped on them for good measure by the advancing soldiers. I found the secret orders written by Gary Noott the previous November. 'Plans for countering a possible Threat from the East' the rubric said, followed by reams of technical data about where OPs should be sited and where LMGs would be able to fire with best effect. In the event the plan was a largely academic exercise; as Mike Norman had implied, there was little likelihood of British success against an invasion force of some thousands of troops. 'We came a good second,' he remarked to me when I saw him off.

Ken and I looked for souvenirs. He took a copy of *Jane's Fighting Ships*, stamped 'Property of HM Government'; I took a penknife, and a bottle of champagne. The champagne, I promised, would be opened only when the islands were back in British hands. I anticipated it remaining sealed for many months, if not years. If not for ever.

We left late on the Saturday night, accompanied by a young girl who had attached herself to us so that she could find her boyfriend, who was one of the expelled marines. We told the Argentines she was a part-time reporter, which prompted them to order her off the islands, just as we had planned. I saw her a few days later wandering the streets of Buenos Aires, disconsolate and bewildered. I never knew if she found her marine. There was certainly little likelihood of her finding him in the capital of Argentina.

The Argentine Air Force returned us to Comodoro Rivadavia once more, and we all spent the next hours telephoning our papers – and, in my case, the BBC – to offer the first eye-witness accounts of the invasion. It was exhilarating and exhausting – the kind of work that makes the tedium of foreign correspondency (of which, surprisingly, there is a great deal) well worthwhile.

All that night and all next day we were typing, phoning, telexing, filing – until finally, at about six on Sunday evening, we left again for Buenos Aires, and the warmth and comfort of the tropical autumn, in place of the South Atlantic winter. I had no suspicion I would see the South, or feel the endless chill winds of Patagonia, ever again.

The week that followed dissolved into a blur. There was, of course, a major news story in full spate, with new streams being added hourly: the Task Force was sailing from England, the American Secretary of State was beginning his mission of peace, the Argentine people were in a state of near total ecstasy, there was the British community in Argentina, the Organisation of American States, the EEC . . . newspapers all over the world were despatching correspondents, TV crews were arriving in jumbo-loads, all the hotels were taking on the seedy appearance of military billets as more and more journalists and hangers-on took up residence.

Scores of old friends arrived; the lobby of hotels like the Sheraton and the Claridge echoed to cries of 'Hello again, Bill . . . where was it last? . . . Kampala, wasn't it? Or were we on the junket to . . . ?' An outsider would find it pretentious; but it did happen, and it can be understood by the undeniable fact that circumstances often tend to throw reporters together into very intense and intimate relation-ships in faraway places and then, as rapidly and cold-bloodedly, remove them from each other's company for, perhaps, many years. You would forget a colleague's very existence for years, perhaps – never stumble across him, notice his by-line from time to time – and then, there he'd be in the hotel lobby, a little paunchier, a little older, the man you had sheltered with during some revolution, or had drunk solidly with during some siege, or whatever. Reporters meeting long-lost friends can be a charming ritual, and if it is self-conscious, it is only because reporters are sensible enough to realise how idiotic it must appear to an outsider.

So there was that aspect to that confused week and, for me, the heady and all too ephemeral phenomenon of celebrity. Everyone, it seemed, wanted to talk to me. When we landed at Buenos Aires, a Panorama team was there to pick me up and whisk me off for an interview; when I got to my hotel, messages lay like fresh snow, covering everything. New Zealand Radio, BBC Scotland, Hungarian State Radio, three publishing firms, CBS Television in New York . . . it was astonishing to see the queue of supplicants wanting to know What it had been Like during the Invasion? I did my best, though after a couple of days I did, despite the adulation, weary of it, and when the *Sunday Times* telephoned and mentioned, in as gentle a way as possible, that it might be an idea if I called a halt to the interviews, and remembered who it was for whom I was working, I was hugely relieved.

It was all over on Saturday, once General Galtieri's masses had gathered in their hundreds of thousands to applaud him, once General Haig had begun his exhausting pan-latitudinal shuttling, once the various interviews with the Foreign Minister and the Interior Minister and the departing British diplomats and spies had been completed. I could see a routine stretching ahead now, at least until the Task Force arrived. There was a danger that I would find myself hunting with one of the biggest journalistic wolf-packs to assemble since Saigon, and that I very much wanted to avoid. So I mentioned to the Foreign Desk that it might not be a bad idea if I spent at least part of the next week 'wandering about down south', to have a look at Argentina getting herself ready for the war that at that time seemed possible, but far from probable. The paper said yes, good idea.

That Saturday morning I met two *Observer* colleagues, Ian Mather and Tony Prime. Ian I had known fairly well – we had spent a couple of weeks together in Beirut the year before, and remembered an idyll at a waterside cafe in Byblos, where we sat and watched the blue Mediterranean, forgetting, for a while, the horrors of the war behind us. I had never met Tony; he was a photographer, newly hired by the *Observer*, and for this occasion had flown down from El Salvador. Ian had come from San Francisco.

On distant and moderately dangerous assignments, competition, at least between the 'serious' papers, diminishes to vanishing point. We wondered out loud what we might do the next week – go down south, we both said. Together, perhaps? Good idea, we said. Tomorrow morning's flight to Comodoro, perhaps? Excellent. Okay, said Ian – we'll pick you up at your hotel at ten tomorrow, Sunday. We'll be away for three or four days at most, and then come back here. No need to check out. Better hang onto the rooms, in fact, in case more hacks descend.

I spent much of that late morning strolling around the River Plate docks with David Lomax, the BBC reporter who had interviewed me for Panorama. Curiously – since we were doing no obvious wrong – we were detained, briefly, by police. We were taken by car to a large office block and asked who we were, why we were in this restricted zone, why we were trying to talk to the crew of a minesweeper (which we had been). We told them that the Argentine government seemed eager to let the British press wander where it wished – only the day before General Galtieri's press spokesman had lifted me from the ground in an expansive embrace and pronounced: '*Sunday Times!* You are Most Welcome Here. No Argument with You. You Must Report Everything. Go Where You Wish. You Will Find This VERY EASY COUNTRY TO REPORT.'

And so, indeed, it seemed. David and I were kept for an hour, and then, after our interrogators made a couple of phone calls, we were allowed to stumble out onto the street again, the police shaking our hands, wishing us well, telling us to please enjoy our stay. It would make a nice tale to tell the lads back at the Sheraton, we agreed, and thought no more of it.

Next morning, weary and dyspeptic, I was less than best pleased when Ian rang to remind me of our plans. But as the plane went at noon – we would risk standby, not being in any great rush to head back down to Patagonia – I levered myself out of bed and with a few clothes slung into my small Globetrotter, went off to the airport. There were seats available, and by teatime we were back in the dusty little oil town, watching the army trucks grind their way to the docks, the fighter planes arc through the clear, cold skies. We had dinner with some reporter friends – John Thorne, the BBC's Johannesburg man who I had last known in Belfast ten years before – and, after a very congenial evening in the bar of our hotel, set off the next day, the Monday, for the Straits of Magellan and that island which, from afar, had seemed so wonderfully romantic and so unlikely ever to be visited, Tierra del Fuego.

Things began to go a little wrong within moments of our boarding the aircraft. Tony, reasonably enough, I thought, decided he would take pictures through the plane's window. There was, after all, a lot going on at the various airfields – troops marching up into the back of waiting transports, light tanks buzzing around, anti-submarine planes taxiing along the runways, fighters being armed with live missiles. So he snapped away and, reasonably enough too, was told, politely, not to.

When we landed at our first stop, the southern shanty town of Rio Gallegos, a couple of elderly passengers who had seen Tony taking pictures, complained. The police were called, and an airline official. We were taken to a little office and questioned for five minutes. Passports, press passes, letters from Galtieri's spokesman – they did the trick; but it was evident the people down south were far less sympathetic than those sophisticated souls in the Buenos Aires docks. We were allowed to proceed, but with strongly worded warnings not to misbehave again.

The next plane, a tiny Fokker with – for Tony – tantalizingly big windows – flew over the broad Straits (a couple of warships waited at anchor) and set down, briefly, at the windy village of Rio Grande. Then it was over the ragged end of the Andes, weaving between giant ice-covered peaks and along valleys glowing red with the late autumn leaves. Finally we reached the Beagle Channel – we were only eighty miles from Cape Horn – and landed at the tiny military airfield in Ushuaia, the former prison camp that was now the most southerly town in the world.

Well, at least a by-line from Ushuaia would look exotic, I said to Ian – a rival to be set alongside The Khyber Pass, Heliopolis, and Truth or Consequences, New Mexico.

And the by-line looked like being the most interesting thing about Ushuaia. God, it was a dreary place! Rows of duty-free shops (Tierra del Fuego, starved of development, was trying to attract tourist custom), dirty streets, mean little houses. But the surrounding scenery was magnificent: Monte Olivia, stark and black in the East, loomed over the town, and the still waters of the Beagle Channel reflected the huge peaks over on the Chilean shore.

Pretty but, as we agreed over a plate of *centolla* – the local king crab, a deservedly great delicacy – and a few bottles of excellent rosé wine – news it ain't. We would leave on the first plane next day, and try looking for military excitement further north. At least we had been here, and made the effort.

We spent the night at a grim little hotel, the Canal Beagle (the slick-looking tourist hotel, the Albatross, being unaccountably full, so the staff insisted, rather coolly), and rose at six to catch the flight back to Rio Grande, from where we could get a connection to Buenos Aires once again.

It was cold and dark as we waited for the Fokker. We had a cup of coffee and a loaf of freshly baked bread, and then moved outside to listen to the BBC World Service news. No good, the static was too bad. Then the plane was ready, and, along with twenty or so other passengers, we boarded. As we did so a large, bearded man armed with a Nikon took our photographs. I was still big-headed enough after the last week's celebrity to suppose he was working for some local newspaper, and was recording the fact of three Britons' visit to his town. He was – but for somewhat different reasons.

On the plane I sat next to a pretty young woman, an Anglo-Argentine who was engaged to a sailor at the Ushuaia Naval Base.

Her father had ordered her to leave and go back north. There was likely to be trouble, he had said. The girl was nearly in tears. She had no idea when she would see her fiancé again. I noted her name – Livingstone. It would make a paragraph for next Sunday's paper.

We landed at Rio Grande at 10 a.m., our onward jet due out at noon. We bought new tickets. We mooched around the duty free shops. I listened to the BBC for a while outside, but it began to rain, a thin and cold drizzle that, whipped up by a cold southerly wind, sent me scurrying back indoors. The three of us went upstairs to the coffee lounge; I ordered an orange juice, getting fizzy orange, which I couldn't bear so early in the day. Planes of every imaginable type – or so it seemed to an ignoramus like me – swooshed past on the runways. I took out my tiny Nikon binoculars to watch them. A pilot who spoke English told me what some of the planes were, and Ian and I duly noted the details in our books.

A pair of military policemen appeared at the top of the stairs. We noticed they kept staring at us. Ian suggested I check to see how keen their interest was. I strolled past them and downstairs. They were quite indifferent, but they would not return my smile. They simply stared, faintly hostile, but not, I thought, menacing.

Our plane was delayed by an hour. We went downstairs, checked our baggage, waited some more. Tony lit up a cigarette and began pacing to and fro. Ian and I chatted in desultory fashion, wondering how many fighters the Argentine Air Force had, whether the British Task Force would ever arrive . . . when suddenly two MPs and an airline official strode up to us.

'You must go with these men,' the official said. 'The Admiral wants to see you.' I replied that we couldn't go anywhere, we had a plane to catch. 'No, you must go.' I said no once again, and a naval officer was called, a small, fat man with a bandaged hand. 'You must go into this room here', he said, waving at a VIP suite. But we have a plane to catch. 'No', he replied. 'There will be no plane for you. You are under arrest.'

A sudden sinking feeling in pit of the stomach. This was everything foreign correspondents dreaded. Far from home, no common language, police in sunglasses, guns, detention, arrest . . . We stood up, MPs descended on us from all sides, and we were marched into the VIP room. The door closed behind us, a sentry standing imperturbably in front of it. We looked at each other. We were in a mess all right, no doubt about it.

Guards ordered us to turn out our pockets, open our cases. All the grimy detritus of travel – the toothbrush, the wizened bar of soap, the crumpled shirt, the air tickets, the notebook – was spilled onto the floor and laboriously catalogued. No one smiled. Every time we spoke one of the sentries put his fingers to his lips. After a couple of hours of this, and after we had asked everyone in sight to telephone the Swiss Embassy in Buenos Aires to tell them of our fate, we were bundled into the back of a van and taken to the local gaol.

Rio Grande is not the prettiest of towns I know; its police station lock-up is a sad, dreary place. We were greeted by the local comisario as heroes – coffee was handed around, assurances (delivered via a middle-aged secretary who had a smattering of English) that we had nothing to fear, that this would all be sorted out before too long. Our heroic status evaporated as soon as we left his office, however. To the guards, we were common criminals, our only distinguishing difference being that we were sober.

They took us downstairs to the cells – a set of three down a short corridor. Ian and Tony a cell each, I was put in a room without a door, a sentry standing looking at me with alarmed amusement.

The cell was completely empty, the bleak linoleum floor marked and torn, a heap of some undefinable, but rather nasty-looking brown substance in the corner. There was a little window high in the wall, through which I could glimpse blue sky.

I sat on the floor, crossed my legs, leaned back and closed my eyes. This was purely temporary, I said to myself. No need to prepare for a long stay. I could hear Ian pacing back and forth in his cell; at one point I thought I heard Tony ask if he could relieve himself. And then there was a curious trundling noise, and an infernal-looking machine presented itself at my door, towed by a couple of burly guards.

It was a portable generator, or so it appeared to my untutored eye. There were heavy copper wires, two red, two black, terminating in large clamps. My stomach turned to water. They were going to electrocute me!

They wheeled the machine into the cell and turned it on. A low grumble, then a menacing hiss, louder and louder. A third guard came in and, just as I was about to yell for Ian's help – not that he could have done much – the newcomer took a long metal rod from his jacket and attached it to the red clamp. He took the black clamp and attached it to the door, and then touched rod to door – and I suddenly realised, to my great relief, what they were doing. They were going to *weld* something. They weren't interested in me at all!

What they welded was a new door. Since there was no door on my cell, they jury-rigged a new one – one they seemed to have found lying in an adjoining cell fitted the gap where mine must once have been, and so they welded it into place. True, my cell filled with sparks and gobbets of molten iron – but I wasn't being tortured, and when they went away leaving a red-hot and very, very closed door behind them, and in front of me, my principal feeling was one of exuberant good cheer. These weren't the awful monsters written about by Jacobo Timerman (I had read his book *Prisoner Without a Name, Cell Without a Number* some months before, and it sprang instantly to mind every time a prison guard looked askance at me); they were merely rather witless goons in a remote country prison, and we would be as right as rain in a matter of hours. Dusk fell, and it started to get chilly. I whispered to Ian next door, but a guard told me to be quiet. I lay on the floor, idly picking pieces of linoleum from a rotten square. I tried to compute the distance from here to the township of Wall, North Dakota, so I could write the graffito '9,856 (or whatever) miles to Wall Drug', which is the current American equivalent of the British Kilroy joke. But before I had traced my mind across southern Kansas, there was the clang of cell door, the tramp of many boots, the fizz of a welding machine rendered into an *un*welding machine, and the cell filled with men in dark blue uniforms. 'Come with us,' one barked in guttural English. We were hustled out to a bus, driven fast back to the airfield and marched, under heavy guard, to a waiting aircraft. 'Armada Argentina', it said on the fuselage. 'Ushuaia'. The Navy was flying us somewhere, but no one was telling us where.

The officers – unsmiling, unpleasant and clearly delighted to have three powerless infidels with whom to toy – sat us, as far apart from each other as was possible, in the for'ard section of the little plane. They motioned to us to stare at spots on the bulkhead. We were neither to look to our left or right, nor try to talk to anyone – least of all each other. No one would tell us where we were going, or why. Our watches had been taken away, and no one would tell us the time.

The plane shuddered and wheezed on its way for hour after hour; I guessed around six. When we landed the air was softer and warmer, and there was no wind. I was certain we were back in Buenos Aires – a step closer, to freedom, even if that meant deportation. The guards marched us to a Navy barrack block, where a chef was waiting with three large beefsteaks and bottles of beer. A late night film, an ancient American thriller, was on television. We were shown to bunk beds in a small dormitory. There were no bars on the window. But a sentry stood at the door, an automatic rifle at the ready. We heard a naval officer who had, it appeared, taken custody of all our belongings, talking excitedly over the telephone. 'The matter is a Naval matter alone,' he seemed to be saying to someone; and from his tone that someone seemed to disagree. Well, we said to one another – by now, with steaks and beer inside us, much relieved and more cheerful than we had been all day – it will all be resolved tomorrow. And we climbed into our bunks, and fell asleep.

Dawn confirmed our destination: we were, indeed, back in Buenos Aires – in fact we were at Ezeiza Airport, the very place where we had landed ten days before. We were going to be deported! Tremendous! And we spent an excited few hours watching the big jets taking off and landing – Lufthansa, Swissair, Pan Am and, yes, a United States Air Force Boeing, clearly carrying flunkies from the Haig peace mission. There seemed no doubt about our fate. Except – why were they taking such a terribly long time?

The day wore on. Sentries came and went. Footballers played outside our second floor window, and schoolboys trailed home from their lessons. No one came to see us, other than a guard who brought in food – spaghetti, and then, as the day wore on, bowls of soup. We sent out messages – what was happening? No reply. Nothing, except that late in the evening there was a distinct cooling in the mood of the guards, and we were ordered to be removed to another, much smaller cell. The door was double locked from the outside, and when, at one stage, we opened the window for fresh air, there were shouts from below and a sentry ran up and bolted it shut. We slept uneasily that night, not at all sure that the freedom we had so confidently anticipated the night before was quite so readily available.

On the Thursday morning we were woken early. A young officer came into the room and, in broken English, gave us the most depressing of messages. 'I am sorry to have to tell of you that you must go back to the Territory of Tierra del Fuego – you must come with me now. Pack your bags.'

I felt as if I had been hit with a two-by-four. Back to Tierra del Fuego? Two thousand miles away? Why, for God's sake, we kept asking. The man had no answer. It was orders, he said. They want you back there. We spluttered our protests, but to no effect. Sentries to the fore and aft, we were marched through a hangar – crammed with aircraft being overhauled presumably, I supposed, for the coming confrontation – and back onto the old bone-shaker 'Ushuaia'. Two civilian officials were on board. They spoke some English, explained they were from the security branch of the Defence Ministry, and that they had been ordered to escort us to the City of Ushuaia, and the court of the Judge of the National Territory. There were, it appeared, procedures that had to be followed; the Navy could not have jurisdiction over our case, it was explained. The civil judge of the place in which we had been arrested was insisting on reviewing our case – so back we had to go.

The southbound journey was altogether more pleasant than that of two days before. There was food on the plane. We were allowed to sneak a look at the coastline beneath us – and when we stopped to refuel at the naval aerodrome at Bahia Blanca we got something of a view of the ships and the blessed military preparations for which we had been so keenly searching so brief a time before. It all seemed quite irrelevant now.

The escorts were reading a copy of *Gente* magazine – one of the Buenos Aires weeklies that had interviewed me during my brief excursion into glory after the invasion. They were tickled pink at sharing an aeroplane with a person whose photograph and whose words were in one of Argentina's most popular magazines, and I was asked for autographs. The irony of the situation – that my fans were keeping me prisoner – did not escape me.

We landed at Rio Grande, the town where the arrest had taken place, and went back to the same cells where we had been detained. But first, a large meal – beef steak, inevitably – and red wine; and in the cell, styrofoam mattresses and sheets. When we woke at 5.30 a.m., on the Friday, our mood, once again, was upbeat. After their rather indifferent start the authorities were eager to show how pleasant they could be, how good they could be. We kept telling each other, as the little plane bounced its way back across the Andean chain to the little port of Ushuaia – the capital of the *Territorio Nacional* – that what we faced there was no more than a formality. A day at the most, and this little misunderstanding would be quite cleared up.

Our arrival at Ushuaia soon dispelled that naïve notion. There was great excitement at our arrival. A long motorcade was waiting for the plane. Each one of us was pushed into a separate car, with three guards in each, and the whole procession took off at a greater speed than this sleepy little town has probably ever witnessed on its rutted, frosty roads. At the police station, a dreary collection of breeze-block and two storey buildings opposite the town's little power station – it was on a hill just off the town's main street – was a crowd of local reporters and cameramen. One by one we were ordered from the cars, and had to run the gauntlet of the press. For the first time in my life I knew how it felt; flashbulbs popping in the face may be all right for a film star, but for a prisoner, it is trying in the extreme.

The prison governor and local police chief introduced himself: Comisario Barrozo, a plump, friendly man with a cheerful face crowned by a magnificently caricaturable moustache. He did not speak a word of English, however. No one did. He and a group of civilian prison guards motioned us upstairs, and locked us into cells – separate, each with a bunk and a window high up on one wall. The door, firmly locked behind me, had a spyhole, and every few moments it flicked back and a large eye – or, more probably, a succession of large eyes – peered through at this curious new trophy that had been captured.

Half an hour of frightened wondering, and my cell was opened.

The photographer, the same bearded man I had seen snapping away with his Nikon as we left the Ushuaia aerodrome on the Tuesday morning, was back. He wanted to take more pictures; first with my clothes on and then, to my considerable chagrin, without. I kept my underwear, and thus a little of my dignity, and told the man I would not lie on my bunk and have him click away as he wished. He seemed annoyed, but neither he nor the rat-faced guard brought in as his escort – a man I christened 'Ratso' there and then – objected. They just shrugged their shoulders, and let me be.

A doctor came next, checking wind and limb in a somewhat perfunctory manner, I fancied. He spoke some English, and asked a series of rather inane questions. What day of the week is it? How many days are there in the month of April? How many minutes in an hour. Of course, I twigged in a second. This was to test my mental acuity. As he left I cursed myself; if only I had said there were ninety days in April, this was a Sunday, and there were five minutes in the average hour, I might have been set free there and then.

My next visitor – my position in the row of cells was that closest to the entrance gate, I gathered, so visitors would arrive at my door first – was in full naval uniform. He was a tall man, with greasy, lank hair, deep set eyes and an impressive filigree of dimples and deep cleft around his chin and jawbones. This was Captain Juan Carlos Daniel Grieco, Marine Captain and Chief of Police for the Territorio Nacional de Tierra del Fuego. An important man, no doubt about it. Comisario Barrozo positively cringed behind him, and Ratso tugged at his forelock whenever Grieco chanced to look towards him.

'How are you feeling, Mister Winchester Repeater?' the captain asked, employing a joke I hadn't been privileged to hear since my school days. 'Frightened,' I replied, truthfully. I was shaking with anxiety, and I felt that I needed some reassurance. 'Don't worry,' he said, with a broad grin. 'Everything will be all right. Have faith in us.' And my door was locked. I heard him making the same inquiries next door, and at Tony's cells. I fancied their replies were less slavish than my own. It was a bad moment: I thought I was going to crack.

Then some food was brought: meat in a crinkled batter, it had the aspect of an elderly person's feet. I was hungry, though, and it didn't taste too bad. I sat on the edge of my bed, wondering what next, when the door opened yet again. Guards ordered me out and along the corridor, through the barred and padlocked gate and into Comisario Barrozo's office, a place crammed with books and dominated by a desk awash in paperwork, and by a huge colour television. Standing by the desk, and looking vastly important, was a portly, balding man of sixty in a three-piece suit. His magisterial appearance gave him away: this was Señor Carlos Sagastume, Federal Judge of the National Territory, and the man to whose presence we had been summoned.

'Fear nothing,' he said, in halting English. 'You must have faith in Argentine justice. Please go and tell your friends that I will be investigating you over the next two or three days, and that you have nothing at all to fear. We are living in a civilised country.' I was ushered from his presence, and taken to the other cells to report the conversation. After a morning of grimly unpleasant reality this, at least, seemed a small morsel of comfort. And when, a few minutes later, we were given back some of our belongings – a couple of shirts, two silk cravats, a thriller entitled *The Eye of the Needle*, a toilet kit, and, incredibly, my Sony short-wave radio receiver – and allowed back into one cell together, life appeared to have taken on some appearance of normality.

The judge looked through the door once more. Interrogation, he said, would begin on Monday morning. Until then, relax. I took him at his word, lay back on my bunk – for which the guards brought sheets, a single rough blanket, a pillow and a mattress from which greasy horsehair spilled in huge tufts, and over which some previous owner appeared to have spilled a moderate quantity of blood – and started, quite contentedly, to read.

Shortly before 19.00, just as it was getting dark, it occurred to me we might try and listen to the radio – after all, if the prison authorities had decided to let us hold on to our radios, they must have known we would listen to whatever we might pick up. Reception in the cell was non-existent; but I soon discovered that if I stood on the end of my bunk and poked the aerial through a tiny gap at the bottom of the tiny window, I could hear London, very distantly. The manoeuvre, perilous though it might be, also afforded the possibility of a view, across the lower part of town, over at the airport runway and the docks, and across the Beagle Channel to the mountains of Chile five miles away. The lights were twinkling, and faraway mountains were bathed in the rich red of the dying sun. If nothing else, I mused, we were in the prison which, as well as being the world's most southerly, must also have had one of the world's best views.

At seven, we heard the distant strains of 'Lilibulero', and the comforting time signals from Greenwich. The news, all about the still gathering storms in the South Atlantic, had one unexpected – but blissfully welcomed – sentence: 'Concern is being expressed,' the newsreader intoned, 'for the whereabouts of three British journalists in Argentina. Their papers have not heard from them since last Sunday, and they were last seen in Patagonia on Monday.' At last! Someone had noticed we'd gone (Ian was sure it would take the *Observer*, which has a somewhat informal attitude towards it correspondents, at least a fortnight to get itself worried). But by the same token – what bastards the Argentines were! They had promised us, one official after another, to let the Swiss Embassy know of our fate. I had told everyone I had seen that we were all family men, that if nothing else our wives and children should be permitted to know what had happened. But no one, it seemed, despite all the extravagant promises, had done anything. 'You can't trust them an inch,' Ian said. And I had to admit, for all my optimism, he was right.

It was much later, and we were about to get into bed, when Captain Grieco appeared at the cell door. He raised his finger to his lips. 'Be quiet. I have a friend to see you.' And behind him was a young man with dark hair and a thick moustache who introduced himself as Anton Foek, from – of all places – Surinam. He was a stringer for an Amsterdam paper, happened to hear we were in prison, and decided, with the perfect logic of a hungry stringer, that he could make a dollar or two filing a story to Europe about us. He had already talked to the *Sunday Times*; they sent their best wishes, he reported, and two or more of them were coming down to Argentina as soon as possible.

Four hours later we heard the results of his work: the BBC reported, in the 19.00 bulletin – which we heard at 23.00 – that 'three British journalists, reported missing since last Sunday, are believed to have been arrested on espionage charges . . . they are being held in the Southern Argentine city of Ushuaia . . .' Donald Trelford, the *Observer*'s editor, had issued a statement insisting we were 'totally innocent'. It all made sleep a lot easier.

Next morning, the Saturday, Anton was back: a team of four reporters from our papers was on its way: Cal McCrystal, Isabel Hilton and Ian Jack from my office, the Latin American correspondent from the *Observer*, Hugh O'Shaughnessy. From the sketchy notes I made, that Saturday seems to have been an otherwise eminently forgettable day. The prison staff did all they could to make us comfortable. One of the trusties came to the cell, dressed in a red nylon jacket and with a black bow tie. He acted as waiter for the police mess downstairs, and added us to his list of customers; he would bring our meals, and beers. We had a sense of being VIPs, and very pleasant it was, compared to the days immediately before.

Just before we turned in that night a guard passed a business card in to me. It bore the name 'Guillermo Balabán' and the word *'Abogado'*, which my rudimentary Spanish told me meant 'Attorney'. On the back he had scribbled: 'Mr Winchester of *Sunday Post*. I am with Miss Hilton. I see you in morning.' Good old *Sunday Times*! They had even fixed up a lawyer. Pity he didn't know the name of my paper; but I was sure his law was better than his knowledge of Fleet Street.

Next morning, early, the guards came back. Would I come, immediately, to the Comisario's office. A visitor for you. I walked, with mounting, nervous excitement, to the office and there, calm and smiling broadly, was Isabel Hilton – all the way from the office in London.

I hugged her tightly. I hardly knew her, but it didn't seem to matter. It was so good to see someone from home, someone who could console and comfort – because at that very moment I needed both. My eyes filled with hot tears, and I found I couldn't speak. My tongue seemed to have swollen to twice its normal size. But no one minded, least of all Isabel, who must have been prepared for this unseemly – and happily brief – display of emotion. I pulled myself together after a moment, and she told me what had happened.

The paper had indeed hired a lawyer – and here he was, Willy Balabán, a very smoothly dressed and engaging lawyer who worked for *Time* magazine in Buenos Aires. He spoke little English, but appeared very friendly and in total control. Beside him, Captain Grieco and the Comisario faded into relative insignificance. Here am I, he seemed to be saying – big city lawyer, and there are you, small town police chief. You know who's boss, don't you?

Cal McCrystal was on his way from London, along with Hugh O'Shaughnessy. Ian Jack was stranded in Montevideo, with little likelihood of being allowed in by an Argentina that was applying tough visa restrictions to British nationals. Isabel had managed to sneak in under the wire; Cal and Hugh had those talismans that were to prove invaluable to journalists covering the Latin side of the story – Irish passports.

It was at this point, when we became aware of the great juggernaut beginning to roll, that a new nervousness started to set in. There was the interrogation next day, and Ian, in particular, was beginning to worry. In particular, he had remembered a small slip of paper he had left in his telephone contact book – a book that was now, like all our notebooks, maps, passports and other papers, in the hands of the judge. The slip of paper had the address and telephone number in London of MI5 written on it. If the judge saw that, Ian kept saying, he would be in prison for ever. He became terribly, obsessively worried about it. It was quite innocent, he kept saying – 'I only copied it down from a newspaper. But if they find it – that's the end.'

I tried to comfort him, but he was quite inconsolable. He knew the paper was there. It was sure to be found. The prosecutor would know what it meant. He would be instantly linked with an espionage organisation. We would all be found guilty, and locked away for ever. Nothing would shift him from the view. He lay on his bunk, or walked back and forth across the tiny cell – not an easy task, given that it was only eight feet wide – endlessly repeating: 'They're bound to find it. They're bound to.'

So it was a tense and sleepless night for us all. Next morning passed slowly. We knew Willy and Isabel were out seeing the judge, Sagastume, at his office, but had no idea what was being discussed. At four, the guards came and took Tony away. He was the first to be interrogated, and we heard him being marched downstairs, and off to the judge. Ian and I were together, alone; we discussed the kind of evidence Tony was likely to give – he seemed to have some difficulty remembering exactly when and where he took photographs. I knew the police would have developed all his film: let's hope, we said, he hadn't taken more than he was prepared to say he had, and that nothing in his pictures truly did compromise Argentina's national security.

A small piece of paper was pushed through our peephole. 'My name is Humbert,' it read. *'Teniente'* (Lieutenant) in army of Chile. Welcome.' We heard the scurrying of feet and, as we peeked around our door – which one of the guards had left open – we saw a cheery little man wave from his cell door. The first of the other prisoners – all under orders not to talk to us, but evidently eager to get to know us.

They brought Tony back at nine, and put him in isolation in the cell next door. He tapped on the wall, and then, when I was up at our window listening to the BBC I heard him whispering from the window of his cell. 'Not bad!' he said. 'Ian will be called at ten, and you at four. Until it's over I'm being kept incommunicado.'

Ian was plunged into gloom, and slept very little. A note from Cal arrived; he had got to Ushuaia at last, along with Hugh, and both men were staying at the Albatross Hotel. They would come and see us the next day.

At 11.00 next day, the Tuesday, Ian was taken away – something of a merciful release for me, since his worry over this missing piece of paper was becoming infectious. I wished him luck.

By 14.30 he was back – I started to use the 24 hour clock now, since all orders in the cells were issued using that system – and put into the cell with Tony. I heard them laughing: clearly Ian's concern hadn't been justified. If they had found the paper, they never mentioned it.

It was my turn at 18.00. I was marched downstairs, through a great press of reporters and cameramen. I recognised Phil Hayton, the BBC's Johannesburg television man; and there was the TV cameraman who had filmed my Panorama interview in Buenos Aires a week before. What amazing irony. They kept shouting at me – 'Look this way! Give us a smile! How are you being treated? Are you afraid?' I'm afraid I behaved less co-operatively than I might have wished. The police pushed me into the car, and we drove away at high speed through the crowd, and down into the town, and Sagastume's office. Cal and Hugh were there, and there was a warm, if rather brief meeting. Cal said he had called Judy from Ushuaia, and she was well, as were the children. 'She is bearing up very well, and sends you all her love,' he said. And then I went in.

It was something of a surprise to find Isabel in the judge's warm, booklined office, along with Willy Balabán and an attractive young woman who was introduced as Margarita Vásquez, and who would act as the court's official interpreter. Isabel, a very considerable linguist, was also acting as interpreter, and seemed to have already struck up a good relationship with various court officials. When Sagastume came in, all gravamen and dignitas, she adopted a more serious mien, and we all sat down to work.

The interrogation, basically, took the form of accounting for my whereabouts and activities during the previous three weeks – it had only been three weeks since my arrival in Argentina – and reading my notebook, page by page. There were one or two problems: I had pages of fairly detailed accounts of Argentine force levels, aircraft types, missile stocks; I had the names of some British intelligence officials; I had some disparaging quotes about the abilities of the Argentine armed forces. The judge questioned me closely. 'Do you think this information you have is the kind a reporter should have ? Don't you feel you have more in this diary than is consistent with your stated role as a mere journalist? Aren't you motivated by patriotism in your job?'

They were tricky questions to answer. Oddly, however, the trickiest moment came when I turned a page of my book to be confronted with a sentence of vulgar graffito I had copied from the wall of the Royal Marine barracks in Moody Brook: 'The nicest thing about masturbation is that you don't have to look your best.' Margarita Vásquez was peering at the book as I went through it, making sure I wasn't missing anything out. I dreaded the thought that the judge might ask for a full explanation of this coarse sentence; but Margarita allowed me to skip it, and simply blushed, thereby keeping some anonymous Marine's concise observation of the sexual realities of Port Stanley out of the mass of evidence accumulating against me.

The questioning went on late into the night, and began once againt next day, ending just before lunch. 'There are 456 minutes of tape here, Señor Winchester,' said Raul Riccieri, the judge's chief clerk. 'It will all make very interesting analysis.' Then the police drove me back to prison, and, the questioning now over, all three of us were in the cell. As the ordeal had ended, and we had been told to expect the judge's verdict next morning, and everyone seemed to expect that it would be a perfunctory decision to expel us for 'activities prejudicial to the good order of the State', we were mildly euphoric. Cal and Hugh came to see us, and we sat talking with amused good cheer about what would happen next.

But next morning there was no verdict. Ian was called back to the judge's office to amplify some points. Then Tony was called away – having told us he had been less than truthful to the judge in one or two aspects of his questioning (something which infuriated Ian, and, I must admit, irritated me). Some more pictures had been developed, Tony said later; there was some doubt that they had been taken at the precise moment and from the precise place Tony had identified. Could he perhaps explain?

The verdict was due on Friday. At first the police said 14.00. Then they put it back until 16.00. We were finally called at 18.30 – and each of us dressed to the nines to make sure of leaving a good impression on the judge, and on the TV crews, there to record our probable release and deportation. Isabel was in the office, and she was handed three sheets of typewritten documents. She looked bewildered. Where was the judge? He is not here, said Raul; Miss Hilton will read the decision.

And so she began, stumbling through the complex legalism of the document, the tortured preambles, accounts of arcane precedents, short treatises on various points of the Argentine Penal Code. We were, it seems, probable offenders under Section 224 of the Code, which makes it an offence to 'make any sketch, notes, representation or photograph of any building, structure, device or person . . . vital to the national security of the Republic of Argentina . . . .' And to Isabel's mounting horror – and to ours – it was clear that, contrary to all we had supposed, we were not, after all, going to be released. 'Now I, Judge Carlos Sagastume, having determined that there is indeed a case to answer, that these three journalists were motivated by patriotic emotions and had in all probability been on a spying mission, do hereby order that they be detained for preventive reasons, until a later date. . . .'

It was shattering news. We all – Isabel included – sat there feeling sick with horror. As much as anything we were bitterly angry that the judge himself had not deigned to come and deliver his bad news, but had retreated to his lair upstairs, unwilling to face us. We were hurried out, past the TV crews and the blazing lights. Cal and Hugh were in the crowd. They knew, and said how sorry they were. They would come to the gaol right away.

Within moments Cal had called the office in London, and had called Judy in Oxford. She had taken the news well, he said, even though it was late at night, and she might well be feeling low. He had assured her we would be well treated. But he could hardly be sure.

The police gave permission for a press conference, and we were trooped downstairs to face a battery of reporters. I recognised Ken Rees of ITN, John Thorne and Phil Hayton of the BBC; most of the crowd were from Argentine newspapers, and one hectoring reporter in the front row kept asking us where we had left our transmitters, and why we were spying, and what had we done to our code books. It was pretty fatuous stuff, and we kept to standard answers about being well treated, being assured of ultimate vindication, faith in Argentine justice. But we were still bitterly angry and disappointed, and I think it must have showed.

We were, I said at one point, prisoners of war.

The next day, Saturday, was one for sober evaluation of our situation. Cal, Hugh, Isabel and Willy came to the office and, over cups of coffee provided by Captain Grieco – who can never have been at the centre of so impressive a media event, and was duly overwhelmed – we discussed our plight. We were interrupted by a succession of telephone calls. Margaret Mather was the first to call, telling Ian not to worry, and reassuring him about his three children; then Hilary Holden, Tony's young girlfriend (Tony had divorced his first wife shortly before; he had two children); and finally, Judy called from Oxford, just before noon.

It was quite wonderful to hear from her. The line was as clear as a bell, she sounded cheerful and stoical, everyone was well, Biggles (my beagle) kept escaping, everyone in our village of Iffley was rallying round, the paper was keeping in touch . . . 'Why don't you just stick to writing the news, instead of making it?' she said, making me laugh. It was probably the most reassuring call I have ever had – knowing that all was well at home, and thus bringing to an end the awful uncertainty, made the prospect of prison quite bearable. After all, I knew what was happening to me; the thought that Judy and the children, who had no way of knowing, might be worrying themselves to death, preyed on my mind. But they weren't overly worried, it seemed – or didn't show it. And that was a great relief.

There were more calls. Frank Giles, the *Sunday Times* editor, and others on the staff who insisted we would not be forgotten, that all possible efforts would be made to get us out . . . these were a heady few hours, and they were capped in a most bizarre and pleasant way. Captain Grieco bundled us into his car, took us for a tour around Ushuaia and then took us home for tea with his wife and his four enchantingly pretty daughters.

We sat in his living room eating pancakes and a sweet confection called *dulce de leche* (made by boiling condensed milk until it caramelized), trying to teach his fourteen-year-old some English, and trying ourselves to learn some Spanish. He took us to his son's bedroom. It had been converted into a 'war room' with charts of the South Atlantic, and flags showing the latest position of the British Task Force, the Argentine warships and their ground forces on the Malvinas.

There were a number of ships marked as being in Ushuaia harbour: a destroyer called the ARA *Trinidad*, and an old American cruiser, now named after the leader of the Argentine war of independence a century and a half before, the ARA *General Belgrano*.

The final gesture of bonhomie offered by this curiously manic police chief was the most bizarre. We returned to prison at around 21.00 and Captain Grieco said, in best conspiratorial fashion, 'I have a nice surprise for you!' He unlocked a door we had never noticed before, and led us into another wing of the prison, whose walls were decorated with pin-up pictures clipped from the weekly magazines. This, evidently, was the women's wing, and we were to be shown the inmates: two young girls, one a prostitute doing two years for hitting another girl in the eye with a broken bottle, the other a middle aged women doing three years for infanticide (a crime that is regrettably common in rural Argentina, where contraception is generally unavailable).

Captain Grieco opened the younger woman's cell – he didn't knock, or give any warning. She was sitting on the bed, wrapped in a towel, drying her hair. She looked frightened, but grinned sheepishly. 'Take a good look at – Maria Correa!' Grieco said, and then clanged her door shut again. He marched us out of the wing, back to our own, and shut us back in our own cells. 'And now,' he said as he left, 'I think you will be having very nice dreams tonight!' We looked at each other, puzzled. It seemed such a childish way to behave. But Maria had been very attractive, as had the Captain's four daughters. The lack of female company was, we all admitted, getting to be something of a bore.

Sunday morning, 25 April, broke gloomily. I finished letters to Judy and the children, which I thought Hugh might take back with him. (He announced he was going to leave. 'It's a tough world,' he told us. 'You have to be tough.') The Chilean inmate who had sent the note introduced himself to us, and other prisoners – who were doing time for murder or robbery or – in several cases – infanticide – came up to us to shake our hands. They had heard about us on television. They offered cigarettes and soap, we gave them chocolate and biscuits that Cal had bought for us.

We took some time to explore our home, now we knew we would be there for some time. Our cell was one of eight, each identical, each opening onto a long corridor which had a wall at one end, a steel barred and padlocked gate at the other. On the other side of the corridor were three rooms – the *comedor*, a dining room with an ancient black and white television; a lock-up stinking of urine, and worse, where drunks were held overnight; and a room with a rickety table tennis table – the games room, I suppose.

At the end of the corridor was the bathroom – a sink, a crude shower made with a perforated coffee tin, and three holes that served as lavatories – the so-called 'elephants' feet' type favoured in the Indian subcontinent. The place was slimy and filthy dirty, and when drunks were herded in of a morning to vomit and perform other unpleasantnesses, it became markedly worse. The water was usually ice cold, and since everyone tried to hang washed clothing and sheets from wires fixed to the shower pipes, the place dripped constantly. It was never a pleasant place at the best of times, although on those rare occasions when there was a trickle of warm water, it seemed like heaven.

There were more telephone calls. My mother and father called, and we heard that the *New York Times* and the *Washington Post* were both on the case. Then Cal came, and brought a thick red notebook for me, as I had asked. This would be the diary I would keep, and I began to write it straightaway, at about 18.00 on that Sunday, 25 April.

Diary........

SUNDAY 25 APRIL   Rather gloomy beginning, especially since news from S. Georgia rather worrying – said to be a force of British helicopters re-taking it. Chilean inmate says that will be 'very bad news for you . . . ' Father and Mother called at 12.00 – very kind of them, they sounded rather nervous and strained. Father said that ITT and Gould (the electronics companies he works for) were most anxious, and Stella told Cal that he has already started calling *NYT* and *Wash. Post* to ask what they were doing! Typical, but really very nice of him. Ian playing patience, Tony reading *Eye of the Needle*, me a ghastly book about submarine warfare! Rather timely! Cal brought this notebook on this evening, so diary essentially begins today.

All afternoon the atmosphere was very charged with rumours that there had been fighting in S. Georgia. At 16.00 Cal came by to say that the S. of the country had been declared an operational zone and that Isabel – for one – was not being allowed back. Cal was restricted to his hotel, though he could visit us and make essential side trips to shops for us. No more calls, in or out of country, though he got permission to call Isabel in BA (Buenos Aires). Bill McWhirter of *Time* said they had all been told at 13.00 that censorship had been imposed and all telexes must be submitted for prior approval. Comisario Barrozo came with an interpreter – Terry – to inform us that for our own safety we were now being moved to a cell away from the prisoners – Ian objected to this, saying he had made friends with prisoners: I urged a united front, saying we should do as the police suggest, as they are responsible for us. He agreed. Film on TV starred John Mills and Bernard Miles, about dumb child, his horse and falcon, on Dartmoor (?). V. British, which point seemed peculiarly ironic, considering what was going on. BBC reception v. poor, until 17.00 local when it improved and we heard that RM detachment had landed on S. Georgia on Thursday to prepare for landing force which went in earlier today. At 17.15 it was announced that the Argentine forces had surrendered, and that one (of 4) Argentine subs had been severely damaged. We are all wondering what a) short term and b) long term effects of this will be on us – so far all the prisoners look friendly, but the mood could change at any time.

Now in next door cell, separated from the others by a barred door. 'We are the panthers, you are the lions' said one of them after, saying our guards were 'loco'. 'You will be safe here – *nosotros amigos, si guerra, o si paz'* said one – and the guards echoed it. 23.00 – still no news of the surrender on Argentine TV – all that was said was that the CO at Leith had burned his codes in anticipation of 'the final attack'. Ian walks incessantly – he is terribly nervous – probably more sensitive to the nuances of the crisis than T. or me. BBC loud and clear to 23.00 (02.00 GMT): Monday's papers expressing 'concern' about our safety, which is very gratifying. Hope J. and everyone are *'tranquilo'*, and not too concerned. Certainly no change of mood among the guards or the prisoners.

MONDAY 26 APRIL   Woke thinking we should whistle 'Marching Through Georgia', as the news is that islands have been taken, 180 prisoners in custody. But Mrs T. says they'll be returned, while of course we are praying that their return depends on our fate. Knowing Mrs T.'s dislike of the press, she may – if she has the power – let us sweat for a little longer! Cal came by at 11.00 with gifts – cups and saucers, chocolate, biscuits, etc. He had been telephoned this morning by Elaine Davenport (Paul Eddy's wife, an American, with good Spanish, who has been here to Tierra del Fuego before) and was surprised, since no calls allowed to T.d.F. She said she was in a 'special situation', but would not elaborate – we are rather encouraged by this, since it suggests the US is somehow involved. Perhaps the call from the US Embassy. She said that next time she called she would have some *ST* people with her. Good lunch today – hamburger and cheese in a hollowed-out squash. But one sad thing – Castro, a big but very quiet prisoner who had been very good to us, collapsed this morning. He had been complaining of ulcer, or stomach ache – they said, before the ambulance came, that he had a *ataque al corazón* (heart attack). But later he was back in bed, and Roberto said he was simply 'very nervous, very tense . . .' TV news dominated by S. Georgia story, but not sure if all know it's been retaken.

Midnight – another prisoner taken off with bad stomach – '*muy nervioso*' said a colleague. Mysterious: is it the food, or is it the tension? Everyone knows about S. Georgia now – no perceptible reaction, though the radio and TV are full of British 'treachery', Cal says everyone in street most friendly. Harold Briley reported that the Plaza de Mayo anti-British demonstration today was also marked by anti-Galtieri sentiment. Will there be a coup? We all think it is likely. How will it – or anything else – affect our fate? We worry when we hear Galtieri proclaim that 'The Argentine flag will fly over the Malvinas as long as blood still flows in the veins of the Argentine soldiers there . . .', and when we hear Maggie going on about 'time running out', and Haig at the OAS saying the same thing. I thought I heard the BBC say that the 180 Argentine marines captured in S. Georgia had already been handed back, but suppose that is unlikely. Great fun tonight: I was bellowing 'Ullmann' – he is one of our favourite prisoners – just like the guards, and we watched him leap out of bed and into the corridor. We gave him some chocolate to cheer him up. Brilliant day – snow on the Chilean hills magnificent, Beagle channel calm as a mill pond. Radio Oxford apparently rang!

TUESDAY 27 APRIL Another brilliant day, making waking up rather depressing for all of us – it's such a silly waste of time we keep saying. Tony is getting rather angry about it all. Morning depression seems a pretty standard phenomenon here. We all remark on our very realistic dreams: Ian dreamed about being duty reporter at the Cup Final, and I dreamed about getting a 28-day sentence! Both of us wake to the real situation, which was consistently less pleasant. Cal – who had talked to Isabel – came by at 10.30: he's had to buy new clothes, because his natty blue suit was getting grubby. He says the rumour in BA – possibly a steer from London– is that something big may well happen tomorrow, Wednesday (I think it is Wednesday tomorrow: the days merge into one another) – and with Briley reporting the growing anti-Galtieri sentiment on the streets it is possible major changes in whole story are in the offing. We still don't know if the inmates are aware of the fall of S. Georgia – I think they still believe fighting continues. But whatever, there's not a trace of hostility from anyone, guards or prisoners. Cal is talking about getting someone really well-known and powerful – like Kissinger – to plead our case with Argentines. We react very positively to the idea, of course. Cal to see the Admiral, and later, the judge, mainly for reasons of courtesy. Willy Balabán is likely to arrive here tomorrow, providing whatever is in the wind doesn't prevent him.

15.00 Cal back with a real pot-pourri of news. All foreign journalists are having to leave Tierra del Fuego, with almost immediate effect – the South Africans [Philip Hayton's BBC crew – they were allowed to stay because the Argentine government had wanted to keep on good terms with S. Africa so they could use Simonstown as a refuelling base] and Bill McWhirter and all others. Peter Wilsher has ordered Cal to leave, anyway, so that's not so good – though Isabel remains in the country and will – unless she is thrown out – remain the *ST* point-man in the country. At the moment I am waiting for Judy to call – the others here had calls today, but thus far nothing from Oxford. Wonder why? Silly to worry, but the others have such a degree of intimacy with the office, and J. is so (relatively) cut off in Oxford. One of the few disadvantages of living out in the boondocks! Reading a Hammond Innes book which is in its 34th impression – he must have made a fortune from it, and yet it is so bad! Am busily wondering if Max Hastings and Simon Jenkins have begun their book – Max is on the *Canberra*, and, I would think, is writing the first chapters as he goes. Me being stuck in gaol is a rather cruel irony. Cal's other news is that Ian is still in Montevideo and – much more important – the judge has intimated a) that he didn't want to do what he did last Friday, i.e. putting us back in preventive detention, b) that he will give us limited freedom, which may well include permission to visit Buenos Aires, once tempers have cooled in the South Atlantic, and c) most enouraging of all, if the Fiscal (the prosecutor) agrees to the minimum sentence of 2 years, he will suspend it. But – and here's the rub, if the sentence is one day over 2 years, then we will have to serve two thirds of it behind bars. So, looking at the worst case, if we get 8 years, we will be freed (assuming our sentence runs from the day we were imprisoned, which was 16/4) on 15 Aug 1987.

Judy did call at 16.30, all fine – she says lots of pressure at home, my father even talked to Alistair Cooke! She says father's going down very well indeed, which is a very pleasant surprise. She talks of a question in the House of Commons on Thursday, and says I will be stunned when I find out how many people have been concerned – Joe Roberts,[1] Iain Moncreiffe,[2] and all sorts of others. The girls – we have christened them UWAG, the Ushuaia Women's Action Group – meet for lunch at the *Observer* on Thursday. *NYT* and *Wash. Post* both had our story on the front pages, and J. promises the pressure will be kept on, and not to worry.

The judge – or his assistant – summoned us at 18.30 to read the formal refusal of our bail request. But then he said that the 'worst case' was 2 years suspended, which cheered us up. But we decided not to tell Cal, in case the office loses the will to get us out quickly. Matthew Stevenson[3] at home, was just playing cricket with Angus – he is on his way to Paris for an interview with *Reader's Digest* – hope he gets it: Connie and he would love to live in Europe. We have a Spanish-English dictionary now, and Ian is quizzing me – what is 'I have'? (*yo he*); what is 'we have'? (*nosotros hemos*). We really are getting quite reasonable – although we probably will end up speaking a prison argot! Anyhow, we are all much cheered today by the judge's suggestion that we can expect a suspended sentence at the end of this all even if we are found guilty (which is surely unlikely). The story from the South Atlantic gets worse: it is thought we will invade the Falklands tonight or tomorrow. All journalists have been thrown out of Southern Zone (though possibly not from Tierra del Fuego, which is likely to be less involved than Comodoro and Rio Gallegos. (2 weeks in custody).

WEDNESDAY 28 APRIL   Quite an upbeat beginning to the day, although as appallingly late as usual – ten, we began to get up. There was an unusual lot of activity around our cell between 6 a.m. and 8 a.m., which struck us as odd – had the balloon gone up, we wondered? The BBC said only that a total sea and air exclusion zone would operate around the Falklands from Friday, which is only logical. There was also the announcement that one of the

1 My former housemaster at school in Dorset.
2 Sir Iain Moncreiffe of that Ilk.
3 A former editor of *Harper's, New York.*

Argentine prisoners had died 'after a serious incident', which sounds ominous. A British para going berserk? (A S. Korean drunk killed 75 people, it was reported yesterday.) We are all sitting around waiting for Margaret Mather to call – she was supposed to after the Wednesday meeting at the *Observer*, but nothing so far (15.45). A container ship in port, but all Argentine naval ships have cleared off. Film on TV of guns being installed at Comodoro airport; people are getting very twitchy. Badges saying 'Islas Malvinas' given to us today – they have a penguin and a sheep under a picture of Stanley Cathedral – said to be the most southerly Anglican Cathedral on earth. Bill McWhirter of *Time* – such a pleasant, intelligent chap – came by at 14.00 to interview us, said that Argentine authorities had been annoyed by my 'bragging' in an interview in *Gente* that I had sneaked into Falklands by pretending to be something I wasn't. The whole business of whether one has 'Journalist' in one's passport, and whether one checks into an hotel as a journalist or not – we apparently didn't, when we came to Ushuaia – raises eyebrows, and hackles. I hope it is something we are going to be able to explain later. Bill raised matters like this, and said essentially that we were hostages to fortune. He advised against hiring some Kissinger-like figure to try and secure our release, because the Argentine Junta was under pressure from everywhere, on all sides, and their pride was being hurt. The longer we are held, the bigger a story we are in UK and US, he said; but try to keep as small a story in Argentina as possible, so there will be no pride-based objecions to our being released later on.

Ian a great deal calmer today, all of us seem to be settling into the routine of the place, tedious though it is. It is another splendid, crystalline autumn day – if only we were allowed out to enjoy it.

No calls from London today – in fact, no one had any calls or telexes from anywhere – I wonder whether the lines between here and BA have been cut for the duration. The British now seem to be saying that noon Friday is the deadline for beginning operations to recover the Falklands. We are all praying that it's not messy, whatever happens.

Late tonight it was announced that Costa Méndez would stay an extra day in Washington, so there's still hope. A one-hour blackout tonight, and the cargo ship in port left during it, in pitch dark.

Cal left – or at least, his plane leaves at 08.00, so he said his salaams to us this evening, leaving us a bottle of Armagnac, and taking letters to Judy and Anthony Sheil.[1] (Work intrudes, even in gaol.)

Sansul, an infanticidist, left, quite unexpectedly. He explained that no evidence had been found against him. We gave him 2 packets of cigarettes, and 100,000 pesos 'for the bus to Rio Grande'. I think we are regarded as soft touches in prison now! During the blackout Ian remarked on the idiocy of it – stuck in the southernmost prison in the world, innocent, in a blackout, waiting for the Royal Navy to bomb us, handing out cash to an infanticidist! And two weeks ago – a little more, actually – we were just ordinary hacks doing an ordinary job. It's all so bizarre. We all wish Sansul well – he was a little soft in the head, but he was good company, and liked us a lot. Prison solidarity is a fascinating thing: we were all genuinely pleased that he got his freedom. I walked an estimated mile this evening, in a 15-pace figure of eight between the barred door and the wooden one. The water here is very good to drink – soft and fresh, like all mountain water. Comisario Barrozo had us in for a whisky: his interpreter said I looked tired. I can't think why: I sleep a lot, and there is nothing to do. But living inside, in the smoky atmosphere of this prison, does get to me. Tony is smoking a lot more now, and it's making the cell reek with old cigar smoke. Ian seems able to read, thank heavens: his obsession with *paciencia* seems to have run its course. He writes a lot in his journal. I dropped a line to the *Oxford Mail* today, thanking them for their interest. Wonder what they'll do with it. Watched football on TV: Ardiles was playing, in Argentina: also a guest star called Maradonna, who is apparently the one to watch in Madrid. I can't say I'm fascinated, but I hope I get to see it from home this year. The one thing I do want to do, somehow, is get back on the Falklands if the British retake them, and see all those good people I was with at the beginning of the month. Four weeks ago this Friday: it seems an age. If the British do retake it the Argentines will have been there one month exactly. Let's see – 8 a.m. Friday seems to be the deadline. The Argentine radio says HMS *Exeter* sunk, but no word at all on BBC – I suspect propaganda, but you never know.

1 My literary agent in London.

THURSDAY 29 APRIL   A cruel beginning to the day. We all got up late again – mind you, Tony and I were reading until 02.00 – and it was pouring with rain. Ian was cheerful, but then Willy came – he had arrived at midnight, after having to take a car between Rio Grande and here. He told us he was going to appeal against the reasons for the refusal of bail – the papers, he said, had to be sent to Comodoro Rivadavia (goodness knows why) and it would take about three weeks before that appeal was heard. And that merely to establish if we could be given limited freedom. Worse to come: we could be here for three or four months before the case was finally disposed of, even though it is Willy's firm belief that we will eventually get a suspended sentence. It seems crazy to me that if we are going to get a suspended sentence at the end of all this, why the need to keep us in prison at all now, and why the need for so much delay? But Willy did make the point that all this could change if the political situation altered. Cruellest of all, from my own point of view, was the letter that arrived from Anthony Sheil (Giles Gordon) offering £16,000 for Corgi book on the Falklands crisis. I was initially very depressed at the notion that the book would have to be abandoned, but now I believe if we could find a collaborator at home then I could do a good half of the work here and leave the rest to the co-author. I will have to ask for the right to use a typewriter here, of course, and to have access to research materials. But I believe it can be done, and I shall approach the lawyer accordingly. This afternoon the chief did lend me a typewriter, and it was truly a delight to sit clacking away with the old two fingers. I typed a note to Anthony asking for a collaborator, and a covering note to Isabel to ask if she would read it over the phone to Anthony or Giles. No letter to Judy, but then I sent one with Cal yesterday. Bill McWhirter came by with *Scoop*, *Put out more Flags* and *Gaudy Night*, which we fell upon with great enthusiasm. Then Captain Grieco – now in khaki battle fatigues – gave us coffee while an ANSA[1] man and photographer wanged away. We had reservations about doing it, especially after the *Siete Días* interview[2] and, even worse, the piece in *Radiolandia 2,000*, which captioned our picture 'The

1 The Argentine national news agency.
2 This magazine interviewed us just after our arrest.

Guilty' and photographed the notes Ian and I wrote to the families.[1]
It seemed an amiable enough chat, and we managed to get over our
dismay, anxiety and anger, all at once. The photographer let Tony
take a picture of the Captain – T. felt so good to use a Nikon again,
it was a delight to see.

Had another visitor – James Brooke, a pleasant young chap who
is the newly-appointed, Rio-based *Miami Herald* Latin America
bureau chief. He was very friendly, says he is going to 'Punta
Arenas Chile' tomorrow. He's lucky to be here at all – there are all
sorts of restrictions on the press here now with rigid censorship.

Sansul is back! He explained he had spent the 100,000 on food,
cigarettes and drink, had slept out in the rain last night, and was
back in the cells until 06.00 tomorrow just to have a warm place to
sleep. It is actually nice to see his funny, lugubrious, El Greco face
again, and we'll miss him when he goes.

Ian is reading *Scoop* – read some of it out loud, and we all laughed
till tears ran. It is just so perfectly written, every line honed to
perfection. An old Walter Matthau, Carol Burnett film on. *'El
Mundo Espectáculo'.*[2]

Now the balloon goes up, or so it seems. We impose our total air
and sea blockade at 08.00 local tomorrow, and the Argentines have
just announced they will impose a similar blockade, from now (I
think). So any vessels in the area will sink each other, or so it looks.
Brooke said Haig was coming back to BA, but so far the BBC has
not confirmed it. According to the press review, two papers
reporting from Washington that Reagan is ready to swing his
allegiance firmly to Britain's side, which means US-Argentine
relations will deteriorate. Willy came – he is off, back to BA
tomorrow morning – to give us some marginally better news. First,
that the prosecutor wants an independent arbitrator to assess the
importance of our military information. Second, the judge told
Willy that we will be freed on $8,000 (100,000,000 pesos) bail once
the international situation has calmed down. So that is a relief, if it

1 The reporters had asked if we would write brief notes to our families at home. We
jumped at the chance, and were very hurt to find that the notes had been
photographed for the magazine, but never passed on. We vowed to strangle the
reporters concerned!

2 The evening entertainment programme on Ushuaia Channel Eleven (*Canal
Once*).

is true. Willy has been over optimistic before, mind you, but equally he has been – like this morning – the bringer of bad tidings. So, a good/bad day, full of interest, as is often the case. Tomorrow, the last day of April – four weeks to the day since the Argentine invasion of the Falklands – the action begins, or so it seems. All of us will be crossing our fingers.

FRIDAY 30 APRIL   Now this – at least as I write, at 13.00 – really is a boring day. No calls, no visitors, nothing. We read, Ian plays patience, we had conversations with a couple of our fellow-prisoners (and our Spanish really is improving – we had a long discussion about the cost of housing in UK and Argentine, the number of rooms in my house, the size of the garden and so on). The *Miami Herald* man has not come back so far and, thinking black thoughts, we rather suppose he won't come at all. A pity: I thought he was a nice chap.

13.50 Tony got a telegram from the Chapel at the *Sun*, wishing him and the two of us well. Tremendous! a link with the outside world again.

And at 14.00 even better – or even more interesting, anyway; we're not sure if it's better – the United States (according to the BBC) has come down squarely on the side of Britain in the Falklands crisis, and has imposed military and economic sanctions on Argentina, and has offered Britain material aid (I wasn't sure if that included, or specifically excluded, military aid: I rather fancy it excluded it.) My immediate reaction was that this would bring a speedy end to the crisis, that the Argentine troops would withdraw with great loss of face and that Galtieri's government would fall as a result. Ian is not so sure – and I admit my reaction was spur of the moment – and feels that Britain can now afford to offer magnanimous enough terms so that the long term aspects of the problem can be tidied up and the Galtieri government can be seen to have recovered some of its dignity. But how, in the short term, will the Argentines react? Will there be an ugly reaction towards us, for example? Will our case drag on precisely because of this turn of events? It is the precise opposite of what happened over Suez, *n'est-ce-pas?* The Atlantic Alliance, and Europe, have been greatly strengthened by what has taken place now. So the Falklands crisis can be seen as an important turning point in geopolitical alliance-building in the 1980s – I don't think that's putting it too strongly. Would that I were a leader-writer tonight!

The 02.00 Papers review amply confirms that – though the *Express* biliously complains that the Americans should have come in earlier on our side, and this would have ended a long while ago. The *Scotsman* predicts a long stint of negotiation now, which is, of course, less than ideal for us. But I think the Argentines will want settlement, along the Haig lines, soon; after all, the longer they delay, the more powerful our fleet will be, and the greater the likelihood of a humiliating defeat. Schlaudeman, the US Ambassador in BA, went to see Galtieri at 3 a.m. today and stayed until 10.30 – 7½ hours of dawn (or *madrugada, en castellano)* talks.

We were asked down to the judges's office to be told – as we had been warned – of the appeal against our bail denial. The court that hears this is in Comodora Rivadavia, so it will take some time. But we don't think there's any chance of bail until the political situation shapes up.

We asked the police office why no phone calls – and the police admitted that there had been so many from all over the world that they had simply banned them all! They didn't bother to tell us![1] So then they said that calls from certain people – family etc., friends, all from specified places – could be made, though they have to be kept short. It seems to me the police are going against the wishes of the judge, so we'll have to watch that.

James Brooke of the *Miami Herald* did come back, so I was right to think he was okay. He took $100 of mine to convert into pesos, and some letters. He, or Bill McW., will return tomorrow. The court interpreter, Margarita Vásquez[2], lent us lots of English classic books and some cassettes: I'm seriously thinking of getting another Walkman 2, especially if they are cheaper here. It would be nice to listen to some decent – or pleasant – music. The other prisoners tend to play old disco music, which is a bit wearing. An ancient

1 The only phone was in the detectives' office. If they felt like arbitrarily refusing to take the calls they could – and did. On scores of occasions when Judy phoned from Oxford she was told that I 'was not available'.

2 Señor Vásquez was a local civil servant; his wife came from an educated Buenos Aires family, and was well-known to the local court officials – one of the few Ushuaians who spoke English.

Barbara Streisand film tonight; and all the newsreaders are looking very cowed at having to present the grim news about America's change of mind. For us, not too bad a day: for Argentina, a grim one. Tomorrow, another month – Labour Day, too. Wonder if I'll be home in time for Mother's birthday, a month from now?

SATURDAY I MAY   Another brilliant morning, though the three of us woke in less than good spirits – the tedium is getting us down, I think. But at 11.00 a lawyer I knew in Atlanta telephoned: she had been trying for days but the police had said I was 'not available'. Now we seem to be allowed calls again, though for only 5 minutes at a time. She said that we were on the Today show, which is good news; we were in the front pages of a lot of newspapers, too. She was keen to get Gerry Spence[1] on the case, and I told her what section of the Argentine Penal Code we have been held under, but I would rather the *ST* and *Obs* did their own legal stuff first. Now that the lines have evidently been opened again it is likely we'll get calls from home: I hope so. I'd like to know what's happening in London. Was there a question in the House, for example?

13.00 We heard Swedish radio announce the bombing of Port Stanley airport – we had thought something was up, as we were woken by men whistling at 07.30 and words like 'fuerza Británica . . .' etc. It seems – now we have heard VOA, [Voice of America] though not BBC – that Vulcans from Ascension, covered by Harriers from our aircraft carriers, bombed the airport early this morning. The Argentines say 2 of our aircraft were brought down by AA, but MoD denies this, and says the operation was 'successful.' VOA corr. in BA says all information up there is coming from a press centre, and why that information can be broadcast and published. Certainly the 'Canal Once – Ushuaia' report seemed pretty sober stuff: they had obviously hunted around for anti-Thatcher material, and only found one thing – a Welsh TUC motion condemning Maggie! We think at the worst that the attack on the airport was designed to force the Argentines into a corner, so they will have to accept the Haig proposal – abandoning the islands with US observation, and leaving a tri-partite administration on the

1 Spence is a well-known and flamboyant Wyoming lawyer about whom I had written in the *Sunday Times Colour Magazine* about a year before.

islands while talks on sovereignty continue; we don't think – unless Maggie really is appallingly jingoistic and bombastic – that the bombing is the precursor to an actual invasion. The Argentines have got to be allowed to save some face. But now we wait – exciting times, I must say, and we seem to be far better placed than the hacks in BA to get a feel for what is going on. Yesterday's chat with sad little Margarita Vásquez, when she said 'Argentina seems to lose everything she is involved in – every dispute goes against her – we don't have enough land for our people, or to maintain our self-sufficiency' – was much more illustrative of the Argentine attitude to all this than any number of briefings in the Casa Rosada.

We learned later that Bill McW., and James Brooke were thrown out this morning – presumably the reaction to the US sanctions.

George de'Ath (the South African cameraman) and his two colleagues are still here, but they are afraid they'll be tossed out too. One of them gave me $500, which will be helpful. (I had given $100 to James, but he was turned out before he could change it, and presumably still has it.) Then the translator, Margarita Vásquez, and an English girl from Birmingham called Jane Scotti (née Wood) brought books, magazines, tapes ('Chariots of Fire') and an electronic chess game. They also agreed to do our shopping for us – loo paper and such stuff – and to buy a Walkman on my Diners Club card. They're only about $90, says George (though Walkman 2 aren't available.) And then Judy called – she had been trying for a long time, and was delighted to get through. 'The magic word is "*esposa*"[1], she said. But we could only talk for a couple of minutes – an air raid warning sounded and the police got me off the line p.d.q. But she said all sorts of things were going on – Rob Cowley at Random House[2] was said to be exerting all kinds of pressure, though I'm not sure of what kind. It was good to speak to her – and they are all well, apparently, and cheerful. Cal got back today, and will see or speak to Judy and the others at length over the weekend. She said she found Hugh 'a bit abrasive', as I had warned her.

Later Ian dropped a terrible clanger. Tony was talking about George de'Ath saying that fighting was still going on in the Falklands. 'What does he know; he's only a cameraman?' said Ian.

1 'Wife'.

2 Who were publishing my book on the British aristocracy.

Predictable reaction from Tony who said, 'Come on, I've done some good work.' Ian realized immediately, of course, and tried hard to row back. But the split between us writers and Tony is very evident – a pity. He is sketching happily all day now he has a pad, and draws very fair copies of portraits in the *National Geographic Magazine*. We wait now for calls from Margaret and Hilary – it's been a little unfair, me getting so much attention.

What a terrible, terrible waste of time prison is! Whatever else this experience may have taught me – about, for example, how much longer I want to be a reporter, if this kind of thing is going to happen every few years – this will be paramount: locking up able-bodied, able-minded men who are manifestly not dangerous to society, but are merely inconvenient misfits, is about as great a crime in itself as whatever it is that brought them here. Their minds and bodies just waste away as they mooch around aimlessly: public works programmes, something unpleasant and deterrent, maybe – but not this gradual erosion of a man's sense of society. Howard League for me when I get back.

News from the Falklands bad: and quite the opposite of our earlier prognostications. The Royal Navy has been bombarding Argentine positions on the Falklands and there has been a fierce aerial battle above the Task Force. Two Argentine planes – Daggers – said by London to have been downed. Four British planes said to be ditto by BA, though the BBC corr. on HMS *Hermes* reported that all those that went on the Port Stanley bombing mission returned safely, with one slightly damaged by anti-aircraft fire. I would tend to believe the BBC – it is giving equal time (though not prominence) to the Argentine claims, though BA is giving no time at all to British claims of success. It is beginning to look as though a landing is going to be attempted, so bloodshed is on the cards. A great tragedy looms, I fear – odd how one's appreciation of this war changes about hourly. General Galtieri is supposed to be addressing the nation on TV soon: every hour or so there is a message from the Junta – a torch, surmounted by wings, a rifle and an anchor, is shown, and a deep voice-over intones the sombre news of 'victory' and 'heavy fighting' and 'British treachery'. But at the moment, it's 'Mork and Mindy' dubbed. I don't know which is worse. Many *Manchester Guardian Weeklies* to read, and do crosswords in. Jane Scotti who brought them, said I had a familiar face – I fear it is the old 'anonymous looks' again, as I don't think I know her from anywhere.

One note of possible interest: a constant and very tedious feature of TV recently has been a 30 sec. 'Unity is Easy' spot featuring 'Our repossession of the Malvinas is a sign of the unity and friendship for all the people of Argentina.' Now it has been dropped, and there's a new message exhorting Argentines to show unity and energy and a lack of factionalism. No mention – in any of the spots so far tonight – of the Islands.

Galtieri went on TV at 23.50 – not an impressive sight, with three military attachés standing like zombies behind him, and two toy soldiers of the palace guard on either side. He said they would answer force with force – at first we thought it was an official declaration of war, but it turned out not to be so. Bed tonight with talk of war in the air, but a general assumption – in our cell, anyway – that Argentina would be forced to the negotiating table in a matter of days. Pym, in Washington, says much the same – that is British policy. 'The Ladykillers' on TV!

SUNDAY 2 MAY   Woke late – we were watching television until 02.30 or so, although Alec Guinness and Herbert Lom don't come over terribly well in translation, so we didn't watch the entire film. Blustery morning – the wind coming from the East (or that quarter, anyway) which is unusual. Tony got a phone call in the very early morning – it was his first wife, which was a bit of a disappointment for him. So today I know that both of the others will be very anxious about getting their calls – I'm luckier at present, having had two yesterday. News from the Falklands more or less as it was last night – details of airport bombing and of later bombardment from naval $4\frac{1}{2}''$ guns 'to prevent repairs.' Pym sees Haig at 10.00 EST (I am writing this at 09.55 EST, noon Argentine time). *Sunday Times* has an exclusive saying 22 SAS men have been on Falklands for the past three weeks, having been dropped there by parachute right at the beginning of the crisis. I can hear from the TV in the other room that the Junta is making yet another pronouncement, to keep up national morale, I suppose.

20.15 Generally down day. Margaret did call, but Ian was limited to only 5 minutes – and probably only spoke for 3 or 4 – and came back unhappier than when he went for it. Since then, no other calls. It is clear that, without telling us, we have been limited to much less communication with our families than the judge initially promised us. No beer at dinner tonight,[1] and no visitors. The screws, in short, seem to be tightening. Is it because of the situation in the South Atlantic? We have to assume it is, though without any hacks here at all – the South Africans were thrown out last night, it now seems – it's a little difficult to tell. Today all was quiet around the Falklands – Pym saw Haig, and professed himself still to be keen on a diplomatic solution to all this. So we wait for the crisis to – in Ian's words – 'bottom out'. The sooner the better: at least our situation is rather better than that of the Royal Marines: they are away for an indeterminate period, and may not come back at all. We'll get home sooner or later – just for now we have to batten down the hatches and weather this storm – if you can call the lessening of privileges a storm – while it plays itself out. All power to Pym's elbow!

I had a thought later in the evening. It must be clear to sensible Argentine military officers that the Falkland situation is unwinnable, especially as the delay goes on – *Canberra, Fearless,* etc., get to the South Atlantic, etc., – and that Galtieri's pledge to fight to the 'last drop of blood' will result in a) loss of the Falklands, b) decimation of the Army and Navy and c) Argentina being treated like a pariah by much of the world. If the Galtieri government refuses to change its stance, will any level-headed military men seek to force it to, or even take over the government itself? I would have thought that conversations in officers' messes just now would be fascinating. But whatever happens it will have to happen quickly – otherwise the British will attack and the decimation of the armed forces will begin. I realize this is sacrilegious and heretical, but that's my theory. Have started reading Dorothy Sayers, *Gaudy Night.* Jan de Harley's *Captain* was surprisingly good; I'd like to read more of his books. It was thoughtful, touching, exciting and, of the genre, well written. but I fear *Gaudy Night* will be bad for nostalgia. 'Lenny'[2], which is what I've christened the Uruguayan giant next

1 Thus far one of the prisoners who acted as waiter for the police mess would be allowed to bring us a can of beer each evening.

2 After the character in Steinbeck's *Of Mice and Men.*

door, plays Olivia Newton-John endlessly, other characters include a pleasant guard we call 'Ratso'. Anyway, one more day down. How many to go?

MONDAY 3 MAY To see Comisario Barrozo this morning – in great trepidation, to work out why we appear to have lost some of our privileges. B. assured us we hadn't: that our situation remains the same, no matter what happens on outside. The communication problem was dictated by Buenos Aires – the same rules apply to us as apply to the other hacks. So we have made an arrangement whereby the wives can call at 20.00 – one 15 minute call a day, to be listened to by George, the ice-cream salesman and interpreter. So whenever the first person gets through this new arrangement will be explained. We got beer for lunch, too – so our feeling is that things are looking up a little. Fingers crossed.

Things continued to get better during the day. Jane – dear, delightful Jane Scotti – came by at 16.00 with all the goodies we asked for – bananas, oranges, grapes, loo paper, etc., money changed; the price of a Walkman (990,000 pesos); and a loaned tape player with five tapes she had specially recorded for us – Brandenburg Concertos, Haydn trumpet concertos, *Messiah*, etc. So now we have music, and later today (perhaps) I'll be able to strap on a Walkman again.

Jane brought with her 'Charlie' – a court official, a very pleasant, rodent-toothed man who had been with Sagastume – the blessed judge – on the first day we arrived here. He was most pleasant and helpful, and sorted out one or two small matters about the waiter, etc.

I slipped away at 17.00 to hear the 20.00 BBC – news of the sinking of a patrol vessel, the missile damage to another, the possible torpedoing of the cruiser *General Belgrano*.

At 17.30 Tony got a phone call from Hilary, at which he put over the details of the plan; but he was dismayed and alarmed when he was suddenly pulled away from the phone and pushed out of the room. He said that the police were listening to the radio, and that suddenly they became very agitated and 'emotional'.

Then, at 17.59 the BBC had a special news announcement, and we heard why. The Argentine government, it seems, has announced the 'presumed loss' of the *General Belgrano*, the 2nd biggest ship in their Navy, with a crew of 1,000. They said that 4 to 5 ships had been searching the area where the ship was missing, and no trace had been found, or rather 'circumstances suggest it may have been lost . . .' This is terrible news: if 1,000 people have died it places this in the category of a very nasty war indeed, and – incidentally – makes us vulnerable to all sorts of nastiness. Surely, surely, this, if it is true, this must bring Galtieri to his senses. Presumably it was a nuclear submarine that did the trick – 24 hours ago, according to some reports – since they can outrun almost any pursuit vessel, and are quiet and full of all kinds of technological advantages. There's some dispute – it'll become clearer later, about whether the loss was in the British exclusion zone (the patrol vessel was, apparently) or in the Argentine's own exclusion zone which is 200 miles around S. Georgia and S. Sandwich islands as well as off the Argentine coast. If it was the latter, it makes it a little easier to explain, because one must presume the Argentines fired first. Still, it's a bad business.

I must try and write more clearly! Sitting listening to the tape of 'Chariots of Fire', feeling very sad about home being so far away and so seemingly unattainable. All the reports from London now talk of the 'deep depression' in Whitehall, and the feeling that this crisis is going to drag on for months – well maybe not that long, but 'a long, drawn-out affair.'

Ian is more upset than I am by the loss of the *General Belgrano*, which seems more or less confirmed. Humbert, the Chilean, can scarcely conceal his glee, and comes into our room giving a conspiratorial thumbs up. He and the Uruguayan 'Lenny' spend a lot of time together – pause there while we had blackout, caused not by an emergency, but by a faulty fuse. Humbert, who is an electrician by trade, repaired it, and we had light again after ten minutes or so. In the meantime we had candlelight in our cell, which made it seem a little cosier. We have just been playing 'Jerusalem' to Humbert, who looked very serious and reverential when we told him it was church music.

I could have hugged Jane today – she comes from Birmingham, is married to an Argentine named Scotti (I imagined there must be all sorts of tensions inside a family like that at a moment like this. One of her neighbours said 'You're not going to the prison, are you?' in a tone of disapproving disbelief.) A cup of tea is being brought just now – no milk, something we haven't had since we've been here. I miss milk a lot. I've just realized. A glass of cold milk now would be much appreciated. As would glasses of champagne, claret, sherry, port – shepherd's pie in the kitchen at home, Tusker bounding about on the sofa, licking my face madly, Biggles wild and excited and then flopping down exhausted – Rupert poking his head around the door – 'Hi!' – Angus mowing the lawn, Alex and Karim off on their bicycles to play football and Judy, steady as a rock, in the middle of it all.

Later news about the *General Belgrano* is not good. An Argentine spotter plane is said to have found some lifeboats – Humbert says 128 survivors, 1036 dead and missing. His figures are never very reliable, but somehow I get the feeling he is 'in the ballpark'.

Ian has just observed that if we stay in Ushuaia next month or so and then get back to Britain in the autumn we will have three winters in one year! Depressing, huh? Tony talked to Hilary today (he was roughed up slightly when the guards heard of the *Belgrano* sinking. He came back white and very shaken) and told her of the 20.00 telephone rules. No one called today, but let's see about tomorrow.

TUESDAY 4 MAY   Well, I suppose it was predictable. at 11.30 this morning George, the interpreter, came with a very long face to tell us that because 'we had written things for outside newspapers' – a totally false charge, except for my note of thanks to the *Oxford Mail* – all our privileges were being withdrawn, with immediate effect. All our money has been taken away; we have no English books anymore – though I see one copy of the *Guardian Weekly* is still under the bed – and we have to eat with the other prisoners, and eat the prisoners' food. Also, perhaps worst of all, we have to get up at 06.00 to answer roll call! No phone calls, no letters. What do we have left? We have our radios – that privilege will be the next to go, I fear, and we will miss it very much. We have each other, for the time being. We all feel very down and shaky – that's been my response all along, to shake and shiver whenever there's bad news. This is the end of three weeks in custody, the beginning of our fourth week.

We'll come through it, I know. Tony Gray, Peter Niesewand,[1] Tony Allaway. Lots of journalists have been in far worse states than we have. Obviously – and George confirmed it – we have had our situation altered because of the sinking of the *General Belgrano*. It really was a ghastly incident – it took place 30 miles east of the tip of Isla de les Estados, and right outside the exclusion zone. Some 400 have been picked up, and reserve planes talk of another 15 lifeboats spotted – so perhaps the loss of life is not too terrible. In Ushuaia the real regret is at the loss of the patrol boat, which has a crew almost totally from this station. That's probably why things have turned so sour. BBC says we have bombed the Port Stanley airstrip again, and another smaller one. My guess is that the mood in Britain will change now. The French have said they are 'stunned' by the attack, and have suggested that EEC sanctions be lifted; the Americans, too, have expressed concern. Pym told the Commons that there was no intention to inflict 'humiliation' on the Argentine Navy, or on Argentina, but to bring them to their senses. My guess is that a lot of people at home will now rapidly lose their stomach for continuing the fight, and that we, rather than the Argentines, will back down. It doesn't seem worth it – perhaps if we suffer a loss now it will rub this in. Anyway, as of now – 13.15 – we're pretty stunned ourselves, but determined to stick it out and behave decently to everyone. Prayer seems in order.

19.00 Another terrible blow: HMS *Sheffield*, a Type 42 destroyer launched by the Queen in 1971, was set on fire and sunk[2] inside the exclusion zone. Nott, in a late night statement in the House, said 12 seamen were missing and other casualties were likely. Grim. Grim. The bulletin began 'There have been major developments in the dispute . . .' and how right they were. These body blows are awful, we just rock with the punches, wondering how on earth two governments can go on slogging at this, losing men, rending families, costing the taxpayers untold millions. The other prisoners

1 Peter, who had become a very successful thriller writer, died in Ireland in February 1983.
2 'The Shiny Shef' was actually sunk by the Royal Navy some days later as she was being towed home for salvage.

don't seem unduly dismayed – 'two to one' said 'Jack Nicholson'[1], and said the loss of the *General Belgrano* meant less as it was so old, but HMS *Sheffield* was very modern. We may worry about our situation, but how awful it must be for the wives and children and mothers and fathers of the dead and missing. Surely – but I've said this before – surely it'll bring them to their senses! We just must batten down the hatches and pray.

We think of nothing other than how this is going to end. At worst – for us – 4 years in clink. At best – a speedy resolution of the crisis, bail for us and then a quick trial. But at least we are alive and a dozen families, or more, back home, will be going to bed in tears, knowing that their lives are ruined, for the time being. War is so senseless. Why are they doing this – as Ian says, it's like two spoiled children fighting over a doll, ending up tearing their clothes, bloodying each others' noses, ruining what might once have been a close friendship – and tearing up the doll in bits, too. Everyone knows that sooner or later the Falkland Islands will be Argentine territory – how are the mothers and wives of today's incident going to react when they see the Argentine flag flying over the islands in a few years' time. What did their sons and husbands die for? What the bloody hell was the point? I'm not a pacifist – not yet. But I could become one very quickly indeed.

Grim night, although intellectually we all agree that the sinking of the *Sheffield* possibly brings peace a little closer – cries of horror from everyone. This last note is being written the next morning (Wednesday) as the guard switched out the light at 22.30 or so. We kept up listening to the BBC, with Nott saying that 30 were presumed dead on the *Sheffield*. Is this the crisis bottoming out? I hope to God it is.

Tripe for dinner tonight, by the way! After all these years![2]

WEDNESDAY 5 MAY Tony's son's birthday – he's rather cast down, understandably, that he can't send a card or any other sort of

---

1 His real name was Salis – doing a long stretch for grievous bodily harm. He had the same manic appearance as Nicholson in the film of Stephen King's novel *The Shining*.

2 Judy had, despite my pleadings, never given me tripe at home: it had become a standing joke.

message out. We were woken at 06.25 after a pretty awful night – it sounded as though the police were having a party all night. It's now 07.45, and it's still dark as velvet. From 06.30 until now we've just been sitting around chatting – not too disconsolately, as we are so perplexed at getting up so early we are struck by the adventure of it all. We can try and listen to the 11.00 BBC news to see if there are any overnight developments.

I taught Tony to repeat *'Mi hijo es diecisiete hoy'*[1] and try it out on our colleagues.

I was sitting here just now – it's 12.45 – and thinking, however pathetic it sounds, that I'd like nothing better than to have a good old fashioned bawl. There are all sorts of tensions building up inside me, and I know that a good cry would make me feel better. All three of us feel similarly sorry for ourselves – it's not just me. Outwardly, in fact, I think I'm in rather better shape than Ian, who is dreadfully moody. On the surface I'm quite calm, but inside I'm a bag of nerves. 'You'd never have thought he would have been the one to crack first!' – I can hear people saying that. Except of course I won't crack, but it is very difficult looking back in this diary to the entry about missing Rupert – that makes my eyes prickle. I suppose it's best not to think about the outside, except to derive some cheer from the certainty that an awful lot of people are rooting for us. I wonder what the papers are doing for us. Is there, for instance, an American lawyer on his way? Are the Swiss doing anything? We feel sure that something is going on outside, though it is awfully infuriating not knowing what it might be.

Later in the day – it's now 16.00 – I began to feel a bit better. Blood sugar levels, I think! Or hormones. Or even bloody bio-rhythms. I told Ian I had to bite my lip to stop the tears at lunchtime today – I think he has felt much the same too. Tony says the 'shakes' that we experience when things go really badly are just controlled aggression.

News from home is a little tiny bit better. No reports of further action – though there are here – and Pym and Haig are both saying that the naval losses in the South Atlantic show that negotiations must begin urgently. The new 'Peruvian Plan', which has been bruited in Washington and New York, is beginning to seem a basis

1 'My son is 17 today'.

for talks: there would be a cease-fire, withdrawal of troops (and the Task Force? that's not clear); some internationally supervised interim administration; and negotiations on the question of sovereignty. It is that last that will stick in Argentina's craw – they'll only accept it if there is a sub-rosa promise, guaranteed by the UN (?) that they will win ultimate sovereignty. How to advance a formula that will allow Argentina to save face – that's the problem. But it is a ray of hope: let's pray there's no sudden deterioration in the military situation.

A number of Argentine naval vessels came in Ushuaia port today, loaded with survivors from the *General Belgrano*. Landing craft went out to meet them, presumably to off-load the survivors, of whom there appear to be about 750, or most of the crew which the Navy admits was on board. It seems about 30 died on HMS *Sheffield*, which is said to be still afloat, and had not sunk as reported last night. A frightful tragedy, whatever condition the ship is in herself.

I thought I'd try and chart my moods from now on, and I'll try and devise some form of chart. It will be difficult to gauge just where I should begin it – if it is to run sequentially it will have to start a number of pages back from the end. How many, that's the question.

16.00 – new rumour and slightly dismaying development: we were moved back to Cell No. 1 again, back where it all started. No basin, less room, less freedom. But I don't read anything sinister into it. Grieco's friend – a man arrested for passing bad cheques – has been moved into our room, which clearly was the 'privilege suite'. It simply underlines the point that we are to be treated like everyone else.

Four South African journalists are said to have been around the gaol today, looking for us, but if they were here – and it was 'Jack Nicholson' who said they were – they weren't allowed to see us.

Peace hopes are rising steadily. In New York the Security Council is meeting, and Haig and Pym are talking peace. But what do the Argentines want? Will they accept the 'Peruvian Plan'. I'm sorry there are so many questions in this, and so few answers. But I shall live in hope. '*Paciencia*', says one of the prisoners. '*Tranquilidad.*'

20.30 Well I'm afraid I did shed a few tears – not too

disgracefully, but perhaps it has cleared the system. I was sitting playing chess on my own when Ian came in – I had decided to say 'present' instead of '*presente*' at roll-call, and Ian decided that the better thing to do was just remain invisible. Well, I laid into him – lightly – about how we had supported him when he was gloomy back in the early days, and then I just dissolved into a few minutes quiet weeping – will we EVER get out? I can't say I'm ashamed of myself, but I feel a bit wet (literally and figuratively).

Football tonight – Argentina versus Bulgaria, a dress rehearsal for the World Cup.

Late this evening another journalist was brought in. An Argentine named Manuelo, a freelance for a magazine called *Norde*, published in Chaco province. He was picked up for writing the name of the military governor of Tierra del Fuego, and for making some not-totally complimentary remarks about the police. He'll probably only stay in for a day. The irony is – and Cal will appreciate this – he was the journalist who asked all the really tough questions at the press conference on the day we were slung in clink after the judge ruled there was a case to answer. But he's a nice, cheerful chap, who is as certain as we need that this will all be over for us just as soon as the political difficulties are sorted out. He speaks French, which I can understand fairly well. He says the total complement on the *General Belgrano* was 1042, and that 800 have been picked up. John Nott says 20 are missing from HMS *Sheffield*. Adding the crew of the patrol boat sunk, and the crew of the three (?) aircraft shot down, that suggests casualties of about 275 already – a heavy toll. Someone pointed out that at this rate of attrition it will be the most costly naval battle ever; soon the total dead will exceed the number of people on the Falklands, who we are fighting for. Or are we fighting for a principle? The *Daily Mirror* editorial today, by the way, was most eloquent.

The BA football field's centre that we see on television is dominated by an advertising sign saying 'Thompson and Williams' – who says links with Britain won't endure? When all this business is over the two countries will resume their intimacy without a moment's hesitation.

I find I care much less about the book now. Freedom seems a million times more worthwhile than an advance from Corgi!

What a dreadful predicament and what a saga – one minute a brilliantly vivid Panorama interview and the next you're under arrest. I'm glad to hear you're in good spirits and I just hope you get back to (currently cold, grey, rainy) England very soon. What started as a rather bizarre game of diplomacy – admirals in the studio with toy boats and submarines zooming around relief models of the area – is obviously turning very sour. On verra. Good Luck. . . .

   With love, Cathy [Collis]

THURSDAY 6 MAY Up at 07.30 – later, because (I think) last night's football match reverie went on very late. The score, by the way, was 2–1 to Argentina. I've cheered up a lot today, Ian is very down, although as I write this (lunchtime) he has cheered considerably.

Diplomacy continues, and no more military action, thank goodness. Mrs Thatcher says no cease-fire until a pledge of withdrawal; Argentina says no withdrawal until guarantees on sovereignty. A pretty wide gap to bridge. But Costa Méndez is going to New York as soon as the Security Council meets (it is due to meet either later today or tomorrow), and on balance things look a little better.

We had our English books back today – temporarily – so we could sort them out according to their owners. It was wretched: it seems the pettiest of things to have done to us, to forbid us to read in our own language. I still have one book and a *MG Weekly*, its crossword proving irritatingly intractable. Ian and I wondering just what our papers are doing. My guess is – not much. They must realize that since the loss of the *General Belgrano* the mood will have changed. They'll have spoken to Isabel and, perhaps, to Willy, so they'll have a fair picture. They'll know, for example, that travel down here is impossible, and that it's not possible for anyone to talk to us. So they'll have drawn some conclusions, which will be broadly the same as ours – that until there's some resolution of the crisis, our position remains fairly grim. Yesterday that made me gloomy; now, I'm quite accustomed to it. It's the new body blows that hurt, and which take time to assimilate.

Not particularly encouraging diplomatically. At about 19.00 we learned that Argentina had rejected the so-called 'Peruvian Plan', which was just the Haig plan with another name – withdrawal, international administration followed by talks on sovereignty. Obviously the Galtieri regime would turn it down – they're not going to withdraw their troops unless they get guarantees about sovereignty – my own feeling is that the British should offer guarantees, at least under the table. But then what would the Argentines be able to sell to their people? How would you assuage Argentine pride? Anyhow, the plan has gone down the drain: Pym said it was a shame, because a cease-fire could have been in force by noon Friday. But in fact we all knew that the 'Peruvian Plan' had been rejected by Buenos Aires last Sunday, and the fact that two senior military men had gone to Lima on Monday (?) was regarded with far too much optimism by the British. Now there's only one plan left to go: the 'secret' United Nations plan which Pérez de Cuellar has suggested. Both Britain and Argentina have said they will take a positive attitude to his offer to be a mediator, so possibly something will emerge. But the cell consensus is dubious – the positions seem so far apart, and the political leadership in London and Buenos Aires so intractable, that more killing seems in order. What if the British re-take just one of the Falkland Islands – West Falkland, say? Could they use it as a bargaining chip? My feeling is that these Israeli-built Mirage fighters are proving themselves so effective – the film of the missile attack on the *Sheffield* was quite extraordinary, apparently – that Britain will have to consider bombing the coastal airfields to stop the attacks. And that could mean full scale war between the two sides, with ghastly consequences for us all. We were put to bed, lights out, at 22.30 by 'Hot Lips', as we call one of the sterner guards.[1] '*Silencio*', he said – but in fact we chatted on, like schoolboys, until after midnight

FRIDAY 7 MAY   Up at 06.00, on the dot, full of trepidation about the Pérez de Cuellar plan. Kissinger spoke out against Britain's action – we laugh at the possibility that this was his way of securing our release!

Then at noonish we learned that the British were stepping up the pressure even more: the total exclusion zone was to be extended to

1 A great zombie of a guard whose lips were unusually disgorged. We named him after the nurse played by Loretta Swit in *MASH*.

within 12 nautical miles of the Argentine coast – still more depression. Then I lost 4 games of ping-pong on the trot, and a game of chess against the computer on level one! I just cannot do well at competitive sport – what deep-seated problem does that relate to, I wonder.

Then, at 16.00, a series of events which totally lifted our mood. Wonderful.

First, the ANSA (?) photographer, Villa-Lobos (any relation, I wonder) and the curly-haired reporter arrived to see us. We were shown to Barrozo's office – great fear that we were being sent elsewhere – to find Barrozo, Grieco – in his khaki uniform – and the two journalists. We were given whisky (we were reluctant at first) and told all sorts of things. First, Barrozo explained that our loss of privileges had nothing to do with the charges levelled against us – it was totally to do with the sinking of the *General Belgrano*. (Grieco said she was hit in the boilers, and two decks above, a sailors' mess and the officers' mess, burst into flames, which is why so many of the injured had been burned. Grieco himself had been involved in the rescue, and two boats had come to Ushuaia with survivors. One had died in hospital here. They talked of huge waves, freezing weather during the operation which Grieco said, was very efficiently organized.) The interview was long and friendly – their last, under the headline '*We are only journalists*' appeared in 105 newspapers, they said. In the middle of the chat we were told that a representative of the Swiss Embassy had come to see us. Terrific news! We hurried through the rest of the interview and pictures, and then the Swiss, a lovely little man named Werner Ballmer came in. He was allowed to stay and talk for as long as he wanted, in a private room. He couldn't have been nicer, and a greater comfort. He had seen the judge (and he had had a terrible, two-day journey down to see us, through Chile, down to Punta Arenas, then by road, in thick fog and rain, slippy roads, across the Magellan Straits to Rio Grande and Ushuaia) after a quick shower and shave, and then spent at least an hour with us. Mr Pym had apparently written a personal letter to the Swiss Foreign Minister asking for all possible help to be given, so Ballmer, after arriving in Buenos Aires to be one of two in the British Interests Section of the Swiss Embassy, left to come down here. Marvellous of Pym, of the

Swiss in general, and of Werner Ballmer. He asked about our conditions – which we were frank about – and then asked for a shopping list. (Barrozo by the way, had said we could give him lists of anything we needed, and we would in addition be escorted to shops to buy clothes and suchlike.)

So we told Werner of our impending shortages – loo paper, razors, toothpaste, underpants – and he promised to bring them. (And, being Swiss, the first thing he offered was chocolate!) He was keen for us not to get our hopes up, but said he felt our case would improve markedly as soon as the political situation did. He left, promising to see the judge with requests for our books each in English, access to family and so on, and he will be back tomorrow. We can also write home, and he will take the letters back with him. He's off to Bern on Wednesday, and can take the letters then.

Well, next – a telephone call. '*Dos minutos*', said Barrozo. It was Elaine Davenport, Paul Eddy's wife, ringing from the paper! First she floored me by saying they had heard rumours of our impending release! A stumer[1] methinks. But then she gave me news, and I gave her lots, telling her about our change of conditions, the visit of Werner, etc. Clearly – although it didn't occur to me at the time – she was doing a story on us for the paper – an Exclusive for us this week. I was in fact allowed to speak for ten minutes (Barrozo kept putting his finger to his lips – 'Don't tell anyone I let you use the phone!') before the chief said I had to get off the line. Lots of efforts on our behalf. My name in *Private Eye*, about a book deal! Elaine said she'd call home – and Margaret and Hilary too, bless her.

Then – it gets better – I had another phone call, this time from Villa-Lobos, to ask 'Did the authorities tell you what to say to us?' To which I replied no, of course. It was good of them to ask.

Finally, Tony had a letter from his former wife, Frances, in Alton, Hants, with letters from his children. Lord Snowdon has been broadcasting about us apparently.

At the moment we are having an animated conversation with three of the prisoners – our colloquial Spanish really is coming on. I'm explaining the English rabies laws to 'Jack Nicholson', who wants to export 2 greyhounds to London!

1 A Fleet Street term meaning a wild invention.

SATURDAY 8 MAY   Up at 06.45, guards reasonably cheerful. I was writing letters until 01.00, then finished them off this morning while we waited for Werner. We swept our cell out and tidied up, and then wrote a semi-formal private 'report' for the Swiss. Werner came at 11.00, loaded with goodies – including, for me, a pair of blue check ladies' underpants! He had meant to bring two pairs of men's, but one of them turned out to be tiny and obviously constructed for a woman! But he's coming back tonight or tomorrow, so we can exchange. He is an incredibly nice and friendly and genuinely kind man, always doing his best to please. I wonder if he's done this sort of thing before? He was explaining the strict neutrality of the Swiss in matters like this: he was under great pressure to do a favour (unspecified) for the Governor of Tierra del Fuego, but didn't want to for just the reasons that he didn't want to be photographed with the two Argentine journalists yesterday. He is scrupulously fair without being in the slightest bit pedantic about it, and we are – as we told him to his face and in person, extremely grateful for all efforts. Captain Grieco came in at 11.45 and showed Werner our cells, the loos, etc. – and I think there may be some improvement. He was astonished we had no facilities for exercise at all – in Swiss military prisons, he said, you have to give a prisoner half an hour of exercise daily after four days. The only bad thing he brought for us were 100 Gitanes for Tony: this cell begins to smell like a French brothel!

Captain Grieco was very depressed (although friendly to us) and said he had no sleep last night. He was deeply dismayed by the extension of the total exclusion zone to 12 miles off the Argentine coast, and said that last night coastal radar showed British vessels very close to the limit, and it was only on the direct orders of BA that Super Entendards with their Exocets (like the one that destroyed HMS *Sheffield*) were not sent out. The Royal Navy will never know how close they came! Grieco thinks Mrs Thatcher is lunatic and thinks it will take years for the relations of ordinary Argentines and Britons living here to be brought back to normal, and this depressed him deeply. He said: 'Your government just does not undestand that the Argentines will NEVER give up the Malvinas now! Every last Argentine will die for the cause of keeping what is rightfully ours'. And on the question of the extension of the exclusion zone, he was very angry. 'We are not wild animals. we are not NIGGERS. We are not people who can be pushed around. It is monstrous for us to have to obey a British rule like this – who do they think they are?' He thinks – as we do – that the situation will get still worse. The Harriers with their improved Sidewinders have apparently reached Ascension, so the battle lines are shaping up. Our position, though, is rather better, methinks.[1]

22.50 Werner came back this evening, reporting great success in his conversation with the judge. We can get one phone call a week from our wives – Tuesday, Thursday and Sunday, we think. We can have our English books back. We can shop. He brought me (from Jane) a Sony Walkman 1, razor blades (he cut his finger on one), soap, coffee, chocolates. Two Christmases in one day! He said we could not go outside for exercise, which is a bit of a blow; we can send and receive letters – so all told, better news on the practical front. But Ian sees it as institutionalizing our position here, and he's been suffering the same kind of depressing worries about 'will we EVER get out of here?' that I suffered earlier in the week.

Negotiations drag on in New York. Argentine television is on all night, with a 24 hour long 'crisisathon' (as it would be called in America I imagine), presenting live news from New York and all over on the progress of the talks. War, Ian and I feel, is but an inch away, and we are crossing our fingers that, if it happens, it will be brief. We fear – and Grieco fears, too – a great loss of life. How terrible that governments get their young men to die for their arguments – you can be sure Thatcher and Pym, Galtieri and Costa Méndez, will live to tell the tale of this crisis. A lot of younger people won't. Adjourning now for the 23.00 (02.00) BBC news.

Bath

Dear Mrs Winchester,

You don't know me, but I heard of the difficulty you are having trying to get through to your husband in detention in Ushuaia. I want to assure you that it won't have anything to do with your husband's circumstances. For years the telephone system in the Argentine has been very inadequate. *There is only one thing to do.* Keep on dialling *without ceasing. You will get all sorts of noises, engaged sounds, and a woman's recorded voice*

1 In prison: we felt that we were in a more secure position than we had been.

saying 'you have the wrong number, please check and try again'!

Take no notice. Just keep on dialling (30 or 60 times is sometimes necessary). Get friends to help you. On other occasions one gets through straight away! (Perhaps it is when someone else has given up). I am convinced one must never stop dialling, for someone else will get on to one of the few lines there are.

I phone to relations weekly, and find Sunday, and between sunset and midnight best during the week. Have the authorities told you to ring at any particular time? There must be someone always on duty. Try dialling during 9, 10 or 11 p.m. (which is after office hours) when the lines are not so congested. No doubt if you have been given the number for Ushuaia, and that of the 'prison', you can dial straight through after the code for Argentina (= 010541). This is nothing less than what the operator in London's 'International calls' will be doing anyway.

I write in haste hoping to catch the Saturday post to you. I was in Ushuaia in April '80 and would be very glad if I could help you in any way if you would care to telephone me.

Yours sincerely E. Joyce Cassels Mrs

P.S.   Do you have Spanish speaking friends to ask (once you do get through) for Señor Winchester, or one of the others with him to be allowed to speak to you? If you have children the Argentines will be all the more helpful in enabling them to speak to their father.

New Delhi

(To the Minister of Justice, Argentina)
Your Excellency
Viva La Argentina!

In India we are fully aware of what is happening in Malvinas. Your Ambassador in India H.E. Dr. Escalante who is highly respected and is a great friend of India is doing a great work. He is working very hard and conveying to our people the rightful stand taken by your brave people.

We in India are fully aware of British Imperialists. We suffered under them for hundreds of years. They divided our country as a parting gift. We are still paying the price for this. We appreciate and understand your feelings. We had the same problem in our country – Portuguese enclaves of Goa, Daman and Diu – we could solve it only by action and not by negotiations. We support your cause. We wish you a great success in your fight for your rights.

While expressing these feelings which are heartfelt and sincere I am pained to read about detention of my friend Mr Simon B Winchester. I have known Simon for many a years. He was correspondent for the Guardian *in New Delhi. I know him as a friend, as a journalist and human being. He values ideals of liberty and democracy. He is a man with a great soul, dedicated to his profession – journalism, a good husband to his wife and loving father to his children. I pray to you, Your Excellency, to release this fellow human being and end the agony of his wife Judy and children.*

I pray for your success and happiness of people in Argentina! Jai Hind. (Viva la Inde!)

Yours very friendly,
Gobind T. Shahani
Assistant General Manager, Bank of Tokyo Ltd.

SUNDAY 9 MAY   This is turning out to be a tedious day – as Sundays in prison must perforce be, I suppose. The guards woke us at 09.30, though, which was charitable of them. The so-called 'crisisathon' was not shown continuously on the Ushuaia TV station, for some reason or other. There was a film which Tony watched for a while, and then everyone went to bed. I lay in the dark listening to the music from *Chariots of Fire* until about 01.30. Araucaria crossword is proving very tricky indeed. I did one of his in about 45 minutes the other day, but this one (in the *MGW* of 4 April) is awful: one clue which was good was: 'Return the cap and apply a thin solution of turpentine' which was *terebinth* (Beret back + anagram of thin = turps).

The news is fair to middling. The British have attacked Darwin and Port Stanley again, prompting the Junta announcements to talk of invasion, and prompting both Nott and Pym to issue denials in London (on Weekend World) and in Belgium (where Pym addressed a generally sympathetic meeting of the EEC Council of Ministers at Liège – I remember when Judy and I stayed at the Holiday Inn there, when I was doing the Mosel wine story – a much nicer kind of story altogether!) But although Señor Ros, the Argentine Deputy Foreign Minister, has complained, he said the talks with Pérez de Cuellar would still go on. That's a blessed relief, because it is crystal clear that if these 'make or break' talks do fail,

85

military action is both inevitable and immediate. We ought to know by tonight I imagine, and the tension is still very high. 'Jack Nicholson' looked sick as a parrot this morning after hearing the Junta's announcement that Britain had begun its invasion, but mainly, it turned out, because he was afraid that the Ushuaia Airport would be bombed, and that the prison might be hit. I assured him that in the unlikely event of an attack, British pilots were well trained, and would not, in any case, strike at a prison that held three British journalists! He seemed convinced by this somewhat unconvincing explanation, and has been cheerful ever since.

I wrote additional letters to the children and to my parents. One day I'll get a letter from them, maybe. Although in a way I hope not, because that will imply a long stay here. I'm afraid in my letter to the children I offered some details of what was probable at our Heathrow arrival – I told them no blatant display of emotion in front of the TV cameras! A little arrogant to suppose there'll be any interest at all – but looking at this in a strictly journalistic light, there's bound to be. Anyway, writing it must have encouraged the children a little, I imagine. It certainly helped me. Page 69 – what a nice number!

Werner came back at 19.30, quite stroppy (though not with us). The guards wouldn't let him visit us, and he had to insist – Vienna Convention, or whatever – on access to us. The little, curly haired guard had, so Werner said, been very rude to him, but Werner was taking none of it, insisting that we insist on our rights. He said that if we do not get the various things that have been promised the Swiss could make a formal diplomatic protest to Argentina, which they would not like. W said he had passed details of the new telephone arrangements on to Paul Eddy, who called him this morning (and passed on his regards, those of the paper – bless them! – and families.) We shall, if the system works, talk first to one of the three on Tuesday night. Werner was on Ushuaia television late this evening, but the guards came in the middle of it and hurried everyone off to bed. Why, I'm not sure – I can't think that Werner would have said anything in the slightest bit incautious or undiplomatic. He is the perfect example of a diplomat's diplomat.

Bed, then, at 23.00, and a hilarious game of Twenty Questions until about 00.45.

What I have seen of spring this year, I saw in Oxford, that day I spent with Judy and the children. There it seemed as though summer was to be the result of some natural logical progression. Here in Brooklyn the norm has become what I used to think of as an English spring. The skies are leaden. The temperature is fickle. And rain is intermittent. Connie and I have just returned from a walk through the neighborhood. Not much to report, except that the bar where you announced you would be happy until 3 a.m. on any given evening is still flourishing and awaits only you for it to be as it was the night we sat at the end of the bar and watched a bartender actually crush ice without a machine. In the United States that doesn't seem to happen very often . . .

Cheers, Matthew [Stevenson]

Oxford

. . . I think about you quite a lot – how courage and determination to make the most of the situation must be stretched to the limits by the cramped surroundings and the constant proximity of your fellow prisoners – how bravery and philosophy must be constantly undermined by childlike waves of frustration & despair. I think I told you that my exhibition in London in October will be about all the work based on my work in prisons & mental hospital. I have thought a lot about the problems of living within contained conditions – be they physical or mental and can only wish you courage to be able to cope. . . .

I got up at 4.30 & went down to Magdalen bridge, which was packed with students. The early morning light was beautiful and the dawn chorus was starting. We could vaguely see tiny boys up on the tower & waited expectantly for the 'heavenly voices' of the choristers. The long wait was punctuated by the usual undergraduate paraphernalia – one carried aloft on the shoulders of a friend exhorting us to vote now for our next prime minister – 'a blue hot-water-bottle' (which he was carrying) & also to BOMB KENT!! – (the reasons being vague). The strange masks of the Morris dancers moving slowly through the crowds with their silent pagan smiles. Suddenly, an enormous peal of bells rang out repeated three times from Magdalen Tower & we realised that in the furore at the base of the tower no one had heard the fluting trebles of the choristers. (I believe those sensible people who had stayed at home heard it all quite clearly on Radio Oxford.) I wandered up the High St, listening to the jazz & rock bands &

ended up in the Emperor's Wine Bar (opposite Balliol) looking out of the top window straight onto a dancing group of students – one dressed as a bee, one as a fairy (with a green face) one wearing two black plastic bags & one as a golliwog. – They danced furiously for hours to a trad. jazz band & then collapsed on the pavement. I then went to two strawberry & champagne parties & a bacon & egg party & then collapsed into bed exhausted. – So ended May Day 1982.

I had an interesting meeting with Andrew Motion, whose poem 'One Life' I am hoping to set – I've done the drawing of 'papilio dardanus' having tracked it down in the dusty attics of the University Museum – range upon range of Victorian collectors boxes smelling of mothballs & labelled in that faded black-brown ink. I subsequently went to a poetry reading given by Andrew, James Fenton, John Fuller & Craig Raine. Andrew Motion had been to the printing workshop earlier and we'd talked about the poem. James Fenton read a new poem which was lovely, and light & entertaining & made people laugh – it was a good opener. I'll send it to you when its published. I drew all the poets in my sketch book . . .

One terrible twist to the landlady saga was that while in this position of being dependent on taking in students in order to pay the bills, I discovered to my horror that I had rats in the cellar! I was greyfaced with anxiety at the thought of having to explain to 'Nelly' (my incredibly glamorous French student) the situation with the rats & spent hours trying to discover if I could smuggle the Ratman in while she was at a lecture. It proved to be quite impossible so, prepared for the worst i.e. all my students packing their bags & rushing out in horror, I finally broached the fact, tentatively, that I thought we had a mouse – or even a rat – & I would have to get the environmental officer in to investigate. I looked up to see Nelly, her eyes misted over in affectionate nostalgia 'Raaats', she cooed in a soft French drawl, 'I love rats. We had rats in our house when I was a little girl and my brother & I used to play with the rats.' – Suddenly I felt I should apologise for being such a sadist as to be planning their demise, but I was so relieved that I felt like bursting into hysterical laughter.

–I hope this letter reaches you.

from Helen [Ganley]

MONDAY 10 MAY Woken at 07.30 – a pleasant change. I up-braided Ian, rather harshly I felt, for his over-cautious attitude to the Walkman demo tape which, ironically, had the sound effects of Harriers at Farnborough. Ullman was playing it very loudly, and Ian was worried that it might be used as evidence against us. So I got it back from Ullman, and snapped it in half.

Instant coffee, instant milk today at breakfast – a great luxury.

At 10.00 – exactly; so I didn't hear the 13.00 BBC news – Werner came for what is likely to be his last visit. He brought table tennis bats and balls, and chocolate – Cadbury's. He cleared up one or two points – he had made good friends with the man from last night; he expects that the first of the phone calls will come through tomorrow, so I'll try and pen a note to Barrozo warning him that a call may come through. As of this moment – 13.45 – we've not heard the BBC yet – interference is very severe, and there is a ship in harbour that emits a radar pulse. Later, I expect. The weather today is overcast and autumnal; wonder what it is like back home. Did I enter that Paul Eddy rang Werner yesterday? It is really good of the paper to take such a continuing interest. Werner who has served in New Zealand, Morocco, China and Cuba, and is now in Bern doing personal work, says he will be coming to England on holiday this year, and hopes to see us there. When he left I had the genuine feeling that he really cares about us, and will be thinking of us personally, as well as officially.

He says the Swiss are already making arrangements for the South Georgia prisoners to be given back to Argentina, under strict orders that they must not be returned to military service for a specific period. The details are being worked out now – they may have to be exchanged in a neutral third country, which would be logistically difficult for them. If they went to Switzerland, say, it would mean a journey of about 20,000 miles from South Georgia to Geneva and then to Buenos Aires. Better than being a prisoner, I guess. Werner made it rather clear that in strictly legal terms we can't be swapped for genuine POW's, as we have to face a legal process. But un-uniformed spies on the *Narwhal*, the surveillance trawler captured in the exclusion zone yesterday – that might be another matter.

Werner mentioned that Sagastume seemed a fair and honourable man, and that the intention at the moment was for us to be sentenced – if guilty – to a two-year suspended prison sentence. To me it is ridiculous to think that, in purely legal terms, there's a chance of being found guilty: but a suspended sentence is better than a real prison term, I suppose. Werner also said the judge assured him we could be freed on bail if the situation calmed down. But would we stay in Ushuaia, or BA – or be allowed to return to London? So far, that's unclear. But being freed on bail to go to the UK – that would put us in a very peculiar limbo-like situation. We all agree that, as of this moment, we would return to prove our innocence, though the political mood of Argentina might be a factor in any decision. But as we are innocent, I'd like the record to show that. Pride, for one thing; and a desire to return to Argentina one day, for another.

Grieco came by while I was doing my mile walk and brought a telegram from Antonia, of all people. ('Thoughts of colleagues with you, love Antonia') How kind of her to remember. It's difficult to see when it was sent – the number before 'Londres' is '294' – surely it couldn't have been sent 11 days ago? I must remember to check with her. Sansul, I see from my diary, has been gone nearly 11 days: it seems like only yesterday he was here. Grieco was gloomy: he said the British were delaying the UN talks so that the second part of the task force could get down to the Falklands. But if so, why are the Argentines still negotiating?

(Pardon the writing: I'm in bed – 22.50 – and lying on my back.)

The news is frustrating: Anthony Parsons says that the next 24 – 48 hours will get to 'the heart of the matter', but he has no idea whether the Argentine Deputy Foreign Minister, Enrique Ros, really has the authority to negotiate, or whether the Junta will say no to anything that in any way tampers with sovereignty. Pym, talking to the House of Commons Select Committee on Foreign Affairs, said that Britain was fairly relaxed about the sovereignty question.

At 19.40 we were all herded into the corridor while our rooms were searched. We thought the radios, our diaries, the brandy (Cal's farewell present) would all go. But in fact they didn't touch our room – they were looking for money possibly stolen by the little waiter. He is terrified, and sent us a pathetic little note begging us to 'save him' by saying we gave him $27. He's only got 6 days to go before he's released (a robbery charge, it seems) and is frantic with worry that he may not make it.

TUESDAY 11 MAY Woken at 06.45 (although a very noisy drunk was brought in at about 01.00) and lay warm and snug in bed until 08.45. Ian as usual got up feeling fairly chirpy, but declined rapidly thereafter – blood sugar level falling off, I guess. I did exercises after making my bed: knee bends, a few press-ups (killers) and those exercises where you twiddle your extended arms in gradually nearing circles. Writing this listening to a borrowed cassette of 'the squeaking Greek' – isn't that what they call Demis Roussos? Ian is trying to get a transformer for his Sony radio to conserve batteries: I don't see the point, so long as batteries are freely available, but he seems keen. Nothing much on the early morning Argentine news. I guess it's just talk, talk, talk in New York. All our fates are in their hands, I suppose. I broke a cup this morning; hope it doesn't bode ill.

A busy – and therefore pleasantly diverting – afternoon. At lunch time the two men from *Siete Días* (the one which wrote the ludicrous story about a transmitter, etc.) came by to interview us. First I gave Barrozo a note I had painstakingly written, asking for the guards to prepare for a telephone call; then we asked for our books back (we got all those that had not been given away: *Eye of the Needle*, *Gaudy Night*, *Merchants of Grain* and a book called *The Greek Treasure* by Irving Stone). Then after lunch we wrote an article for *Siete Días* – usual sort of things, plus sympathy for the *Belgrano* sinking, etc. At 16.00 we went back to Barrozo, who was with George, the faithful interpreter – Barrozo asked us to write, rather than type, the article – for our own protection. Then back came the two *Siete Días* men: we told them – the reporter was really slimy – why we were angry at their first report; and they took the article, translated it into Spanish so the Comisario could hear – he liked it very much. Photos etc., then they went to drive to Rio Grande. Next, George de'Ath and his interpreter (South African Radio) came by with apples and chocolates – very kind of them. They say that the mood of the hacks outside is both incredulous and sympathetic – they've just woken up to the fact that, as George said 'You're really in gaol – they're not playing with you . . .' Everyone is very sorry for us, it seems. Now – will we get a telephone call? This is the next crucial test – but even if not, we can wait for Thursday and Sunday. Time goes past quite quickly now we are in a routine (although today's has been pretty severely interrupted), although it seems much faster in retrospect than at the time.

22.06 YES! A call did come through from Judy, at 20.06 – right on time. Perfect line. Fifteen splendid minutes. She and the children are all fine, though Rupert is taking it all rather badly – nightmares, etc. If he has been so badly affected, maybe he feels closer to me than I once thought. Perhaps when I get home he'll be the one who is most affectionate and pleased to see me. Maybe, in other words, we'll grow closer, and that's no bad thing. *Eh bien* – complicated world. Judy sounded splendid. Biggles ate weedkiller in the car, staggered about, had to be rushed to the vet and pumped out and have a drip put on him overnight. But he is fine now, except he has bandages on both front legs, as though he'd made a suicide attempt. Judy said she had 'stood the American mortgage company on its head', whatever that might mean. Apparently some problems from that quarter, but not to worry, she says. Also there was a bitchy piece in *Private Eye* saying that Frank Giles was all set to fire me because I had gone to the Falklands without permission and hadn't filed for the *Sunday Times* at all! What nonsense. Simon Hoggart apparently had told Ingrams that it's quite untrue (as I trust it is). I asked her to ask Frank to try and send a telegram to say it isn't so, because it is worrying – although it isn't really because I know it is untrue. Judy says the Director-General of UNESCO has asked the Argentine Government for our release, and the Government in BA says it is reviewing our case. So that's something. Judy also said the UN 'at a very high level' are involved. RTE[1] has apparently been extraordinarily energetic, and only today Inder Malhotra was in touch from India. Looking at the three of us in this grim little room, it is difficult to imagine we are the focus of such great international interest. A great fillip for all of us, and even now, 22.25, we're all talking about Judy's call.

In the Falklands a British ship destroyed an Argentine tanker in the Strait between the two islands: it blew up as it was running away

---

1 Radio Telefis Eireann – Irish state broadcasting organisation, with which I had a long and friendly association.

– a great fireball indicated it was probably fuel oil or petrol. Very courageous men, taking a tanker through the British blockade – 'They could have been saved if they had surrendered' said the Task Force Commander, and warned Argentine ships not to run away.

WEDNESDAY 12 MAY   Today is Tierra del Fuego Police Day, and we were allowed two extra hours in bed as a privilege! It was very pleasant and in fact I lay in bed until nearly eleven, reading *Gaudy Night*. I wrote a note to Barrozo, thanking him for last night's telephone call and warning him of the next call on Thursday. We're all still very high on last night's call, and expect to be able to tell Werner – who ought to ring today – that his arrangements worked out perfectly.

A generally slow day, with nothing of interest – not compared with yesterday's hi-jinks. From BA we heard of the travails of other hacks. Julian Manyon and two technicians from Thames TV were picked up outside the Foreign Ministry – abducted, just like the Bad Old Days in Argentina. They were found six hours later, stark naked, in a village 30 km outside BA. They had been robbed of everything – cameras, money, etc. It sounded quite terrifying, though a great tale to tell in years to come. Two *Newsweek* men had similar troubles, and two Norwegians were thrown out of the country. Someone else had a problem as he was trying to get out to Montevideo, but I didn't get his name or exactly what his trouble was.

Line-up brought by a guard who made us shout out our number in Spanish. I stumbled over '10' — (*dias*); Ian said '*diez et uno*' (for eleven), and Tony, best of all, should have said the Spanish for twelve, but instead said 'Fuck Knows!' The whole process ground to an immediate halt! Everyone collapsed with laughter.

No word from Werner, but I did have a telegram from the wonderful Isabel in BA, commiserating on the first month of detention (how many more?) and promising much was being done on our behalf, not to feel abandoned.

In NYC the talks continue. Pym, in London, spoke of progress; Enrique Ros of a 'very important day'; and Pérez de Cuellar of 'progress – hope to have this stage of talks over by the weekend'. But BBC correspondents are not reporting great optimism.

The interview with Werner was shown on *Realidad '82*, the

93

lunchtime nationwide television programme. We have noticed that nearly all the guards go out of their way to be friendly. One came and had a long chat with us, which Ian and I were able to follow in considerable detail. Our Spanish is coming along pretty well, though Hugh (who is back, apparently, in BA) would doubtless pour scorn on it.

The British used Seahawk to shoot down two Argentine Sky-hawks (the BBC says they have 60 inland, 15 on the aircraft carrier). The British lost a Sea King, which went down in the sea, but of its own accord, it seems. The crew were all saved. Argentine TV is giving graphic illustrations of what the citizenry should do in the case of a bombing attack – it upset 'Jack Nicholson', who, I think, is actually very scared that this prison will be bombed.

Three inmates – one woman and two of our colleagues, including 'the ferret',[1] went to BA for psychoanalysis. A long way, especially as they have to come back again.

It is getting quite crisp and cold outside, from the air one feels during the BBC broadcasts.[2] There was a stiff Westerly blowing today, and there were lots of white horses in the Beagle Channel: it must be awful out in the Atlantic proper. The BBC defence corr., by the way, said that the Skyhawks had been trying to attack *Broadsword* or *Brilliant*, both about 30 miles west of the Falklands. This indicates a probable plan of the British – to move on West Falkland first, and then to stop and call for negotiations again (this is presuming of course, that Pérez de Cuellar's proposals fail, which at this stage looks a little unlikely, we hope). The *QE2* apparently left Southampton today, with 2000 troops aboard. Her 'luxury fittings' are swathed in khaki, and her outside-swimming pools have been decked over for helicopters (a lot of helicopter activity here today, by the way). She should reach the South Atlantic in ten days. Argentina has warned that any vessels bound for or connected with the Task Force are liable to attack – imagine what would happen if the *QE2* were to be sunk by an Argentine submarine!

1 A tiny prisoner, always friendly, who darted in and out of other cells, perpetually inquisitive, and clearly quite mad.
2 When we listened to the BBC we stood and poked the aerial through a hole in the window. We thus got , for a precious few minutes, a taste of the outside air.

THURSDAY 13 MAY   Nothing today – slow and steady, as we wait for the New York negotiations to produce something. Pym, in the House, spoke of 'the most difficult stage' of the debate; and in Buenos Aires General Galtieri, speaking to Julian Manyon and his crew – they had been stripped naked by robbers yesterday, and Galtieri went along to apologize – said that Argentina 'could sit down with Britain and discuss our ultimate intention, of sovereignty over the Malvinas . . .' It sounded the first indication of Argentine flexibility we have heard so far – quite unlike Costa Méndez, who trotted out the usual formula of the Malvinas 'now, tomorrow and always Argentine . . .' So perhaps there is some room, after all. No news from the Front, except that the Royal Navy now talks of three Skyhawks being shot down in yesterday's actions. Only 80 to go!

Late last night the Federal judge, Sagastume, was on television, and there was a rush of prisoners (well, Jack Nicholson, actually, and Humbert this morning) to say *'Buenas noticias para usted!'* It seems that the Cámara Federal – not exactly clear what that is – has been approached about our case. There were indications, though based on what I'm not clear – that we could be freed before long. Nothing is fixed or clear, but it looks as though some of the external pressure is having its effect.

17.04 – the 20.00 BBC news seems better. Mr Pym spoke of the way in which British military pressure was making it more difficult and costly for Argentina to maintain her grip on the Falklands; Mrs Thatcher said that there now appeared a genuine desire for accommodation with the British, and, perhaps most heartening of all, General Galtieri told Julian Manyon *et al* – to whom he apologized for their having been roughed up in BA yesterday – that he wanted an honourable settlement with Britain, and that talks about the long-term future of the islands would be acceptable. But the Argentine flag would always fly on the island, he said. The developments may, of course, come to nowt, but they look fascinating. I'd love to be in the Foreign Office or at the UN, and know exactly what went on.

23.15. Well, Ian didn't get his call after all. It was awful for him – and I imagine for Margaret, too – when the minutes ticked away. Did she try, and get a busy circuit? Did the policeman on duty refuse to take the call? Was the phone busy? Whatever, it was a disappointment for us all, but particularly for Ian. We'll compose a note to Barrozo tomorrow – that'll take up more time, too – and ask what happened. Will she have the nous to call tomorrow? The next scheduled call is Sunday, and it would be only fair if Margaret were allowed to call then. If all goes well it should be Hilary next Tuesday, and Judy in a week's time.

Also, we had a much better translation of the judge's remarks on TV last night, and it was far less optimistic than Jack Nicholson reported. The judge simply said that the papers were at the court in Comodoro Rivadavia – that is where the *Cámara Federal* is, and that our appeal for bail would be decided in the next couple of weeks. But it does seem apparent that the judge, in common with everyone else, thinks that we can be disposed of quickly once the situation at sea is better.

On that score, John Nott was in a belligerent mood in the House today (the 5th debate), saying the Argentine forces were 'beleaguered' in the Falklands. I guess they must be, if the 'net is closing', as Nott says it is. British air defences seem a lot better, too – I wonder if the Super Etendards will go up again and put an Exocet through *Broadsword* or *Brilliant*, the only ships equipped with Seahawk (as the BBC reports). The papers detect a split between the Pym (settle, compromise) faction, and Thatcher. The *Telegraph*, *Mail* and *Express* are predictably keen to press home our military advantage, and retake the Falklands and re-establish British administration. Reagan said an interesting thing at a White House press conference today: 'The main problem is the intransigence of one side, Argentina. They wanted guarantees of sovereignty before negotiations, and I gather there has been some progress on this point, so we can only hope and pray'. Does he know what he's saying? That's the trouble with Reagan – he speaks without thinking (though not as often, or as indecorously as Ford!) *The Times* smells a rat in the UN talks – Argentine delaying tactics, it wonders? I doubt it. The longer we wait the more troops we'll have in the area, the hungrier (for food, fuel etc) will be the garrison on the Falklands. *The Times* seems misguided. I hope so.

Dear Mrs Winchester,

I write on behalf of Oxford City Council and, I am sure, on behalf of the people of Oxford to express our deep concern at your husband's continued detention in Argentina.

With your husband's arrest, I was suddenly made aware of the discomfort, the hazards and the actual danger faced, particularly by correspondents on foreign affairs, in bringing to our attention what is happening world-wide.

As far as the Sunday Times is concerned, we read it in the comfort and safety of our Sunday morning breakfast table and, perhaps, never think at what cost this is possible.

I offer you and your family our support and sincere good wishes in what is surely an exceptionally difficult and worrying time for you.

Yours sincerely, Olive Gibbs, Lord Mayor

FRIDAY 14 MAY   Woken at 07.00 this morning by the guard I call Charlie Chaplin[1] – he was quite friendly. It's almost as though they have all had instructions to be nice to us. I stayed on in bed, while Ian – as usual – got up and bustled around. At 08.10, Werner called from his house in BA. He said he had tried in vain all yesterday – the circuits were very busy. He had in fact tried at 07.30, but had been told (erroneously) we were all asleep. Anyway – I told him about Margaret not getting through – so it was arranged that he would call Isabel or Hugh (or, he said, a cable to the FCO) and see to it that Margaret got the word that she was to call tonight and tomorrow until she gets through. Possibly, Werner said, it was the difficulty of getting lines. But it was so easy for Judy, I said, I felt it was the police. So we decided to write another note to Barrozo, explaining last night's problem, and asking for the officials on duty tonight to be prepared for the call.

Werner had managed to get out quite early – except that his '13.30' flight from here left an hour earlier, and he had a panicky time rushing for the plane. But it took him to Comodoro Rivadavia, and after a night there he got to BA next day (Tuesday?). He said he was a little upset by an article, presumably in the Sunday Times – presumably by Paul Eddy – saying that our conditions had de-

1 A very small and precise-looking guard with a Chaplinesque moustache.

teriorated: I think this must have related to the talk I had with Elaine Davenport that first day Werner came. In part, then, it was my fault, and I trust it won't do us any harm. I said to Werner 'You never can trust these journalists . . .' and he laughed. He is off to Switzerland today, so that means Judy and the children will get their letters on Monday or Tuesday. Did I mention that the letter I sent to Judy for the *Oxford Mail* had been on the front page? A rag-out of my signature, and the text of the letter below it. It is most touching, the way Oxford is taking a real interest in the case. In *Gaudy Night*, Harriet Vane and Peter Wimsey have just punted to Iffley; that made me feel most odd. But I've no doubt the intimacy that derives from living in a small town is good compensation for the distance from the metropolis. Does North London take Ian and Tony to its collective heart in the way Oxford has, seemingly, taken to me?

According to Werner, the hearing on our Comodoro Rivadavia bail appeal is, or was, due this week, and Willy is somewhere in the region. So we may see him. There's been a great deal of air traffic in and out of Ushuaia already today (it's 11.45) and so for all we know Willy may be on his way here. He has been cast in the role of Job's Comforter has old Willy, always appearing to bring us gloomy tidings.

No shower this morning: the water is absolutely scarifyingly freezing, and my face tingles with incipient frostbite even after a modest shave. But we are keeping both ourselves and our clothes clean, I'm glad to say, and apart from needing a haircut I'm looking reasonably well turned out. *Gaudy Night* is coming on fast: I really don't want it to end. So beautifully done, and of course the Oxford reminiscences are so evocative. 'The bells chiming the quarter in a tumbling cascade of friendly disagreement'. How I remember that!

Now it's 20.35, and I'm writing this as Ian has, at last, received his telephone call. How marvellous for him: he must have almost despaired, and it wasn't until 20.30 that it got through. I'll report on his mood later.

Earlier we had a nice surprise: Grieco called us in, gave us beer (with Barrozo and Grieco's son[1]) and put through a call to the Sheraton in BA so I could speak to 'an old, old friend', Jennifer Siebens. I had no idea who it was, but it turned out to be the CBS

1 An amiable boy of 20 who had been working on his car all day and smelled tantalizingly of engine oil.

'fixer' who set up the interview with Bob Schieffer. She called in Bob, and then ran down (11 flights, I think!) to get Isabel Hilton, who spoke to both me and Grieco for a few minutes and will be allowed to call back at 20.00 on Sunday. It was too rushed to talk in detail, but she did say that a lawyer-colleague of Balaban's was on his way here to see us – courtesy call, is all, I think.

There were letters and cards for Tony, and two cables for me (both sent on 10/5 – four days ago – and received on 12/5, thus taking 2 days to get across Ushuaia) one from Cal, bless him. Norine[1] was having her farewell lunch; I'll miss her like mad. And to say not to worry about the *Private Eye* piece of 'mischief regarded here with contempt and amusement . . .' Also there was a cable from John Pilger – how nice people are to send such things! I really love Fleet Street, and all hacks! Bob Schieffer was nice, too. I miss hacks, the best people there are (Judy and the children aside).

Grieco had some fascinating gossip. A British ship sunk, plus one other severely damaged. HMS *Hermes* hit by two Exocets, and Sandy Woodward – GOC Task Force – was dead, either suicide or natural causes. Also he said the number of Skyhawks downed on Monday (?) was 4, not 2 as reported by BBC (actually they said 3, 2 shot, one crashed).

Finished *Gaudy Night* – truly one of the most delightful books I've read for a long, long while. She is a total genius. Now I'm starting a Donald Zec pulp novel, *The Face*, which Angel (?) of *Noticias Argentinas*[2] lent me. He visited for 5 minutes tonight, and took away a shopping list, as we're pretty short of most things now. Supper excellent – pasta, meat, rich gravy, bread. I'm starting to like prison food, though Bob Schieffer asked 'how is your weight doing?'

The midnight news from London was less good. Sir Anthony Parsons and Nico Henderson were being recalled for consultations this weekend: Pérez de Cuellar speaks of 'difficulty in bridging the gap' though 'we're still in business'; Galtieri, on Peruvian TV, said that Argentina made some concessions, but would not concede on the sovereignty issue.

1 One of my dearest friends, a Dubliner who was the Foreign Editor's research assistant.
2 An Argentine news agency.

Ian's phone call lasted 15 minutes, and really cheered him up. All are well, pressure reported from the International Press Institute (Frank and Donald went to Madrid to get a resolution passed), the OAS (journalists!) and the American and Canadian Journalists' Association. Cal had been advising the womenfolk on how to play the publicity thing – was Judy on radio or not,[1] rather confusing. Anyway, pressure continues to build up through various respectable international bodies, so that can't be bad.

SATURDAY 15 MAY   Hot water this morning! And in great abundance too – perhaps a result of our whingeing note yesterday. So I shaved, showered, washed my head – Head and Shoulders shampoo, now – and washed my two sheets, which were getting a little grubby, to say the least. Also my tan trousers, the ones which Cal bought over a fortnight ago (it is more than a fortnight since he left – how time flies when you're having fun!)

Ian says that Hilary Rubinstein[2] has been inquiring about a book.

We got up pleasantly late again – call, and *forma* at 09.15. Then I clambered back into bed, snoozed till ten, had a cup of tea[3] and chatted. Ian is very concerned at the lack of sugar and coffee, and grumbled about running out of everything. I said I was sure George de'Ath would do some shopping. 'Eternal optimist' said Ian. 'Eternal pessimist', I said to him.

Watched *Tarzan* on the old Montgomery Ward television that's in the *comedor*. At least, half an hour of it, it really is dreadfully bad.

Almost as bad as the Donald Zec novel I'm ploughing through. It's called *The Face*, and it has a very poor attempt at imitation of the language of the Michael Herr book, *Dispatches*. It is almost embarrassing to read it – the way you feel when a really poor comic comes on TV, and you know everyone in the room is cringing. Well I got a bit of that feeling reading it alone in bed last night.

It now seems (according to the 17.00 BBC news, through extremely heavy interference – jamming?) that British forces 'recap-

1 Judy had said she had been on The World at One, or so I thought.

2 A London literary agent.

3 We had a one-bar electric fire which we laid on its back and balanced a steel water jug on the grille. After about an hour, if we managed not to kick it over, the water would be hot enough for tea.

tured' an island off the West Falkland island, that an ammo dump and several Pukara aircraft had been destroyed. I'm not sure if the raiding party stayed there or not – is it, technically, an invasion, or just a raid? Parsons and Henderson are back in London, both pouring cold water on stories of the talks breaking down. Pym promised the Scottish Tories – God, how awful and unrealistic they are – there would be no sell-out, and that Britain had not once backed down on its demand for an Argentine withdrawal. Did I mention Grieco's depression at the *QE2*'s departure? He, as a professional soldier, is faced with the realities of the situation – like losing a lot of men and ships, and seems less happy at the prospect. Who can blame him?

16.30, and the other two are sleeping like babies. Ian said he was very cold, and so the new heater was on full blast. It is like a brothel. But I've made up some more milk powder and have a jug of water on to warm up, so they'll wake up to some tea and presumably feel a lot better. How we all spend our time says something about our differences, I suppose. I read a great deal and I find I can really lose myself in the pleasure of a book – even, as with the Donald Zec monstrosity, with a bad book. I play ping-pong, even though I usually lose to Ian, it doesn't really bother me. Patience, usually for about half an hour at a stretch. Chess, I've really given up, because I cannot – thus far, at least – make my mind work in the necessary way. Ian plays a lot with the computer chess game, though he usually loses, and I think losing casts him down a great deal. He plays ping-pong and patience, too, and sleeps (like now). But he finds it very hard to read for long at a time – in fact he is finding this imprisonment, and worry about it, has made him lose his powers of concentration. Tony, good old Tony who hasn't a worry on his mind, I'm sometimes forced to think, sleeps or 'chats' – he doesn't understand a word – with the other prisoners. We learn that he spent two 28-day periods in the glasshouse during his national service, once for stealing a leg of lamb from the cookhouse! He's the most surprising photographer I've ever met on one of the 'quality' papers; but he must be good at his job, or the *Observer* wouldn't have hired him. Ian, deep down – well, perhaps not so deep – is very angry with him for 'getting us into this mess.' I'm not sure that I wasn't an equally contributory factor and so, too, was Ian himself. But in his angrier moments Ian blames Tony, and it's not too healthy. I've just been washing clothes and sheets and making milk – damn it, at times like this I quite like doing domestic chores.

21.30. Well, the BBC reports the attack on Pebble Island as having destroyed eleven Argentine aircraft, together with ammunition and radar. The commandos were helicoptered in from a cruiser. The Chilean Antarctic Survey has said it will offer a vessel to transport Argentine wounded 'if necessary' – so the Argentines are clearly worried. But Galtieri, talking to Mexican TV, says 'our casualties are 400 – but we will fight even if there are 4000 or 40,000, and not just for six or seven weeks, but six months or six years!'

Two more nice things to break up a dreadfully boring afternoon: a telegram from Pat Ferguson,[1] a playback to Ian saying 'you are on page one', but giving the additional and extremely welcome news that the *New York Times* had (today) called for our release. That, I feel sure, is most important, and we're very grateful. A letter to Abe Rosenthal[2] soon, I think. And the other nice thing was a card from Matthew Stevenson, written in Paris at the end of last month, saying he had seen the family in Oxford, all, including the dogs, were well, and that the house looks wonderful. 'I am doing what I can in New York' he says.

Bed at 00.15, after a perfectly dreadful 1960s British film about some Etruscan statue in a London museum that comes to life and does dreadful things to people. Really bad, but the limited dialogue meant that Ian and I could understand a good deal of it. We watched in the Ferret's room, they drank maté. It was cosy and warm, and a pleasant Saturday night. Back to reading the dreadful Mr Zec!

SUNDAY 16 MAY   Late lie-in. Hot-lips woke us at 09.15, but left us for another hour before coming back and chatting to us about capital punishment (none in Argentina) and police pay. He is the

---

1 The *Observer's* deputy foreign editor, would always send 'playbacks' to foreign correspondents, telling them how their story had been used in the paper that night. Playbacks are always great morale boosters.

2 Executive editor of the *New York Times*, a man I knew vaguely, and had the greatest respect for.

moodiest of the guards: he does a 12 hour shift every other day, and has been in the police force for 4 years. We finally got up at 11.30 – until then the prison had been deliciously quiet, typically Sunday. Now there are cassette recorders and radios playing, and prisoners chatting in the shafts of northern sunlight. For prison, it's quite pleasant. Today, we have three possible diversions planned – Hilary should call at 20.00, Isabel at 21.00, and a possible beer with Grieco during the afternoon. A perfect autumn day – Beagle Channel smooth and cold, clear blue sky, and the Chilean mountains touched with pink as the sun rose this morning. Just now – noon – the sun is as high as it gets (which is not very in this latitude) and so the rose colouration has gone. There's still not much snow on the peaks: they're clearly not granite, by the way – some of them are sharp, aiguilles-like, most dramatic, and probably either basic, or metamorphic rocks.

19.00 The Comisario came by in the middle of the afternoon to ask what shopping we want done – he took the list, and one of his men came by an hour or so later with the results, fruit, biscuits, chocolate, coffee, *dulce de leche* . . . very nice of him. Then we listened to the BBC news: not so good, both sides seem to be digging in hard. The Junta here is meeting tonight to work out its 'final response' to London, and Sir Anthony Parsons and Sir Nicholas Henderson are in London, where the mood (on TV, anyway) seems very bellicose. Nott on The World This Weekend (?) when asked if the Argentine flag would ever fly on the Falklands again said 'No! Never!' The Foreign Ministry issued a clarifying statement – Nott is an ass!

Then at 18.30, Isabel-of-blessed-countenance rang from BA. Her view of the South Atlantic situation is rather pessimistic, that there's got to be more fighting before talks in earnest will start. But she said that the pressure for our case is starting to take effect: Pérez de Cuellar, she said, has taken a personal interest, as has UNESCO, the IPI etc., etc. She said that Willy argued our case at the Comodoro Rivadavia court this past week, and she was wondering if the judges there might take a decision based on the pressure from outside. The court, she implied, might be the next opportunity for a 'review' of the case. Fingers crossed here!

Later, dear George arrived with a pile of books from Jane Scotti and Margarita Vásquez: all Good Works – *The Alexandria Quartet*, Katherine Anne Porter, Thomas Mann, GBS plays (which Ian and I would like to read), Saul Bellow, Aristotle, Morris West and an obscure (to me) book on Tibetan mysticism. If we're here long enough I suppose we'll get through all of them. But for now they look rather formidable.

Hilary did manage to get through at about 20.30, just the same nerve-tightening delay that Margaret had suffered on Friday. She seems fine, and had rung the others today, but as always with Tony most of the talk seemed to be taken up with sentimental guff rather than anything we wanted to know. He managed to speak for about fifteen minutes, with no problems, so it looks good for Tuesday, and Judy. Isabel is due to call on Wednesday at 20.00.

The BBC had a very dramatic report of the Pebble Island operation from Brian Hanrahan – but on a destroyer, not on HMS *Hermes*. Is *Hermes* still alright, or was there anything in what Capt. Grieco said the other day? Are the naval commanders telling the hacks all their plans, in the knowledge they can't file it? It'll be interesting to talk to the lads later. What is Max doing on the *Canberra*? Funny, I've lost all interest in doing a Falklands book just at the moment, yet I was so keen two weeks ago, wasn't I? This experience now, for me, makes the actual crisis fade into much less significance. But it'll probably swing back. Another call came for me just now, but I've no idea who it was, because the guard we call 'How Are You?' – as he says that on all possible occasions – had to radio the Comisario for his permission, and the Comisario was nowhere to be found. I wonder who it was. Could it be who I think?

(Later.) It was Willy Balabán, bless him. He says that the decision at the *Cámara Federal* in Comodoro Rivadavia will come, probably, on Friday. Was Willy optimistic or pessimistic? Fifty:fifty he said, infuriatingly. After his optimism three weeks ago I have to regard his guarded – or any other kind – of optimism with some reserve. It just means the week will be even more tense. 'I hope to see you very soon with good news . . .' he says. We daren't hope.

Terry Wogan, Hilary reports, may give us a mention on his programme tomorrow – woolly pullies by the ton, I expect!

MONDAY 17 MAY   I wonder what he said[1] – Terry Wogan, that is. While I remember, yesterday or the day before I thought I had lost my contact lens (left eye) and had a moment of panic. But just as I was reconciling myself to the loss I felt a slight discomfort in the side of the eye, poked around, and there it was. It was almost the most pleasurable thing to have happened that day.

This morning, after a latish rise – 'Hot lips' is quite a pal these days, though his moods are unpredictable; we got up at 08.30 this morning – Ian and I read GBS's *Man of Destiny* out loud, standing side by side by the bunks. Ian was Napoleon and, variously the lady and the lieutenant; I was the lieutenant, the strange lady, and her doppelganger and Giuseppe. It was great fun. There is a long speech by Napoleon where he describes the British, and the way they always (in matters of Imperialism, and everything else) manage to have morality on their side, e.g. they send a missionary in to bring Christianity to some people they wish to conquer, wait till the missionary is attacked and then send a military expedition, 'in the name of Christ' to save the missionary and, just by happy coincidence, to annexe the territory. The speech should be pinned to Maggie's desk while she plans her Falklands expedition – it's a tidy, though of course cynical rationale for what London is doing right now.

Tony is not so well this morning. He has what he describes as a 'rheumatic' right shoulder, and has some difficulty moving it. So he is sitting pressed against the radiator in the *comedor*, seeing if warmth will improve it. He is very quiet today – the aftermath, I suppose of his chat with Hilary. I miss Judy, of course, but just for now I feel she and I have both adjusted well to what's happened. I long to see her again, and the children. Will the dogs remember me?

17.50   A nothing sort of day. Parsons is back in NYC, but there is no optimism anywhere. A senior Argentine foreign ministry official is due in NYC later today to give Perez de Cuellar the 'definitive statement' of Argentina's position. On the islands, a destroyer shelled Port Stanley and Harriers did aerial reconnaissance. An invasion seems to be shaping up.

1 I had sent a telegram via Herr Ballmer to Terry Wogan promising that if he asked listeners for woollen pullovers for us, we would bring some penguins back with us. The point of the cable was to show London we were still in good spirits: I had no idea Terry Wogan would actually mention it on his programme.

At 17.45 I was called in to see Barrozo: a small parcel had arrived for me from someone called Martinez in Caracas. I don't know anyone in Venezuela, so Barrozo (whose wife: a pleasant, small, dark-haired woman, was in his office) said he will open it with '*due precautions*' and then give it to me. I said to him, '*Si es bomba, tú has; si sapon, yo hay!*' And they all laughed. Who on earth knows me in Caracas? I told the others it's probably some tall blonde who got a crush on us on TV and sent us the soap 'with which I've just lovingly washed the inside of my thighs . . .' Ian says he's writing all these sexual fantasies down in his book.

The Junta is up to Communicado Number 72, I think. The music – very strident, imperious – makes us laugh. We wonder if, as the invasion begins, the announcements will become even more forceful, culminating in an announcement from Galtieri that he has retaken England and captured the Queen.

19.50   On balance, thus far, a depressing day – perhaps because we had expected something – the cards from our lawyer – and they never came. Or not so far. And the news is pretty indifferent, which adds to the feeling of lowered spirits.

20.30   Hugh called Ian from Buenos Aires, but got cut off twice – though Ian didn't find this particularly sinister, as everyone in the room where he took the call was very friendly. The only message Hugh had time to pass on was that the lawyer's assistant had passed on the letters and cards to the Judge today.

The news is now terrible pessimistic. 'The tide is against peace . . .' says Pérez de Cuellar, and everyone seems to think war is imminent. Foot has asked for a 48-hour delay after a breakdown of the talks (if that is what happens) so that Parliament can consider invasion, or whatever. Sounds pretty impractical to us. Tony seems a little better, though he was in bed early. Tomorrow, if I'm lucky, Judy will call. I must write a note to Barrozo about it, the parcel of (?) soap, and the wanting letters.

London SW 19

You seem to have been there for so long, but you are certainly not forgotten, either in the newspapers or in our – my especially – thoughts. Judy said she was able to talk to you last week. She's remarkable – a tower of strength. Oh what a party we'll have when you get out! I've no idea when

or if this will reach you, but it's to show that you are not forgotten, even though you are so far away. No point in writing about the events, so instead I'll report that England is suffering from a plague of greenfly – i.e. that summer seems to be here at last. I went to N. Norfolk this last w/e to stay with some friends who have started a trout fishery there. It's a big project, with 5–6 lakes being dug out & prepared for different types of fishing. It's hard to see when they will ever get their huge investment back, but meanwhile they live in a beautiful area – buttercups & kingcups in the fields, lazy cows, hedgerows that haven't yet been butchered. And I took the 2 boys (5 & 3) on a long walk to see the local pigs & thought not for the first time that perhaps my life needs to change direction! We drove back through Thetford Forest, which I'm always writing about in the magazine as if I knew it intimately. I love trees, but most especially at this time of year. All this chatter I realise looks like gloating – I'm sorry. But it will be waiting for you. . . .   Take care dear Simon – v. much love to you & the others –
Juliet [Walker]

TUESDAY 18 MAY   What seems to have the makings of a slow day. It is half past noon, I have showered and shaved and have washed two shirts and a pair of extraordinarily uncomfortable Argentine smalls, and Ian and I are sitting on our bunks, drinking a cup of coffee, waiting for lunch and the first news of the day – the BBC 16.00 bulletin, and the 13.00 Realidad '82 lunchtime ATC[1] show (which is really quite well done). I got up late – 11.15 – after watching Roque[2] mend our electric heater, which went 'pooff' this morning. I've finished the Morris West book *The Ambassador* – very pretentious, a poor book – and had a desultory look at Dan Morgan's *Merchants of Grain* (which reports the payment of a $60 million ransom for the two grandsons of the founder of Buenos Aires Bunge Corp.). But it looks too heavy, so I am trying Saul Bellow and *Henderson the Rain King*. Also, a note to Barrozo, which I'll write after lunch.

1 Argentine Television Color, the main TV network.
2 One of the more unfortunate inmates, a forlorn little man who had attacked an officer while he was in the army. Roque was subject to the most terrible depressions; but when he was cheerful he was a splendidly clever and bright conversationalist, a great trickster and storyteller – my own favourite among the twenty prisoners.

18.10   I wrote it, and within a few moments I was summoned to
the presence to be given seven letters which had been in his file – for
goodness knows how long. None for Ian, sadly – three for Tony and
four for me: Simon Hoggart, Matthew Stevenson, and a card from
some people in Laugharne, Carmarthenshire, who had apparently
written to me when I left the USA. They wrote to offer hospitality,
which was very kind; Simon's letter was very typically Simon, written
from the Benson Hotel, Portland, OR., and full of his plans and
schemes and successes. It was nice, of course, and it is churlish of me
to be less than delighted by it – but the fact is, I am in a totally
frustrated position professionally, and for him to tell me about his
Punch articles, and his microcomputer magazine contributions, is a
little irritating. What a pig I am! Matthew's letter by contrast, was a
model of kindness – it is full of the kind of information I was
delighted to hear, and ended with him saying that he'd testify for me
anywhere, any time, no matter what the cost. That is real friendship,
and I'll not forget Matthew for it. Sorry to be so rude – '*grosero*' –
about Simon H – it was good of him to write.

On the 20.00 news the BBC talk about what sounds like a new
Argentine counter-proposal 'to narrow the gap . . .' Could it be? Is it
a trick? Delaying tactics? The British are now said to have troop
transports in the area, so the Argentines have good reason to be
feeling nervous, I would suppose. But let's not get any untoward
optimism: we've been disappointed far too often.

Next – will there be a call from Judy?

22.45   Yes, she did – the lovely lass! She got through in six
minutes; I told her I loved her and was proud of her. She was
thrilled, and that I had heard such good things from Simon and
Matthew. Then her news: all well, Rupert and Biggles better;
Private Eye printed two letters, one from Cal, one from Susan
Hillmore, denying last week's story; Walter Cronkite, Seymour
Topping *et al* are putting pressure on Galtieri; Balabán is flying to
Washington to meet the *Sunday Times* lawyer; *Time* magazine says
we may shortly be handed over to the military for 'a swift
deportation'. Too much to take in all at once – it makes one gasp,
the way the world has rallied round.

Then, Comisario Barrozo handed me more goodies: soap from
Juliet's sister in Caracas (which the police half destroyed, thinking

it might be a bomb!).[1] And piles of cards and letters from hacks – all the *ST* people, (2 kisses from Sally Soames – wishes from Hugo Young, Phil Knightley and David Robson *et al*). They sent three cards, one for each – drawings by a cartoonist. Very nice and professional. A very funny card from the assorted hacks in Montevideo. (Nothing from the hacks in BA, though – very odd?), letters from Hugh O'Shaughnessy, Balabán's appeal in Comodoro, letters from *Observer* people, clips from the *Observer*, a Servob,[2] the splendidly wittering editorials from the *New York Times* and the *Washington Post* and reports from those papers. Press handouts from the Committee to Protect Journalists in New York, telegrams from the Sao Paulo Journalists Association, the Commonwealth Diplomatic Correspondents Association, and so on and so on. It is really splendid. We are all excited and touched – people like Bob Low – whom I've never met – really are rising to the occasion. On balance, then, a great and hopeful day, though as I write this I must break to hear the 02.00 BBC news. Fingers crossed, once again.

23.15   The Argentine proposals were presented to Perez de Cuellar a few minutes ago. No details – but Enrique Ros, when asked if they were final said 'there is no such word as "final"'. But Mrs Thatcher has warned that Britain will not stand for 'repeated Argentine prevarications' – and it is announced today that *Canberra* is on the scene, Harriers are down on a container ship, and Sandy Woodward has ordered 'action stations' or something similar, meaning that Merchant Navy commanders must do as Woodward wants. Let's see what tomorrow brings – peace or war? Letters from home (ruefully, I note I've had none so far, while the others have had plenty). This is going to be a tense few days, though this particular one has been feeling pleasant, and exciting.

WEDNESDAY 19 MAY   I'm sitting in the *comedor*, a little wall-eyed because one of my contact lenses is steamed up, or whatever (Ian calls it 'oiling'). The tape player is playing 'Chariots of Fire', yet again. It is a cold, greyish morning, a first winter's day type where

1 I was given an envelope filled with Palmolive soap flakes, the fragments of two bars that had been sent. I used them for washing shirts in the slop-room bucket.

2 An *Observer* Foreign Service piece, which *Observer* correspondents usually file for overseas clients on Tuesdays.

there has (probably: it's difficult for us to tell) been a moderate ground frost. From the windows of the *comedor*, across the tumbled ruin of rust and debris that is Ushuaia's power station (with MAN diesel supplementary generators outside to provide power as the town got larger), the Martial Mountains are covered, once again, with a dusting of snow. It is difficult to say with any precision how high the peaks are. Mount Olivia, to the east of town – we can't see it, but we have a tantalizing glimpse of its northern slopes – is 4,500' high; so my guess is that the jagged Martials are up to about 3,500'. In fact, the ridge that overlies the Martial glacier looks similar to the Snowdon Horseshoe, in scale as well as shape. There is snow now down to about – if my estimate is right – 2,500', and I'd imagine that from now on it will creep ever downward as winter takes hold. The guide book[1] speaks of the Ushuaia Snow Festival in July and August – ugh! Cross-country skiing, snowmobiling (another ugh! discovering that they have found their beastly, snarling way down here too – ruining the wilderness everywhere), downhill skiing (a nursery slope to the west of town, they say) and 'skating in Ushuaia Bay' are all popular pursuits in the Southern Winter.

I wonder if we'll see the Aurora Australis – it'll mean I have seen both, in that case, as I could see the Borealis in Greenland. From what I recall they say the Southern lights are not as impressive, although that sounds like nonsense. We talked about seabirds today – which bird is it that spits oily vomit at you, and lives in Northern Scottish islands in great abundance? I plumped for gannets or guillemots: Ian said they were fulmars, which were also, he said, the most numerous seabirds in the world. Is this right? Ian has just come in to tell me that he almost got a hat-trick at patience – three cards remaining in the third hand! You can see how 'teejus' life is these days if this is our primary excitement. I've begun, with some trepidation, *The Alexandria Quartet*, having put down Saul Bellow with boredom and disgust. (I cannot think what the Nobel Prize Committee can have been thinking about). As with the last time I read one of the AQ – I can't remember which – I find it so terribly rich it is exhausting and overpowering. But it is so obviously good

1 Written by a local American resident, Natalie Goodall.

and great (and no! not because I've been told to think that: it *is* marvellous) that I feel I must take the opportunity to persevere with it. Typically of course, we'll be released while I am at the best bit, and all my good intentions will vanish in the excitement of return. That, though, could well be an age away: no news yet on the British response to the 'new' Argentine document, if indeed it is new. But, my God, the Argentines on the islands must be scared: as must the British troops on the waiting ships. To know that some of your number will be dead in just a few days – no matter what nationality, it's an awful thing.

To have volunteered, and now to be preparing for slaughter for a cause in which you have no personal interest – it is so ghastly. Politicians do terrible things to the young. With Mrs Thatcher it is either no job, or a job for which you can go and be killed. That was clumsily put, I realize, but when I come to read this book one day I think I'll know what I meant. And as I write, 'Jerusalem' is playing on the tape – sentimental, stirring, so very British, and that's what these boys are dying for, or what they think they are dying for. But what, really, will they die for? Mrs Thatcher's re-election? How cynical can one get? Anyhow, Ullman has come in to ask me for a map of the Falklands. He wants Umbert the Chilean to tattoo it on his back tonight – every night Umbert gets out his pins and inks and tattoos seahorses and octopusses and swords on the backs and arms of the other prisoners; the results are spectacularly ghastly and, so it seems from the anguished looks in the bathroom of a morning, agonizingly painful. Downstairs I hear the bread – long sticks of pseudo-French loaves – being delivered: the day begins.

15.40 The news worsens. Mrs Thatcher says the Argentine plan 'is not encouraging'. The Ministry of Defence has taken over a BBC transmitter on Ascension to broadcast (at, I think, 08.15 and 23.15) in Spanish to the Argentine forces on the Falklands. The BBC say their broadcasts from the Ascension relay may be affected – we'll try to rely on 15.24 and 6.02 MHz, or the Americans. I've sent a note in to Barrozo telling him about Isabel's call, and also asking if Margarita Vásquez, or Jorge, can come in and read Balabán's Comodoro Rivadavia appeal for us. I hope Barrozo isn't getting pissed off by my daily notes – I said that to him (though not so inelegantly) in today's.

The military in Buenos Aires say a British invasion can be expected tonight – a five-pronged attack, they say (though how they can suppose that, or anything, I've no idea). All told I must say the news looks bad – I hope neither side humiliates the other totally – a bit more killing, and then some talking, seems to be the order of the day. Mrs Thatcher says a UN Administration in the Falklands would be acceptable; yesterday, though, Pym said that if we did go to war, all concessions offered by the British would be withdrawn. But – I wonder. Do the Argentines perhaps plan to surrender the islands without a struggle? They could; and the troops come home, just as the South Georgia detachment did, as 'heroes'. The benefits of a controlled press!

19.40   The situation is still graver – and I have to come back to my point around the time of the *General Belgrano* and the *Sheffield*: a lot of people are in a far worse state than we are. Many children are going to be fatherless, many wives husbandless, both in this country, and back home. Unless there is an accident (or an 'accident') we will all get out of this before too long. But not for now. General Galtieri has cancelled a BBC interview, suddenly, because of 'grave developments'. The Security Council is meeting, in informal session. The Pope has called for a Mass for Peace with British and Argentine cardinals – an unprecedented happening, and one that is bound to symbolize the the futility of what seems about to happen. We are hunkered down here, waiting, waiting. I am due to speak to Isabel soon – will she get through? And the first of the Ministry of Defence broadcasts from Ascension is due to broadcast in about 15 minutes, at 23.00 GMT (20.00 here).

Judy said yesterday she has good and bad days, just like us: but she sounds strong and wonderful, and I feel increasingly loyal to her. She's a damned good woman, and I love her for it, and for a million other things, too.

Well, it's 21.30, and Isabel didn't get through, though a pleasant and affable Barrozo popped in to say it would be all right if it did come. The BBC is reporting a 'crisis atmosphere' in BA, with all the country's war preparations complete. But Pérez de Cuellar says that although everything is in a 'dangerous' state the negotiations will continue for another day or two. Some hope! The MoD radio station on 9.710 MHz – it is called Radio Atlántico del Sur [RAdS], and its existence has prompted protests from the NUJ and the ABS – is broadcasting away, with the government promising not to involve the BBC in any way. The government has taken over one of the (apparently) BBC transmitters on the island, and before the midnight news there was an announcement that listeners on 11.75 MHz might experience reduced power. Surely the soldiers on the Falklands, for whom RAdS is beamed, will be ordered not to listen to it. If they do, MoD promises (according to the BBC) no propaganda, just 'factual' news to counter the 'wildly inaccurate' accounts they have been getting recently over Argentine radio.

22.05 – I take it all back: Isabel did call just now, nice as ever. Willy Balabán flies to Washington on Tuesday, to have a conference with William Rogers, a former US Under Secretary of State, who has been hired to work on our behalf! How good the *ST* is. I suggested that Friday's hearing on Comodoro will be tinged with politics, and she agreed. Much love, books being collected; letters from US for me (from 'a gentleman' Isabel says) and a letter from the collected hacks is on its way, but got lost last time! Isabel is a dear.

00.40 Playing cards till now; then Barrozo came round, wine as usual – but we thought we'd turn in.

The Sunday Times, *London*

I was astonished and delighted to get your letter, dated 8 May, this morning. Bravo for the Swiss Consul. You are entirely right in attributing his visit to F. Pym, to whom I wrote a personal letter (Trelford associated himself with it), asking him to go to the utmost efforts to stir up the Swiss. This he did, with great alacrity, alerting his Swiss opposite number in Bern, with the results that we now know. I have written back warmly to thank him, because I think this really was a worthwhile initiative which paid off in real results.

For the rest, you will probably have heard of the multifarious efforts being made on your behalf, for the wide spread international support – IPI, American Press Associations, British Press Associations, individual editors, leaders in other papers etc. etc. – which the affair has attracted. Journalists may be feckless and difficult people, but my God, when something goes badly wrong, they certainly know how to rally round the flag. When it is all over, we shall have many people to thank.

Meanwhile, I am very glad to gather, from the tone of your letter, that you are in good spirits and in good health. I wish we could get copies of the paper to you. You would see how very well we have been covering the Falklands affair, in a manner which, I think, puts us well ahead of all our rivals. We have, of course, been running a weekly story about you and your comrades.

I will write again to the address you have given, and have encouraged other members of the staff to do the same. It will be interesting to know whether the letters get through.

Always remember, that no experience lasts forever; everything has an end. I feel as sure as I can about anything that we shall see you back here before many moons are past. But as to when that will be, I am not a prophet, nor are you.

Thank you again for writing, and please write again when you get the chance. I will keep on sending you letters.

Yours ever, Frank
[Frank Giles, Editor]

THURSDAY 20 MAY   I feel so sorry for the prisoners when they fall into depressions: they all do, at one time or another. Today it's Jack Nicholson – he stayed in bed most of the day, or wandered around, unsmiling. 'Olivia', too – the chess player – spent nearly all afternoon walking grimly up and down the corridor. Goodness knows what precipitates it, but it really is sad. And poor Humbert, the curious Chilean: he's just been told he's not going to get out for another 28 days, while he had been expecting to be free yesterday. He, though, seems quite stoical about his ill-fortune.

As are we – though ever more bored. The situation is now almost totally hopeless – Mrs Thatcher told Parliament that the Argentine response was tantamount to a rejection, and she in turn says Argentina's demand are quite unacceptable. Argentina has turned to the USA for help, and Pérez de Cuellar still has a plan of sorts to advance. But Britain and Argentina seem to be hopelessly at odds – for one thing, Argentina wants to flood the Falklands with its citizens, presumably so that in any vote by Falklanders on a later settlement, Argentine claims to the island would be locally upheld. What a brass neck! They also want the Task Force to go back to Britain! So it looks like war. The Foreign Office steer seems to suggest that the troops will go for one island at a time, or one bit of territory at a time, rather than an all-out assault, because the British are supposed to want to limit casualties (on both sides, I suppose). There is every expectation of a pre-emptive strike against the Royal Navy to delay or forestall an invasion. We'll possibly know tomorrow, or even tonight. A Sea King helicopter crashed on the north side of the Straits of Magellan, in Chile. No one knows if the crew is alive – they found a tent! Have they been picked up? What were they doing? One theory suggests they were reconnoitring the airfields on Tierra del Fuego – that includes this one here. The Chileans have protested, not unnaturally. God help the crew if they're found. They'll have some explaining to do!

Two letters: Bruce Norman and (bless her!) Cathy Collis[1] – lovely to hear from both of them, although Bruce's note was a catalogue of woes, his sickness in central America. Cathy's letter was a gem, full of news and good wishes. It was real Dorothy L. Sayers material, beautifully written, full of interesting observations – the Barbican Centre, Billingsgate, the BBC, Cathy's search for a job. I wrote back, giving her what passes for news from me. But I don't expect I'll have a chance to post it for a little while.

It's 19.50 now, and Margaret should call. Let's hope she has better luck than last week.

Yes, she did – and there was a reporter from the BBC Today show there, so the final five minutes were given over to an interview, with Margaret playing the reporter. Ian told all about us reading Shaw and Sophocles (!), and spelled out our condition in some detail. The call came at 20.25 so she didn't have too bad a time getting through. Then a game of doubles table tennis, and some delicious rice, milk and cinnamon, which was splendid.

George came and read the translation of our appeal for bail, the decision on which may be given in Comodoro tomorrow. He said – but one doesn't want to get optimistic at all – that the arguments sounded very good, and it was possible that the courts might sit up and take notice.

Meanwhile, Argentine Television says that Britain has 'broken

---

1 Bruce is the editor of a BBC2 history programme I worked for, and Cathy the assistant producer of a film I had helped make for him.

off' the negotiations – no explanation at all. So the war of words that is the inevitable precursor of a real war begins.

The Sunday Times, *London*

It seems absurd that we have never spoken, since we both do the same kind of work at the ST. *I have worked for the paper since 1966 and left Insight last summer to return to writing under my by-line again. I have admired your work from a distance and would like to have known you better. Now of course I have to resort to a letter written from a distance of 8000 miles or more. I have been listening to Elaine Potter who sits next to me telephoning newspaper editors around the world to see if they would join a committee to help campaign for your release – a non-political committee, she stresses, campaigning solely on the issue of press freedom. Ben Bradlee said yes instantly and so did the editor of the* Sunday Telegraph. *She is now waiting for 14 people to call her back (must be a record). . . .*

With every good wish, Peter Gillman

FRIDAY 21 MAY   Each morning starts the same way. A guard comes round banging on the cell doors and yelling '*Arriba!*' – 'Get up!', and, sleepily, the prisoners get out of bed and wander down to the bathroom, clean their teeth (with their fingers!) and then swab out their cells, and the passage, with Jeyes Fluid (a smell I'll not forget in a hurry). Then most of them go back to bed – Castro, the gigantic Uruguayan, slumps onto his bed and turns his radio on full blast – the louder it is the more soundly he sleeps. This morning it was just tolerably loud – 'oh, Castro must be half asleep!' someone said. After about 09.00 the new shift comes on and shouts '*A forma*' and we all line up to shout '*presente*' to our names. Then the place quietens down as most of the prisoners go back to bed – I do. At about eleven I get up again and go down to the bathroom, which is usually deserted, and I shave, and – if the water is at all warm, as it was this morning, I have a shower. The water is very soft, so it lathers very quickly. Then I go back to the cell, either to play patience (as now) or talk until lunchtime. Today there is an air of miserable expectancy, half because of the proceedings in Comodoro Rivadavia, half because it looks as though the balloon is about to go up. Except that on the 04.00 news – which Tony and I listened to, as we had been chatting late into the night – there was talk of a 'new' Peruvian plan. Probably it'll get about as far as the last one – which the Argentines rejected. Today might tell.

The attack begins. Six landing parties of 200 men each were on the Falklands early this morning – one R/Marine Commando established a permanent position with heavy artillery, vehicles and anti-aircraft equipment, on East Falkland, and five other parties are still fighting. The losses are already considerable: 5 British ships hit, two seriously; 5 Daggers, 4 (?) Skyhawks and 2 Pukaras wiped out. 2 Argentine helicopters; a British chopper crashed, with 21 presumed dead. The British landing parties are not supposed to have sustained casualties – indeed, the Commandos' landing was said to be unopposed – while there are both Argentine casualties and prisoners. Everything is still going on – heavy air attacks from Argentina, fighting on the ground. Nasty. And yet here – although there is increased naval and air movement, it is perfectly tranquil: the mountains seem to hang in the air, lightly frosted against a perfect blue. There are hundreds of tiny white horses on the Beagle Channel, and seabirds are wheeling in the currents, and settling in one large flock about half a mile offshore.

Mr Iten (?) telephoned at 16.35, from the Swiss Embassy (to check on our condition). He sounded every bit as kind and understanding as Ballmer, and sounded optimistic. 'I hope I won't have to telephone you again', he said, cryptically. But I didn't press him on the point, warning him only that we do not like to be made optimistic if we crash down the next day. He said he understood.

Table tennis with Roque, who is really woozy after his tranquillizers. Poor lad – I feel so sorry for him – no friends, no relations, no future. I'd like him to come back to Britain to be a Magan-type figure.[1] To leave him to rot here seems such a cruel fate.

21.06   Five ships of ours damaged, 17 Argentine aircraft and two helicopters destroyed, Royal Marine Commandos and Paras in control around Port San Carlos, at the northern end of the Falkland Sound, on East Falkland.

21.40   A very touching gesture tonight: we were listening to a brilliant piece of description from Brian Hanrahan on the *Hermes* –

1 Magan was an Indian servant of a friend in Belsize Park – an all-competent 'Gentleman's Gentleman'.

talking of the little cottages of San Carlos, 25 adults and six children now under the British 'umbrella' again – when Barrozo came in with three beers. '*Tranquilidad*', he said. '*No temáis nada*'. He may have known the real news, but he told us the 'official' news – 5 British ships attacked, 2 sunk, Harriers, choppers destroyed. Maybe Barrozo believes that, and was being genuinely sympathetic. How very kind. But what happens when he finds out the truth?

Hanrahan's report was masterly.

(Great host of drunks in tonight – splendid noise, shouts, bangs – like Fleet Street.)

Back to Hanrahan: he talked about the landing ship anchoring for 4 hours in darkness; total silence as men clambered down rope ladders into landing craft; flash of White Ensign as craft disappeared towards coast; then ships left – leaving the Argentines to suppose that this attack was nothing more significant than all the other raids. But there was a British settlement back under British control, with no damage done. Then, at dawn, planes attacked: wave after wave of them – one Pukara being chased over a hill by a missile (which got it), then the destroyers, out at sea, set up a 'missile screen' to protect the big ships. 'But some missiles got through' was all he could say – 2 ships badly damaged.

Tonight Pinto[1] came and asked if I could translate a letter into English for him – to go to a girl called Susan Johnson in Punta Arenas. It was a touching little note – for a year, he said, he had 'lived in obscurity'; he missed her – it was three years since he had last seen her. I was glad to write it for him – his miseries are far worse than ours. He used to be a waiter at the Hotel Cabo de Hornos in Punta Arenas (Ian had stayed there once, funnily enough) and tonight he pretended to be a waiter here; taking our order and even recommending the wine, with *centolla*, he said, '*San Felipe vino blanco, seco, frío*'. So we offered him a '*propina*'. He said he would give us '*desayuno en cama*' – '*jugo de naranja fresca, dos huevos revueltos, tomates, tostadas con mantequilla, mermelada de naranjas, café con leche*'. And, he promised '*una señorita linda*'. What fun!

1 A young Chilean in prison for not having the proper papers – the usual way in which people disappear in these parts, its seems.

22/5 I was listening to the Cup Final (a 1–1 draw, with a most exciting extra time) this morning – it started out as a very dull match but, just like Uganda[1] in 1966, it finished as great excitement – when Capt. Grieco came along with a postcard from Juliet, and three telegrams, one – the best yet – from Rupert, saying '*No threes a one and five betas.* '[2] How pleased I was, and I've asked Tony to get Hilary to pass on the message. Ian – rather meanly, I thought – wondered whether school would bend over backwards to be helpful to him, knowing the trouble he is in – but whether that it is true or not, it must have encouraged Rupert enormously, and maybe, as I've remarked before, this experience will change our relationship for the better. Juliet's postcard, pigeoned via her sister Olivia in Caracas, was full of information – there were 361 words on it! Biggles, she said, was the very worst. Capt. Grieco had some interesting news. All Tierra del Fuego is said to be looking for British SAS men who, it is thought, were dropped by the helicopter that came down in Chile (the pilot apparently set fire to it – it settled normally). Grieco said that radar saw the chopper come in, go down for three minutes and start up once again. Did it drop men? Grieco was concerned because Ushuaia has a fuel store and the airport. 'The war comes to Ushuaia', he said. He also said that in the operations room he was listening to British and Argentine operational channels – both in English, with British and Argentine pilots talking – in an unfriendly way – to each other. 'You will go down into the sea', said one Argentine pilot. 'Yes, you will go down with me too' retorted the other. 'Speak in English some more' says the English pilot. 'No, my English is no good . . .' Grieco's interpretation of the news is not encouraging for the British: the detachment on the island (British) is surrounded, has only light weapons and cannot be resupplied. We'll see if that is true later. A score of new inmates today – a stinking herd of drunks, dirty as anything, smelly and awful. They are all together in the ping-pong room (hence no ping-pong! Well no ping – lots of pong!) and pee all over the place. It's funny – the prisoners, of which we're a part,

1 Judy and I lived there when I worked as a geologist, and will never forget sitting in our jungle tent listening to the England-West German world cup final, which was exciting even though neither of us could tell one end of a football from the other.
2 His school results.

formed a tight little community. The newcomers broke that up, and until they become assimilated (they may not; they may be short-stay only) their presence is resented. All of the prisoners are friends of ours now – Ullman, Chino, Pinto, Rocky, Roldan . . . I suppose we'll never forget them. Nor they us. Writing to Pinto's girlfriend was poignant. He came in a few moments ago to look up the English word for '*alegre*' – it is 'happy'. I wonder why. Because we wrote the letter?

The 18.00 BBC news brought word of the 'complete success' of the landing: 500 men, including 3 Marine Commando, 2 Bat of Paras are on the island, secure and advancing. 2 communities are now British. We have lost one frigate, HMS *Ardent* built in 1977; one other ship has an unexploded bomb in its engine room; 3 other ships were slightly damaged. Three of our invading forces have been killed; an unknown number of Argentine casualties, and nine Argentine prisoners taken. We shot down 20 planes (including 4 choppers) – our total casualties are therefore about 50, theirs – goodness knows.

23.00   Just before the BBC 02.00 news, over the crackling of interference, came 'Plaisir d'Amour' – it was lovely to hear it, and so very sad too, for us all – those of us here, and those out in the Atlantic.

I finished the 4/4/82 *Guardian Weekly* crossword: the three last clues had stumped me for something like three weeks! The cleverest one was 'Little Bo-peep's Sheep eventually kills and eats pseudo-fish'. The answer is 'Lampreys' – LAM(B) + PREYS. If Judy had been doing the crossword – Araucaria, of course – she'd have finished it in an hour or so. Tony very angry today – he stamped up and down for an hour, banging the barred door at the end of the corridor each time. We get a little worried he might thump someone one day.

22/5 was our 40th day in the wilderness.

London

Just a quick line before going off to Dublin to continue my Haughey researches. I have, of course, been in regular contact with Judy and know that you and Ian and Tony are well. I realise that although this is basically true you must be going through a very trying period now that the serious stuff is happening in the South Atlantic. However, I believe the campaign at this end is coming along quite well. Magnus, certainly, has never reduced his enthusiastic effort. Some good things have happened: the UN secy gen and the OAS people have acted promptly to draw Argentina's attention to the general concern about your predicament and I think it can be said that you are well and truly in the public eye. Another interesting thing is the Irish factor. I sounded out some people in the Taoiseach's office yesterday and they reacted with considerable enthusiasm to the idea of Charlie doing his bit to have the three of you freed. One aide said: 'Ah sure I'm just about to go in to talk to him now and I'll call you right back.' He hasn't yet called back, but that doesn't mean anything. I think Charlie would see obvious political benefits in being able to say that he beat the Brits over the head with his no sanctions decision but rescued the three British hacks. We would have no objection to him doing just that. I gather the Buenos Aires joke last week was: 'What is an Argentinian's favourite dinner?' 'Pizza and Irish coffee.' I expect they're not in such a jokey mood at the moment.

There is little gossip to impart. I was godfather to Jon Swain's infant daughter at an Army church in Aldershot last Sunday. It was one of those delightful, late spring Sunday afternoons – warmth, a slight haze over the bright greenery, grassy smells, etc. We drank lots of champagne with the christening cake. Jon is terrifically proud of the child. Her name is Pia which is also Pakistan's airline.

Peter W has been on holiday this week, which should give you an idea of how relaxed we have been about Britain going to war. Actually, with Insight composing most of the material in diary form, there are considerable limits to what we in the foreign department have been able to produce. But, despite the obvious vacuum caused by your own incarceration, our coverage has been quite successful. Our circulation rises every week, though we still have difficulty in expanding beyond 60 pages. I do hope the appalling conflict is soon over. The whole thing seems so senseless once anyone gets killed. The popular papers have conducted themselves with unbelievable bad taste. I wonder sometimes if staffers on the Sun might say to themselves on occasion: 'How can I possibly live with myself?' But maybe the answer would be, 'Comfortably'.

Stella and I had a nice lunch with Judy, Margaret and Hilary after I got back to London. I must say it cheered me up a lot, since I felt pretty awful about deserting the three of you in Ushuaia. Apart from anything else it was good to be surrounded by so many stunning women. I think I can understand why the three of you are in such a rush to come home.

The next step in the campaign should be the formation of a Campaign to free the British Journalists in Argentina. This would be an international effort, backed by lots of editors of reputable papers, magazines and broadcasting systems. We would organise press conferences to give news of you, details of the latest representations on your behalf, etc. We are also considering forming a British or European equivalent of Cronkite's 'Committee to Protect Journalists' in America. Elaine Potter is sounding out a number of VIPs to see if they might like to associate themselves with it. I thought someone like Sir Hugh Greene might make a good hon chairman but nothing has been settled yet. Among others being approached are Lord Shawcross and Lord Devlin. It would, I think, be a handy organisation to maintain even after your release . . .

One other point you will probably know about: Anthony Whitaker is travelling to Washers on Monday to meet up with Willie and Rogers. This will be a most valuable meeting and will help us formulate the defence to your best advantage. I probably won't hear the result until I return from Ireland. But, in the meantime, I wish all of you the greatest success in the trial (if things go that far), early freedom and much patience until that is achieved. All colleagues here send their warmest regards.

Yours ever, Cal [McCrystal]

SATURDAY 23 MAY   The British are said to be consolidating their position at San Carlos rapidly, and to have attacked Goose Green, about 20 miles south. Forward sorties of Royal Marines, trying to make contact with the Argentines, are being made. The correspondents say that the locals are helping the troops dig in – even small children are lending a hand! (That sounds suspiciously like propaganda to me, although I have no doubt that the locals are very pleased a) still to be alive and b) that the British have returned.)

This morning, after a slightly liverish start, I lay on my bed reading out loud a wonderful short story by Katherine Anne Porter (author of *Ship of Fools*) called 'The Grave'. It was exquisite, a little gem, and we all enjoyed it greatly. I showered – freezing cold water again – and washed a towel and some smalls. Ian and I then read bits of Natalie Goodall's *Tierra del Fuego* in Spanish, making the English translation as we went. It is a bit confusing when birds described as *'blanco'* turn out to be 'black-throated'! and fish described as *'negro'* are 'white backed'. But still. The *'toro de la canal'* is, as we expected, the 'canal bullfish'. We learned about survival – you eat a lot of *'hongos'* – fungi, but only the mushrooms that have a white top and black gills underneath. Talking of sickness (as it were) both Ian and Tony had stomach trouble after eating some *arrozo con leche* this morning. I only had a mouthful, as it tasted sour; they had a large cupful each, and felt rotten immediately after lunch. What have we to look forward to today? A call for Tony, and then perhaps Isabel in the evening. Also, Ian and I plan to write a note to Grieco, telling him one or two odds and ends and expressing the kind of friendship to him we have made evident to Barrozo.

As the Argentine forces appear to be putting up zero resistance to the British – thus far, at least – and as the Argentine people appear to have accepted, without opposition, the re-taking of South Georgia, could it be that the national psychology towards victory and defeat is no more and no less than their attitude towards victory or defeat in, say, the World Cup? Perhaps they will be able to assimilate a defeat, and say – 'Ah well, there'll be another chance one day . . .'

A few moments ago (it's now 17.30) I was standing at the window looking over at the aerodrome: the landing lights were on and twinkling in the dusk; the snow was crisp in the evening light, and Radio France ('sponsored by UTA and Hachette') was playing Rod Stewart's 'The First Cut is the Deepest'. A tender moment, one I'll remember for a long time. For a few seconds I could forget this awful prison and this ghastly war, and think back to the real world.

Hilary called at 20.40 – giving Tony, and indeed all of us, several minutes of near heart failure. She seems fine; tomorrow the *ST* and *Observer* people leave for Washington DC, with Willy going from BA to meet William Rogers and other unspecified people. We wonder if they'll see Haig – or even Ronald Reagan, through Henry Brandon's good offices. Anyway, it gives us some thing to chew over for a few days more. The news seems good (from the islands); six Argentine aircraft downed in a fast and furious attack on the Task Force, but one more frigate hit and on fire. It's a heavy loss being borne both by the Royal Navy and the Argentine Air Force – but thus far no word of the fate of our troops on the islands themselves.

The MoD has given wide circulation, apparently, to a picture of a Regimental Sergeant Major leaning over a fence talking to a group of islanders, holding a mug of tea in his hand. It's not the British flag, the question of sovereignty that's at stake, the picture seems to symbolise – it's the way of life of the people, which was being forcibly changed by an invading force and which now – so we hope – will get back to normal. But I hope the British don't give, or even try to give, the Argentine forces a pasting. I don't want them humiliated. From that point of view I'm not sorry that a frigate or two has been ruined – it makes the battle seem a lot fairer and more even-handed. But what curiously empty people the Argentines seem to be: all this strutting and pretentiousness and macho behaviour. They're all talk, they're bullies; but when it comes to a fight – so it seems, I may be terribly wrong – they've not the stomach for it. Yesterday the captured troops said they had not eaten for three days: poor things, young conscripts, quite bewildered, used as tools for these asses in the Casa Rosada!

MONDAY 24 MAY The huge Uruguayan who sleeps in the next cell – his name is Castro – has a habit of turning the radio on full blast when he goes to sleep, and turning it off when he wakes. At 09.30 today the prison was totally silent. 'Everyone's asleep except Castro!' Then the radio went on, faintly. 'Ah, he's getting drowsy!' Finally it was turned up full blast. 'Now he's fast asleep.'

The first BBC bulletin – the 15.00 Reel – had John Nott predicting that 'the days of the Argentine garrison on the Falklands are numbered. It can only be a short time before the people of the Falkland Islands are returned to democracy and their traditional way of life.' We all hope this is not wishful thinking on the Government's part.

Tomorrow, we note, the 25 May, is a big Argentine holiday – Independence Day, or something similar. We think General Galtieri could – or rather should – use it as an opportunity to do something decent – either for the Falkland situation, or for ours.

The Task Force Number Two – lawyers – goes to Washington today, according to Hilary's information yesterday. We wish them every success, whatever it is they are trying to do.

21.30 We are all very low today – perhaps the first time since our imprisonment that we have all felt ghastly. Tony and I discussed the long term possibility of being less co-operative – not yet, not without the agreement of the papers and not without a full realization that it will bring, in the short term, vengeful response from the Authorities. But anyhow – it's not for yet, and, indeed, not for a long time. Our feelings were compounded by listening to the 00.30 Radio Newsreel, which had graphic descriptions of the air attacks on the new San Carlos Bay base and its supply base, a vivid piece from Michael Nicholson (ITN's Mike, I assume) on board a frigate (or ship) under attack ('Get down for God's sake!') and a superb piece from Brian Hanrahan, who really deserves an award for his reporting from his viewpoint overlooking the sinking of HMS *Antelope*, the sister ship of HMS *Ardent*, which went down on Friday. Clearly the Argentine airforce is getting through our air defences, learning tricks, though at a terrible cost to their air force, and their pilots. 25% of the Air Force gone, 3 Royal Navy ships, but Nott says more ships have already joined the Task Force, more than compensating for the losses. The MoD says there's been damage to British ships today, though refuses to elaborate – could some more have been sunk? In short, things don't look as if they're going so well for the British today, and that is reflected in our mood.

TUESDAY 25 MAY   Amazing scenes last night. At 03.50, Umbert rushed in to our cell crying *'Explosion! Explosion!'* and we looked out to see the Hotel Albatross ablaze, great flames shooting up from its roof. At first we all thought a bomb had fallen short of the airstrip, or that someone had carried out a sabotage raid, but it later seemed more like an ordinary fire. Mind you – this is 25th May, Revolution Day, and the Albatross was built by the Argentine government – perhaps there was a late-night function there last night, or something important was planned for today. It looks a little suspicious. Very spectacular, the fire raged for about an hour, spreading at one stage to an annexe in the north. This morning the smell of smoke and charred timber filters into the cell; the Ushuaia skyline is a little modified, and the roof of the annexe – which was saved, eventually – is all warped and scorched. Men are on the roof securing its flapping corrugated iron sheets. The BBC 16.00 news talked of the Sea King found near Punta Arenas, the crew having now been spirited out of PA by commercial flight. Did the chopper land men in Tierra del Fuego (an appropriate name, by the way, for a place where the town centre burns down on Revolution Day!) and were they responsible for what happened? Surely they'd go for fuel dumps or something similar – not an hotel. Except I suppose it would do something to lower local morale, and that must be of some importance.

22.30 Isabel rang at 18.30, and I told her that we were all feeling a little blue – she was very understanding and nice. Her impression is the same as ours – that nothing will or can move so long as the military situation remains bad. But she promised us that no one had forgotten us, and that hundreds of people were working on our behalf.

Later, Judy rang. It was lovely to hear her voice, and I'm afraid for a few seconds I was too choked to talk. But I got over it – these waves of emotion are dangerous things, but she is wonderfully calm. Rupert was there too – with him it was difficult too, but I don't think he will have gathered that I'm anything other than very tense. I do hope it didn't upset him. Her news – actual news – was pretty limited. She is having lunch with Magnus Linklater on Thursday to help coordinate all the efforts being worked on our behalf, so that will make her feel even more involved than she is at the moment. She told me about Willy being in Washington today, and she was delighted to hear – what I haven't written thus far today, that we heard Peter Wilsher talking about us on the BBC's Outlook programme this afternoon. He had called Judy this morning to ask what he should say (he had been in the Cotswolds this weekend, lucky blighter!) He also called to say that Terry Wogan had mentioned us on the radio again this week – possibly today. Judy had written to him to thank him for mentioning us on his show last week, and got a response – how nice. (Though for Peter W, who heard the TW mention, it was not so nice; in the middle of it another car ran into the back of his!)

Peter's piece on the BBC was very uplifting: he was difficult to hear – a combination of a 'Cotswold sore throat', and the very poor reception – but said that we were having to fall back on our 'spiritual resources' which is a nice phrase to use. Jon Connell was on the radio too, as well as the MoD spokesman, Ian McDonald, who is a friend of Ian's.

No visit from George de'Ath today, though our letters are all written and ready to go. But he probably had some problems today, his hotel having gone up in smoke. (Cal will be most amused by that.) Judy, by the way, thinks Hugh is a bit of a dead loss; he never told Cal he was coming to BA, and so lost the opportunity of taking any *ST* mail from me!

I have an infestation of intestinal worms, so I have asked Barrozo if I can see a doctor to get the appropriate tablets. Naturally I want to be very discreet about it – the others don't know, and I don't want them to find out; if possible.

The news from the Falklands is less than brilliant: another Type 42 Destroyer has been put out of action, by the sound of things. Sandy Woodward must be getting worried, though no one knows what the Brigadier on land is planning to do. There is a feeling that we are in the worst period, and we are all longing for the consolidation to end and push towards Port Stanley to begin. But, as John Nott said, there'll be no pushing him – he'll go when he's good and ready.

Where are the Super Etendards? And what was the Sea King – now in Chile – doing in the area? A lot of two-and-two-putting-together, leading *The Times*, among others to suppose (perhaps they have a steer) that SAS men landed and blew them up at Rio Gallegos. If that is so, or if there are thought to be SAS men on Tierra del Fuego, it makes our position a little dicey, I would have thought. We have bounced back quite a bit from yesterday's depression, I think. A long stay seems inevitable, but as Judy says 'I've lasted 8 weeks, I can last another eight so long as I know you are well, and well treated. Keep your chin up!' I will my love, I will!

WEDNESDAY 26 MAY   A spat last night, I'm afraid, prompted by me. 'Hot-Lips' ordered us to switch off the lights at 00.30, I, childishly, decided I wanted to be allowed to switch the light off when I wanted – he called his superior, Cosina, who explained the rules. But it was a bad error, and it made us stand out rather ridiculously and be vulnerable to new losses of privileges. We had an argument in the dark – me accusing Ian of supinely accepting all the rules and regulations of imprisonment, and arguing that concessions are only won by the application of pressure. We fell asleep rather unhappily.

But when we were awoken at 08.30 by Hot-Lips he smiled, I gave him a cheery *'Buen día'*, and then, when he came back from waking the others, I apologized: *'Disculpe por anoche'* I said, he came and shook my hand and all has been made up. So we started today off well enough.

Bad, bad news from the front. HMS *Coventry* sunk, with 20 dead, 70 hurt; the merchant ship *Atlantic Conveyer* hit and abandoned. The Royal Navy's 'Day of Disaster' they are saying in London – though Mrs Thatcher promises that resolution is unswayed, confidence uneroded. Like heck! I am sure John Nott and Co. must be terribly worried by what Mrs Thatcher calls 'these grievous losses'. At the UN, a surprise move – Britain and Argentina, both, seemed likely to accept a modified Irish resolution calling on the UN Secretary-General to try and arrange a cease-fire. Would that have happened yesterday, say, when Britain's losses were much less. Thus far 5 surface vessels, lots of Harriers and helicopters; it's an awful toll for such a wretched little war. If Argentina wins, what will the British national psychology be? Perhaps it will make her buckle down and try, perhaps – probably – not.

I sent a note to Barrozo later in the day asking for a visit with the doctor for my 'condition', and also to ask if there were any letters. Within half an hour there was a doctor, who prescribed pills called 'Tru' to be taken in groups of four, each Wednesday for the next four weeks. He said it is not at all uncommon, and that I should not be embarrassed!

Then George de'Ath and his crew came back because he got permission from the Admiral to interview us. This he did – after telling us dramatic stories about their escape from the Hotel Albatross! He had been in one girl's room, his cameraman in another and there were various other girls dotted around the hotel. The alarm was given at 03.00 – they thought it was a diversionary attack by the British, and that something else was in the offing. Some guests were burned, many escaped totally naked! Mass panic and confusion, he said, and 'a number of people all being interviewed by the police.' His cameras – $30,000 worth – escaped, and the next morning the cameraman found his jacket, with his passport, lying, totally unharmed, on the peg in his wardrobe! They are now at the Hotel las Lenguas. They brought food and soap and books, including Norman Vincent Peale's *The Power of Positive Thinking*!

Ian was not too happy with the TV interview – he has been wondering ever since about the wisdom of having done it. I thought it was okay, except we had little to say. Ian was particularly concerned to hear George report he had 'nearly come to blows' with some Argentine military officers who fully believed we were spies. I soothed him a little by pointing out that in Britain there were undoubtedly hotheads too, who would bitterly dislike Argentine journalists at home. Even so, he was less than happy – so what else is new?

Barney Miller on TV here!

The reporter called Angel – *'Apache'* – came too, and asked what I fancied might have been leading questions about 'the possibility of a political end to our troubles.' He said 'You know that the government can decide, whether you are guilty or not, to free you . . . ? Well, of course we know that: but was there any significance in his asking? Clutching at straws as usual, I'm afraid.

THURSDAY 27 MAY A pleasantly late start for the day – it was 'Charlie Chaplin' on duty, and he forgets both *Arriba* and *Forma*, so we lay in undisturbed until long past ten. I had been reading *Charmed Lives* by Michael Korda, until 02.30, in any case – it was a fascinating book, pleasantly written and easy to read – so I was really weary. Also, the four pills I took yesterday to rid me of my little friends seem to have had an effect on me – so all told I felt rather ghastly. But a cup of coffee did the trick – coffee, in fact, has become one of the major pleasantnesses of our day. Mixing the milk, waiting the hour or so it takes for the water to heat up, mixing the coffee itself – all splendidly ritualistic, and we look forward to it.

The news from the Falklands seems at first blush to be rather better for the British – Marines advancing east in the direction of Port Stanley, Paras advancing southeast to Darwin and Goose Green where they are said to be shelling the 600 Argentines from high ground. One report on the 18.15 Reel said that some resistance – tougher than had been expected – had been encountered. Parliament cheered when Mrs Thatcher said the troops were advancing. Everyone here is still very friendly – it is almost as though the guards had been told to be nice during this 'time of trial'.

Toothache tonight, but of a sort I've had before.

Margaret called – an hour and twenty minutes late, really making poor Ian sweat – and told us a) the Pope was involved, via Cardinal Hume (Hugo Young knows him) and the BA Cardinal, whom Hugh O'Shaughnessy knows b) The Irish government is getting involved. Cal is in Dublin, sent a note from his hotel to Charles Haughey and was in to see him in a second! So messages have been passed to the Irish UN delegation in New York, and we'll see if that helps. Judy and Margaret had lunch with Magnus.[1] Tonight William Rogers, Balabán, Anthony Whitaker and an *Observer* American lawyer were having dinner with Bob and Christine Chesshyre! What a small world.

Extraordinary happenings tonight. Barrozo came in to ask how we were, and I asked him about a new work rota that I saw had gone up in the *comedor*. Fine, I said, of course we'd work – it was our duty day tomorrow – but what exactly do we have to do – clean out the passages, the bathroom, the *comedor*, the games room? Barrozo clearly didn't know about the note and was horrified. Straight into his office – coffees all round (after it was discovered there was no beer), and promises that all we had to do was clean our cells, our plates and the shower after we had used it. Long chat, very friendly. Then – at 00.30 – Barrozo's side-kick got all the other prisoners out of bed and into the *comedor* to lecture them on how important we are, how we must be treated well, how we need do less work, etc, etc. We are all hoping that they don't react against us – but I insisted to Barrozo (in pretty fair *castellano*) that we weren't complaining, that we would do what we were told to do. Let's hope the others don't think we're moaning, and that they don't moan about us! We'll know tomorrow, I guess, when we get the knife between the shoulder blades, or the razor blade in the potatoes!

Oxford
I'm going to start this now & then finish it & try & get it away to you by

1 Magnus Linklater, the *ST* Features Editor.

second post tomorrow. It's not that I have news, its just I want to try &
maintain contact so that you won't feel lonely & neglected. I begged a
photograph of you from the office & have that propped up by the alarm
clock so I can lie in my bed & stare at you! It makes you look very wise &
benign & I'm pleased with it. It was an interesting day ploughing through
your file – if it wasn't so tragic it would be ludicrously funny. It still seems
to me that good spies don't write things down! & as for this business of
disposing of mini-computers . . . Magnus was very charming & obviously
very concerned for us as families – he has added us to the list of recipients
of his weekly Bulletin on the Ushuaia Three, & we discussed his idea of a
co-ordinating committee. They plan to launch it with a press conference
featuring the wives. If they do, its only fair to warn you that I shall buy a
new dress!! David Blundy was in the office & was very sweet – he thinks
you have no excuse now & could easily think about your joint thriller! I
also did a piece for LBC with a man named Magnus something who
claims he was on the Journal with you, I'd never heard of him & neither
had James, but then I had no idea James started on the Chronicle – what
a forcing ground for talent! James was more ebullient than ever in a
broadly striped blue & white shirt & a bright yellow bow tie which exactly
matched his hair!

Talking of shirts – Rupert borrowed one of yours tonight to go out to
dinner at Raishmee's house. He does seem most enamoured of her – maybe
it's because she is Indian. I was so impressed that for the first time ever
someone considered Rupert presentable enough to take home to meet their
mother – an acid test don't you know!! I'm hoping we can reciprocate so
that I can inspect her! Oh dear, aren't you glad you aren't that age again?

Friday 1.20 pm, so sorry not to finish last night & as you see I have
missed the second post – however it will be dropped into the box in a
minute as I'm going into Oxford. I shall pick up a US visa application for
my pristine new passport, which reminds me, what exactly do you have
written in yours? I kept telling the paper I was certain it would have
'writer' in it, as in your old one, but I have wondered as there was such a
to-do about it, & reading the article, translated, from some BA magazine
its easy to see why. They were pleased to call you 'bald, with a long,
intellectual face' & Ian as 'gingery with sad, nervous eyes'. Sounds a bit
like Biggles!

Papalmania has hit the country – do you remember when he was in
US? We walked down onto the Mall & bought the badge I still have on

my board. I am very hopeful about our approach to the Pope, & after all he is himself a writer & an intervention of this sort is apparently something he very much likes to do.

Now, World at One is finished, so I'll tear out & do my errands. I miss you & love you, we all do, don't forget it will you? & also remember to take your vitamin pill. I'll write again v. soon, take care SBA, all love, as ever

Judes

Madrid

Mercedes and I went last night to see Chariots of Fire *that splendid film which you doubtless remember with pleasure seeing in England a good while ago. For me it was the second time submitting to the dubbed version which destroys so much but the film is still irresistible. Was England really so golden in the 1920s at least for the favoured few? The dubbing lobby here has a history: the actors and actresses helped the censors under Franco gaily speaking the false translations in the name of morality so that mistresses became 'sisters' etc but, come democracy, they refused to bow out and lose fat extra earnings. So we still suffer them in the name of a film going public which either knows sufficient English or would certainly prefer the original language and to read the sub titles. Alas, we are not Paris where one cinema has the original version and another simultaneously shows the film dubbed in French.*

I thought of you and your strong liking for Gilbert and Sullivan. I am substantially ignorant, though one of my childhood memories is of my father with a fat red album of 78 records of selections from the various operas being played in scratchy tones on a His Master's Voice gramophone.

A few weeks ago I was going through the notebook of personal jottings I kept during two of my years in India: do you remember that visit we made between planes in Lahore one very hot summer afternoon? Desultory conversations in air conditioned surroundings dominated by the pyjama'ed rich Pakistani businessman's wife while rickety figures, the mali and his merry men could be seen through the big glass windows working away in the heat outside. Did I tell you I bought from Oxford by post (for £37) William Howard Russell's My Diaries in India, *written as you know in the closing stages of the mutiny? Disappointing as literature but with a warning if we did not quickly abandon our sense of superiority our days in the subcontinent would be inexorably numbered. His recommended solution was to live up to our high ideals.*

I hope these random remarks on other subjects help transport your thoughts for a while; give Ian (who may remember propping up a European Security Conference bar with me here last January) my best regards. To you all my affection and esteem. Bon courage,
 Richard [Wigg]

 London

I hope this reaches you (or that you're on your way home when it arrives). It's difficult enough to know what to say, except that we're all thinking about you, and hoping that some sense and some justice prevails before long. It must be getting miserable out there: that's the kind of banal understatement these letters tend to contain. Anyway, to the extent that good wishes and kind thoughts can help, you have them, in abundance.

But how to cheer you up? If I could remember enough Wodehouse off the top of my head I'd be tempted to send you a screed – you should certainly concentrate on that kind of memory rather than on some Greene-ish kind of introspection. Knowing your endless capacity for frivolity in the face of doom you'll be OK. Certainly, from reports I gather you've become a ping-pong demon, quite apart from your Spanish exploits. I myself, as you will have noticed, speak my Spanish with an Argentine accent picked up in a little Irish bar at the back of the Plaza Hotel in Buenos Aires, and it wasn't the only thing I picked up there. That was a long time ago, and had something to do with football.

I expect you've got at least a couple of novels floating around in your head, and I hope they're letting you write as much as you can so that some of the frustration can be worked off. Incidentally, your early pieces from BA and the Falklands were used by the Scotsman *(via* The Times *foreign news service) which pleased us all. This whole sorry business has depressed me, but it's a feeble kind of depression compared with the difficulties you three are facing. You'll know about all the pressure being cranked up, and I can't believe it will go on much longer. With the military thing coming to its climax I'm sure the dealing, and your release, can't be far off. We'll have a great thrash when you get back.*

Mind you, a lot of work lies ahead before then. As you'll know we've all been thundering away like the clappers here trying to keep up with events and just to complicate things His Holiness descends at Gatwick tomorrow, ready to stir up trouble in Liverpool and Glasgow. Thank God, so to speak, I'm off on a five-day trip to Scotland, well away from the fuss and from Mrs Thatcher. I will raise a large Laphroaig to you somewhere in the bogs. I hope that isn't too tantalising a thought to put in such a letter, but maybe the prospect will help to keep you going. We still have to do that walk across Rannoch Moor. It's not going to be an even contest: I'm sitting at a desk getting fat, you're racing around a ping-pong table. Still, we'll do it. We might also manage a day at Lords against the Indians – now there is something to look forward to.

Well, I hope another worldshaking event takes place soon: your release. I'm, confident you won't have long to wait, but I'm aware that the days must now be beginning to drag along in an appalling fashion. You've got great reserves, I know, and they'll keep you going. If it's any help, you can be sure that all your friends here are thinking about you and looking forward to welcoming you home. However dreadful this experience, you can always keep your mind on that.

I'll ring Judy this weekend.

Till we all get together again, try to keep your spirits up and remember that we're all with you.

Yours ever, Jim [Naughtie]

FRIDAY 28 MAY A trickle of supplicants came into our room during the night to tell us they were *'enfadado'* – 'angry' – with the police, and, to an extent us, for what had happened. But gradually this morning the mood seemed to clear, and when I went in to the wash, Ullmann[1] was giving his usual morning Formula One sound-and-action show, and was smiling broadly at me. So I think all is well. But when the prisoners were busily working clearing the hall I fancied they looked and sounded rather aggrieved. There is a young – and terribly miserable looking – prisoner in the table tennis room, so there's no table tennis playable. It's a shame because it is the only exercise we get, except for walking, which we'll now have to do as a substitute – one hour at least for me today.

Ullmann, it turned out, never walked until he was eleven years old – he had polio. You can tell he's been on crutches – he has a very developed chest, and upper arm muscles, and walks a little

---

1 Ullmann had a remarkable ability to mimic the noise of racing cars, and would do so as he washed every morning.

oddly. A nice chap, always cheerful, a born loser. I asked Roque the other day if he wanted to come and work for me in England, and he got tremendously excited with the prospect. But he'd be hopelessly unreliable, I suspect – that's the main problem with so many of these prisoners.

A long, tedious day. Roque nearly in tears at one stage, either with pain or because he was upset by what had happened yesterday. It was horrible to see him strike the wall with his fist, bitter, desperate, terribly sad.

At 17.30, Mr Iten rang from the Swiss Embassy, little news, except that they had apparently succeeded in getting an assurance from the Foreign Ministry – for what it is worth – that our case a) will not be dependant on the political and military situation and b) that it will be speeded up because of the length of time we have already spent here. A small ray of comfort. I asked him to call Isabel to remind her to ring tonight.

And she did, at 21.06 – quite cheerful, saying that all the hacks had become terribly bored with the Sheraton and that the bills were gigantic. Her news was what we had heard the other day from Margaret – 'the Holy Father' had become involved, that Cardinals were dashing about interceding on our behalf, etc. Willy was still in Washington and all the meetings there had gone well. Isabel would call again on Monday to tell us what Willy's news was, if any. She rings the Comodoro court every day, she said, to see if any decision has been made on bail.

Mother's birthday on Tuesday, so I asked Cosina if I could send a telegram: I expect Judy will let me know if she got it.

Our troops captured Darwin and Goose Green, according to the MoD in London. Very significant news, we think, since there is an airstrip there, and the Argentine forces in Port Stanley must be feeling increasingly cut off. British casualties are said to have been 'light', which suggests the Argentine army is putting up only moderate resistance – something Galtieri is presumably going to have to answer for in the Junta.

SATURDAY 29 MAY   Snow! When we woke – the others had to get up and do chores at 07.00, as a direct result, I fear, of our little talk with Barrozo two nights ago – there was a covering of about 2″ on

135

the ground and the roofs. A very low cloud – possibly of warmer air, condensing on the now cold land – hung eerily over the town and the Beagle Channel, which was still. Perfect peace – rosy coloured mountain snow, pale misty blue skies.

Then, early afternoon, a mail delivery: a couple of letters for Ian and Tony, and a whole host for me – Juliet, Matthew, Usha Vatsia, Helen Ganley, Isabel, Ken Clarke, Christopher Thomas – it was wonderful of them. They all seemed to think we're being very stoical about it all: I suppose we are, though it doesn't seem very brave to me.

Barrozo and his little daughter came by in the late afternoon, just to find out if we were still all right – very good of him, the 'affectionate courtesy' much in evidence. We told him we were well and happy, given the circumstances – added to that we had a load of shopping arrive this morning – all the usual, plus cheese this time! Matthew, bless him, sent a *NYT* crossword and a map of New York City. He'd know that was the kind of thing I liked.

The news from the Falklands continues to go very much Britain's way: 900 Argentine prisoners have been taken at Darwin and Goose Green, though the CO of 2 Para, a Lt Col (whom, I assume, I have met) was killed in the action. The Argentine media seems about ready to announce the capture: already the people have been told that our beachhead is 4,000 – 4,500 strong, and Barrozo said that a big battle is probably in the offing. The British, he suggested, wanted everything completed by the Pope's visit on 11 June. Perhaps.

Today 2 Argentine frigates came in to port, and, from another dock, an icebreaker converted into a hospital ship left for the Falklands. Clearly they are taking casualties and I only hope the British submarines don't make the awful mistake of torpedoing her! The hospital ship, white with huge red crosses painted on her sides – and one on her bridge – was clearly equipped with a reinforced bow for ice work. She was painted white – presumably not her colour for ice duties.

Matthew reports that Judy is fine – so does Juliet. But how odd that there's still no letter from Judy herself. It is so frustrating it's amusing!

Much jubilation among the Chilean and Uruguayan prisoners at the news from the Falklands. We were mentioned on the World

News – 'good physical condition . . . but depressed at the situation because it will affect their situation.' That was on an Argentine news agency, and it sounds most measured and responsible.

London

I've just heard Mrs Winchester talking on LBC (8.15 am) and she says you're all feeling a bit low. Not surprising: but keep your chins up because we're all thinking of you – and talk about your plight. You'll soon be back on London's dirty streets, dodging the rain.

My husband left at 6.30 am to go to a dog show in Bath. The kitchen is full of chalk – we have to chalk our breed when they go to the shows to keep the coat 'pure white'. It's all nonsense anyway and I know we are suckers to pay the enormous entrance fees and petrol prices to get to these distant Championship Shows. We're 'on the hook' and I don't see us getting off for a while. Last year we made up our first Champion and that was great fun.

We sell our puppies all over the world – for showing, breeding, and companions. We seem to have gained great friends this way.

Do you like dogs?

We've got 9 in all! Our neighbour doesn't like them and they don't like him. You can imagine the fun we have here sometimes, can't you?!

We're coming up to the mad school season. You know, Founder's Day, sports day, PTA meetings, and parents evening with the form teacher. I find them all equally boring and I always feel guilty because all the other mums are so intense about it all.

My son takes 'O' levels in 2 years time. This year we had to choose the subjects. He hasn't the foggiest idea what he wants to do but he does seem to be good at languages.

One daughter is gym crazy and good at Physics but not very keen on school at all. She's going through the stage of liking anything that looks like a man. Make-up, hair, nails etc and last week she had her legs waxed for the first time! 12 years old. I didn't know what male species were when I left school at 17 years still in knee socks.

My youngest daughter is the extrovert. She had just conquered a phobia of being alone at night. She watched Murder on the Orient Express *two years ago last Xmas and ever since then had refused to sleep on her own. Suddenly last week she decided she was OK. Anyway, she's good at dancing and art.*

It's difficult writing to people I don't know but even if you find this all

boring at least it's something different to think about . . .
   Keep the sense of humour going and you'll be OK.
   Littlekiss

SUNDAY 30 MAY   A cold grey day, with the snow looking firmly
established for the winter. We woke at around ten – though they
had been wakened at six – and I ate cheese and orange segments in
total luxury; then coffee. Ian announced that if he were an
Argentine he'd round up all the Port Stanley population and use
them as hostages. He went on to say that 'The Pope needs
Argentina'. Two idiocies, one on top of the other! Wonder what the
third will be? Then Ian confessed that the reason he was annoyed –
and he was, or he wouldn't have said that – was that Tony had been
revealing that he had told less than the truth on his interrogation –
he had, it now seems, told them he had not been in the army, or
wasn't any longer, or wasn't in the reserves. Tony was in a black
mood for half an hour or so, and then it passed away. Later we
heard that in fact our forces had taken 1,400 prisoners – that was
twice as many as we had expected. All the civilian population had
been locked away in the community hall for the last month, and
houses had been looted. The Argentine government said, in an
independent communiqué, that they would pay for any damage.
The Argentine people haven't been told of the loss of Darwin and
Goose Green (or *Ganso Verde*, as it's called in *castellano*), other than
their forces have gone out of radio contact. MoD says the operation
– which cost 12 British lives, 31 hurt – was 'one of the most brilliant
and courageous operations since the Second World War.' Doubtless at home they'll be euphoric, though the Pope's presence might
be calming the jingoism.
   It's now 21.20, and Hilary's call hasn't yet come through –
suggesting busy circuits.

MONDAY 31 MAY   Heavyish snow again this morning: winter is
beginning to have a look of permanence about it. As usual, after
forma I lay in bed (as did Tony who, it turns out, had a vicious
headache all day, and his temper was hardly improved by the fact
that Hilary's call never did get through) and we had coffee and
chatted about odds and ends. Last night, at about midnight,

Barrozo came round, and we had our usual polite chat. He shouts terribly – his poor wife and children must be half deaf.

While I was combing my hair – no; washing my smalls, actually – Ratso came into the bathroom and started laughing at what he said was the attack on the *Invincible*. I raised my finger put it on the end of his nose and said '*No humor!*' which provoked him to begin shouting and threatening. I explained my position – but I rather fancy he will be one to watch if the situation turns out desperately for Argentina. Funny, because at the outset he was one of those who indicated he didn't care, and that he would be '*amigos si guerra, si la paz.*' But that no longer appears to be the case – although in fact it is me that's on the short fuse. Ratso went and told the tall, lean chief that I was in a bad temper about it, and all of us cooled down. I don't care for him, however.

Then two journalists from *Somos*, one looking uncommonly like Paul Connew of the *Mirror* and the other a chap I met with Gabriella Cocifi in the Rio Gallegos airport seven weeks ago today as it happens, came and we sat in Barrozo's office talking only to them. They made it clear it was more of a social than a business call, and that they would only write about us if BA wanted them to. They – or rather, the one that spoke the better English – said he felt sure our situation was linked to the political situation. Oddly enough I – and Ian – could understand the pair of them much better when they spoke slowly in *castellano* than when they spoke English: in other words, we have reached the stage where our *castellano* is better than their English, which isn't bad after just 49 days of this. Ordeal? I still don't think I'd take it out of the category called 'experience.' We heard last night that an English zoologist released from Mozambique had asked, at Heathrow, for 'fish and chips, toast and marmalade, and beer.' That after 5 months of maize!

A curious – but pleasant – afternoon. At about 17.30 we were called into Barrozo's office to find the missing Captain Grieco – looking, I fancied, rather sheepish, about the way matters were proceeding over on the islands. He insisted that *Hermes* had been 'sunk' some weeks ago. But the main point of the visit was to give us mail – letters (lots of them) and parcels of books from the BBC and from Paul Connew in BA, and from a friend of Tony's at home. Harold Robbins, *The Story of the Orient Express, 84 Charing Cross*

Road and many others. Then Isabel called with the bad news from Comodoro Rivadavia that because of the continuing political situation we could not have bail. It was on the 02.00 BBC News, so she got to us in time, bless her! She had had my rather grisly letter, and wasn't at all offended![1] I can't say I was terribly upset at the news – the rest of the day was reasonable – and my pingers and castellano are coming on fine – that I just shrugged and put it behind me. Isabel said Costa Méndez had been asked about our situation at a press conference in BA (by Hugh) and that the Pope was becoming active in our case – 'he'll see the file as soon as he gets back from London' said Hilary.

Then – the best event of the day – there was a letter from Judy, written in bed with Tusker lying beside her. She sounds wonderful – lots of visitors, lots of callers, lots of flowers. People are so good. Tonight I expect we'll hear how she received the news about our bail denial – stoically, I have little doubt. She really is a treasure.

Poor Captain Grieco. As he gave us whisky and read the papers with us – and took a paperback called *Dirty Movies*, the horror! – he looked worn and saddened by the situation – of which, I feel sure, he must be aware. He is full of bluster, of course, but it wavers at times, and he talks, very sensitively, of wanting his wife to call our wives to reassure them, of how we must miss our children, of how his oldest daughter cries over the phone from Buenos Aires because she is so upset at the situation. 'She burst into tears at both the *Sheffield* and the *Belgrano* – "those poor boys", she said.'

Letters also from Frank Giles (who professed to being 'astonished and delighted' to get my letter), from Rosie (or perhaps I said that already), from Peter Chandler, from Peter Gillman – unmet so far, but he told me about being 3 months in a tent on the slopes of Cerro Torre, in Argentine Patagonia. He had self-censored three words in his letter[2], in a passage about who he believed had stolen some strawberries (à la Caine Mutiny) during the climb – I suspect (and I must ask him when I get back) that the words were 'the only Argentine.' Am I right?

1 I had sent her a note telling her how fond I was of her for all she was doing: I felt I had rather gone over the top, as I was almost in tears when I wrote it. I somewhat dreaded her reading it, once I had sobered up the day after I wrote it.
2 Because, he felt, they might give offence if read by an Argentine gaoler.

I read until 02.30, glancing at Judy's letter from time to time: she'll never know what contentment that brought, and what a lucky person I really am. I read the *NYT, Atlanta Journal, Outside* magazine and, now, Cookridge on the history of the Orient Express, a book of which Matthew would surely approve.

Okehampton, Devon

. . . How to begin to write to you anything that is not utterly boring? I was turning it over this morning as I shifted the electric fence for my two cows, and felt I must find the nearest common denominator. Geographically I was never further south than Bahia Blanca, where I spent one or two school holidays a long, long time ago. It was on a handsome old estancia founded by a Scottish family in the last century, and it was winter. I have memories of huge log fires and Aladdin lamps and long sessions with a wind-up gramophone after coming in from riding. And outside, the greyish, wiry grass (I never saw the pampa green, it was always winter) the dirt roads frozen hard, the huge, flat disc of the horizon with far-off groups of poplars like ships on the skyline. And I remember those wire fences bordering the roads, mile upon mile of them, and every now and then the carcase of a horse that had starved, imprisoned there on the road, unable to reach grass or water. Sometimes a living one, or a small group. One used to look away, think of something else. That was easier in those days than it would be now. I suppose there are fewer horses now. I hope so.

Further south I can only go by proxy. At school there was a girl from Comodoro Rivadavia and one from Santa Cruz. It was before air travel, they came to and fro by sea. They suffered badly in the mosquito season, because, it was said, the cold climate had made their blood too rich and appetising, unlike those of us whose homes were in the north and whose blood was thin. No one came from Ushuaia. It was only a penal settlement in those days – for ordinary convicts I think. No one said anything about political prisoners.

I was reared in Paraguay, and Argentina was never home to me although I spent 5 years there. They were reluctant years and I felt as trapped as you do. All my contemporaries had gone home to the war with the British Latin American Volunteers, but my part-German ancestry made me ineligible. My prison was larger than yours, but it was still prison. I used to think that the horizon-line of the River Plate was like a stone wall. Eventually, I saved enough from my reporter's salary (which was microscopic in those days) to pay for my passage, and 'escaped'. The sense of relief was indescribable, but I can assure you that when your time comes it will compensate for all the frustration and the isolation and anxiety you have suffered. Meanwhile, you are not forgotten. People who do not know you speak of you with concern, you are frequently mentioned on the BBC and in the press and I am sure no string is left un-pulled that could possibly speed things for you. In years to come you will look back on this episode and it will not be entirely wasted. Nothing is.

I live alone now, apart from my family of animals – my cows, my dog, my cat and my beloved ponies, in a cob-walled cottage in a tucked-away valley. Dartmoor lies to the south, blue on the skyline. The stream runs north to the Bristol Channel by way of the Torridge. It's a country of great oaks, and wild daffodils, and pheasants that squawk continuously at dusk. Right now the sky is full of swallows. I do not think I shall move again.

Very sincerely yours,
Rosemary Theobald.

Milan, Italy

A piece in yesterday's Sunday Times suggests that you might like to receive letters from anyone and everyone, and I'm sure that sacks full are on their way to you – but perhaps not too many from Italy . . .

So what, you are asking, does she do in Italy. Well, I sell Kraftliner and Kraftpaper, not to mention semichemical fluting for a group of state owned Swedish mills. Kraftliner and semichemical fluting are the materials with which corrugated cardboard is made (for boxes) the Kraftpaper is used to paper sacks (for cement for example), but perhaps you know that.

All this paper is sold in reels 125 cms in diameter, the width of your choice, and comes down from the north of Sweden by rail. Occasionally a waggon goes astray in East Europe and I have fun tracking it down. Does this sound dull? Surprisingly it isn't! though I can't pretend its glamorous.

The purpose of this letter is to break the monotony for a moment, and to say that we are all thinking of you (all three of you). However, I hope by the time this ever reaches you you'll be free.

All good wishes from sunny Italy,
Sincerely,
Elizabeth Fenton

Liverpool

I don't suppose you remember your visit to me but I most certainly do and so I thought I would like to send you this assurance that you are not forgotten. It is difficult to do anything practical to help but do believe that many of us care, and spare time to think of you.

Toxteth soldiers on. We have survived the Queen's visit to open the new police HQ (me in a hat & white kid gloves!), and the Pope & Ian Paisley – with only four arrests. Whether we shall survive Heseltine remains to be seen. We need you back to help us!

With every good wish,
Yours sincerely,
Margaret Simey

TUESDAY 1 JUNE   Mother's birthday. She did get her telegram, and sent one in return. 'Success inevitable, reunion guaranteed' she said. A brilliantly sunny, cold day. (Must NB from yesterday my irritation with Ian: he was writing a piece for the paper. But then I had written a long letter to Isabel, so perhaps the two cancel each other out!)

A fairly uneventful morning: the two reporters from *Somos* came at 09.00 with Nestlé's powdered milk (it really does dissolve instantly – much better than the other stuff) and cigarettes, and took our letters – mine to Judes and one for Isabel, and Ian's two. The news is all of consolidation at Mount Kent – 250 dead in the fighting at Goose Green and Darwin, and the troops discovered a cache of napalm. Tut tut! (It was denied in Buenos Aires.)

Then at 18.30 we were called to see the judge – Sagastume himself, along with Raoul and Margarita[1] – he told us, formally, of the denial of bail by the Court at Comodoro – he had this information in a short telegram from the Court, not giving any reasons – and then went on to explain the worst possibilities for our case. 'Explain the worst case to your wife – then she can only be pleasantly surprised,' he said (more or less). The worst case – according to him, and speaking as of now, is a 3 year gaol term which would equate to 8 months, less the time we have spent in

1   Raoul Riccieri, the judge's chief clerk; and Margarita Vásquez, the interpreter.

prison already. The best case is freedom, of course, and in between, 2 years suspended, or 2 years actual (which would also be 8 months, oddly enough!) Ian is sceptical – but Raoul said that the judge was resisting pressure from the Foreign Ministry and the Ministry of Justice and so 'will not be pressured by any other ministry . . .' In other words he will judge the case on its merits, without any external interference – the independence of the Territorial Magistracy is at stake, it seems.

But he really did seem reasonable tonight – though heaven knows he was before. A Buenos Aires intelligence specialist will evaluate the evidence – the information that Julian[1] gave me, Tony's three-post-warning pictures – and then it's up to the defence. I don't – or won't – think it represents anything but reasonable news.

Then at 20.00 – 20.25 actually – Judy called, the love. She was a bit down, because Anthony Whitaker, back from Washington, had talked about '9 months before the case even comes to court . . .' Surely not. He is a bit of a Job's Comforter at the best of times. But otherwise Judy was fine: a BBC man had taken the letter for Judy and Cathy Collis back, so (since Margaret got her's today) Judes should get her's tomorrow. Biggles can no longer get out of the garden! Tusker is going to have to be plucked! Alex is a little asthmatic as he has been swimming in the river all day (it is half-term); Rupert is smitten with an Indian girl; and Angus is as fine as ever. I talked for 20 minutes or so – the guards were very friendly and gave me coffee. They are all being especially nice.

Cal was on the World at One today. Lord Devlin is probably to be the head of the Committee to free us. Judy said dozens of people in the office hugged her – sexy devil!

NB For tomorrow – a Dissertation on Argentine Justice. Like sewing buttons on custard?

WEDNESDAY 2 JUNE Yes. It does seem a most *peculiar* system. There is no open trial. We've no idea what the prosecutor really wants in the way of a sentence. There was no oath. There's no opportunity for us to defend ourselves – although the defence lawyer can personally submit documents to 'prove' our innocence. All that happens is that the judge sees and reviews the files, and

1 A British friend in Buenos Aires who knew the Argentine military scene well.

then decides on the sentence. Our first impression from yesterday's meeting was that the judge has already presumed our guilt, and it is now a question of deciding whether a two-year-suspended, or a two-year-actual, or a three-year-actual, or a three-years-plus-one-day, or an eight-year sentence is the most suitable. I don't know what to think, and I've even less of an idea what William Rogers is going to think of it all. Should we tell the press about our lack of faith in – or perhaps shortage of understanding of – the judicial system here. A lot of the case appears to be spent attempting to prove that we are not spies – i.e. proving a negative, which is barely possible. Thinking about it, I'm very cross indeed about Whitaker's suggestion to the womenfolk that our case might be nine months in coming to court! I simply cannot believe that this can be true – surely the judge will bow to the pressure on that score, if for no other reason.

Ian and I had words today. He gave his radio to Olivia, and I said I didn't think it was sensible for us to hand around our radios at a time when the prison authorities might be sensitive about the prisoners getting non-authorized information. There was a brief exchange of verbal cannonfire, but he did go and get it back. He was still a little liverish over our wrangling about whether to talk to a reporter from a magazine called *La Semana*: I was (although recognizing the arguments for and against) basically in favour of talking to them; and he was not. I suspect he simply wanted to win one argument after having been forced back on the other. And I say that without malice – simply as an observation of human behaviour. It's probably what I would do if I had been whipped – try to win on another battlefield. Complex things we all are, and yet so similar in our fears and feelings, really. Ian and I tick in much the same way, and I'm delighted there has been so little friction. On the other hand it is true that in the past fortnight there have been a rash of incidents between us, more than in the previous four weeks, and I hope this isn't a trend, because after a few more weeks we could be screaming at each other, and finding life in prison even more unbearable.

It's cold outside, and Ian complained of being cold in bed last night. But it is very beautiful, and the mountains look eminently climbable. News from the Falklands a little vague today – but one interesting development has taken people by surprise. Two senior military officers from Buenos Aires have turned up in New York for talks with Pérez de Cuellar with – as I thought – full powers to negotiate (with him, presumably; not with the British) for a settlement of some sort. Could this be an expression of the Argentines' desire to avoid a bloodbath at Port Stanley, because that, I am afraid, is what looks like happening. The British are now admitted, on Argentine television, to be just 25 km. to the west of Port Stanley, and General Menendez has broadcast to the Argentine troops calling on them to inflict a 'crushing defeat' on the British. There are all kinds of horror stories: napalm stored at Goose Green, a Falkland Islander tied hand and foot, kicked and with a gun in his back because the Argentines said he had talked to the British forces by radio. I hope to God they don't use napalm at Port Stanley – although their magazines accuse the British of using a French bomb – the 'Beluga' – which is prohibited, they say, under the Geneva Convention.

We eventually did see the men from *La Semana*: they took away letters for Judy and David English (thanking him for being on the Committee to try for our release, if indeed he is), and a letter from Tony to Tony McGrath, the *Observer* picture editor. The reporter for the magazine seemed a pleasant fellow, and we talked for about an hour about the political situation – not about our imprisonment. We did, however, ask for an interview with Galtieri – perhaps if they print that he'll be impressed by our cheek! Coffee was given to us during the interview, which was in a private office – the prison clearly still trusts us. To bed late – 01.30 I think. (I have occasional difficulties writing – putting letters in the wrong order – why is this? Something to do with confidence, or writing too fast, thinking ahead of my ability to transcribe?)

London W II

I was very sorry to hear that you had been taken by the Argentinians. It sounds worse than school! I hope that you will be able to get out soon. I've heard the weather is very bad there. It's boiling here. You must be getting pretty bored – what do you do all day? The war is getting to be boring. It's all you hear about on the news.

Get out soon.

Love from China [Williams]

PS I met you and your family in Washington and in Graves Mountain
Inn, Virginia, in April 3 years ago (I was 10) do you remember?
PPS I hope the meals there are better than at school.

Oxford

I begin this letter by reintroducing myself as Manager of Barclays Old
Bank. You will wish to know that Andrew Cavell, my Assistant Manager,
keeps in touch with Mrs Winchester.

My managerial colleague John Anthem has become Manager of our
Summertown branch and his place here has been taken by Miss Pamela
Butt from St. Ebbes. It is a novel experience having a lady manager
working with me – I am so polite it's not true!

Competition between the Banks and Building Societies is hotting up.
We are now quite big in the home mortgage field and the Abbey National
has reacted by making cheque book facilities available. 400 of our branches
are to recommence Saturday opening – I must say I never agreed with the
original decision in 1969 to close on Saturdays. My then Branch, Lewis
Lane, was always packed to the doors on Saturday mornings. . .

We think a great deal about you and your colleagues in your present
difficulties and send our best wishes for your safe return to Oxford.

Yours very sincerely,
H. W. Mitchell

Oxford

Oh my darling – don't think that the great splodges on this page are tears,
nothing so romantic – it is merely an incredibly hot day & I pottered round
& got out a deck chair & thought I would sit in the sun & write to you. It
reminds me of India – a great wall of heat as you walk from our cool hall
into the light, & the ground is parched & cracked, so the marks are drops
of sweat! It's almost incredible to hear that you look at snowy mountains
& that there is snow on the ground & here I sit almost melting.

It's no good. I have had to retreat indoors, partly the heat & also the
reproachful glances of the weeds. We continue to beat them back & pop in
plants to take their place. I fear the winter has blighted the monkey puzzle
tree – all the branches are brown & it does look very sick: I don't much
mind of course! The rose bushes are doing well & seem to have survived
the ice & snow. The field by the front door has just been left & the grass is

147

as high as the fence now. Biggles got into it yesterday & couldn't see which way to go when I called him from the gate.

It was terrific to speak to you last night, to find you so cheerful & to have such a long time together. Its amazing what joy one takes in things that one never thought much about before, i.e. phone calls. Have you moved cells (is it pink-painted by any chance?) I think the jail should be re-named the Ushuaia Hilton – or maybe Intercontinental! Of course now we shan't be able to visualize where you are in relation to the rest of the jail: Cal drew us a detailed diagram showing where you go to answer the phone etc. I also have the view of down-town Ushuaia pinned up on the kitchen door with large X-marks-the-spots on the Jail, the Courthouse & the Albatross (or late Albatross) inked in.

Your letter came today via BBC – oddly enough sent on by Sheila Osborne who was in Washington with John Humphrys – thank you. It is so good to hear from you & good also that you are enjoying writing letters – perhaps you would like to take over from me as family letter writer?! I have all your letters propped up by my bed – it is just like a teenage romance! In fact I remember I used to keep your letters under my pillow so they all got very dog-eared! (I've still got them). In those days you only wrote to me – the boys were twinkles in your eye & as for sending love to Big Tusk – well, I never imagined such a thing. I assure you the dogs are well & happy: they haven't fought for at least two weeks, must be the heat. Tusker comes in from his walk, rushes to his drinking water bowl & just lies full length on the floor to drink! Please don't even imagine Biggles coming to grief 'cos he hasn't & when he did – wolfing weedkiller – I told you, didn't I?

And while we are on the subject . . . I am being honest with you when I tell you all is well, because it is. Of course it is a hassle having to take care of all the admin. that you normally do – it has given me a much greater respect for you. The children are not delinquent & I rather mind you even suggesting that they might be! They do miss you, & certainly miss the contact they would have with you by phone even if you were away on a long trip. Both schools are being specially helpful & keeping a discreet eye on the boys; Alex's mates have been told not to talk to him about you unless he brings it up. Alex has asthma – just the usual – but he has gone a beautiful golden colour with this sunny weather. Angus & Ben have been swimming at Mesopotamia – two sassy twelve year olds, I should think they are a great menace!

Thursday 2.10 p.m. Just been into Oxford to look for a dress for the Sunday press conference. Waited for the bus at Queen's Lane & watched Schools coming out, they looked very shattered poor things. Rupert & Angus start in two weeks.

We have had a very grand invitation from A. Sheil for 18 June, black tie or 'exotic', a dance no less, very near too, at Reading; I should like to go, I've come to know him very well but only by phone. Jonathan Dimbleby & family have moved out to live in Bath. The Chesshyres were going to spend last weekend at Graves Mountain Lodge on our recommendation – I haven't heard how they got on. Bob gave Balaban dinner & thought he was a very dynamic, bright fellow. I went to early church on Sunday; it was a lovely morning & through the open door we could hear the birds singing. We prayed for all prisoners & especially Simon Winchester & his family: I was very touched.

Isn't the Falkland landscape like Greenland? & the houses, it does sound so bleak & inhospitable now though. The BBC have got their Irish passport holders out in BA in force – Róisín McAuley – imagine, & Brian Walker are there now. Christopher Morris carried out your last letter. Are you able to get to a typewriter at all? Cal wonders how your novel/play is proceeding, or how about some short stories – maybe you just plain don't feel creative? I do wonder. I'm sorry this last page has been such a jumble – the phone has rung constantly & I do want to get this into the post today; like you each time I send a letter I wonder if we'll be together before you get it. I miss you & love you very much & we'll have such a good time when you come back . . . take care & be of good cheer, all will be well if you can just endure. Positive thinking as I told you the ill-fated day you left in April.

Much love as usual from RA & A, also from Biggles & Tusker, & all from me,

Judes

The Beverly Hills Hotel, California

Dearest Simon, you poor old bugger,

This note-paper is not meant to upset you, but to remind you of happier days when we frolicked like young lambs by the pool – one of so many good times we had together in this country. You've been on my mind so much I just had to risk the notepaper – and perhaps a US postmark will stand a better chance of getting through than my Brit efforts. Did you ever get the kids' drawings?

I don't know, from the sound of it, how you've remained sane, though the little messages reproduced in the ST *all have a characteristic whiff of world-weary humour about them. That pic, too, is quintessentially you: good to see it stuck on your kitchen wall when we went to see Judy a few weekends ago, though the plan of the cell on the kitchen door lowered spirits again. I guess you must be writing it all down. You deserve to get some kind of compensation for such hell, and a noble book should be one of them. For my part: when you're back, and recovered, ask for any treat you like, starting with a spanking meal at the restaurant of your choice. The dancing girls are already hired and waiting . . .*

I've seen less of you in England than in Washers, but I can't stand the thought of someone I know so well and feel so fond of going through such shit. Yr friends, as you must guess, feel pathetic and powerless; any doubts I may have had about the ST *are quenched by the fact that, were I ever in yr position, Cal and Magnus wd be the two people I would hope would be put on the case. They're doing all they know how. It must surely now not be much longer.*

I much admire your sang-froid, as it seeps from yr published utterances, and I expect to be filled with respect when I hear the grisly details. You're a survivor, Simon, and a wonderfully good-natured one. I pray you don't have too much longer to keep it up. Say hello to Ian for me, and give my best wishes to Tony P. Forgive what I feel is a very inadequate greeting, but be assured that you're constantly in our thoughts and words. You've stuck it with guts and gusto: just think how much better a place the world will be once you're back in it.

With fondest love and fellow-feeling, and the earnest hope that I'll see you again soon:

Tony [Holden]

Leicester

I am writing to express our deep concern regarding the way you and your two compatriots are being imprisoned by the Argentine thugs. My family and I pray for your safe deliverance from the darkness and evil of your present surroundings.

Yesterday the BBC's World at One carried a report upon your plight. The three of you have not been forgotten – efforts are being made for your release. The Pope visits Argentina on 10th June on a visit for peace. We

were deeply moved by his simplicity and humanity. 'May the peace of
Christ be in your hearts and in your homes' was his farewell benediction.

June roses perfume our garden, and the heady lilac scents the twilight.
Norman, my husband, has been planting snapdragons, geraniums, blue
lobelia and phlox in the borders. We love to feed the blackbirds and
thrushes which sing amidst the dawn chorus. Soon the blackcurrants and
gooseberries will be ripe and the birds will share this harvest. I shall be
making blackcurrant jelly and gooseberry jam as we listen to the hourly
BBC news reports from the Falklands. As in 1939 we are again at war
fighting dictators with ruthless disregard for the things we hold so precious.
Your freedom of movement and speech have been stopped – you three are
now following in the way of so many great and wonderful men and women
who over the ages have suffered in this manner. Nothing can separate you
from the love of God and the prayers of his people are with you and for you
all at this time of great difficulty.

We send our love to you all; and the people of England's Green and
Pleasant Land have not forgotten you.

Yours very sincerely, Olive and Norman Walker and Mum who is 90
in October.

THURSDAY 3 JUNE   Up at 09.30 to a pleasant enough day: the sky
in early morning is magnificent, bright reds and oranges over
Falkland way, as if the battle is going on in full technicolor! No
news at all from the islands of any fighting – could it be that the
Argentines are being pressed to accept a peaceful end to this all?
Why are there no reports? If the Argentines were scoring successes
they'd be saying so in Communiqués; if the British were landing
more troops, firing artillery and so on, we'd hear that. All we do
know is that 2 Argentine officers are in New York, Pérez de Cuellar
has 'given up' his mandated peace hunt, Parsons is likely to veto the
Spanish-Panamanian Security council vote, and all the public
negotiations are off. But there was a story in the *Financial Times* this
morning suggesting that Argentina would be willing to accept UN
administration over the islands – if that is true, and if you add to that
Mrs Thatcher's remarks on television yesterday, suggesting she'd
be happy with a multinational force on the Falklands, and that a
battle for Port Stanley could be avoided if the Argentine troops
agree to go, and go within the next ten to fourteen days – if you add

all that together it looks at least possible that a plan could be being worked out while the commanders on the islands stay their hands for a while. 'A lull', everyone says – but why?

As I write this – at 14.25, in the *comedor* – there is a women's TV chat show on, and I must confess to lusting after the various women on it. 52 days have gone by now without a trace of womanhood – I think I can quite honestly say I am sex-starved now. Ian is reading Norman Mailer's *An American Dream* and finds it quite good except for the sex scenes which, he says, are quite dreadful. Odd – and I think I agree with him – what seems nice is simply the company of a pretty woman: bizarre, intense multi-orgasmic sex is of no interest at all. Judy's letter brings her vividly to life, and I miss and want her more than I can say. I must have read her letter ten times so far, studying each line, each word, like a young lover! That's what prison does for you!

Ian due to get a call from Margaret tonight. Perhaps we'll learn a little about Whitaker's scare story, and about how they all are.

Yes, Ian did get his call, after only six minutes waiting – he was very surprised. Basically the news was that Garret Fitzgerald – former Irish Prime Minister and Leader of the Opposition in the Dail – has agreed to chair the Committee to urge our release, and he, and other members of the Committee are holding a press conference at the Hilton Hotel on Sunday afternoon. The obviously good thing about Garret – with whom I had lunch about twelve years ago in the University Club in Dublin, and he may well remember me – is that he will be able to gain access to Galtieri, or whoever replaces him as leader of the Junta. So on balance it sounds like excellent news – all courtesy the *Sunday Times*, so we gather. This annoys Ian a lot – he feels the *Obs*. is doing nothing much. He is haunted by the remark in Frank's letter that Trelford[1] has "associated himself" with Frank's personal letter to Pym, the one that got the Swiss so deeply involved in this case.

But Ian was a little downcast – close to tears at one point, I felt – after having been told to put the phone down by one of the goons. He only got about 8 minutes, I think: the trouble with Ian is that he refuses to make a fuss about anything, and is full of his determination to 'blend into the woodwork'; I can see why he feels like this,

1 Donald Trelford, editor of the *Observer*.

but on balance I am in favour of keeping highly visible. A good example of the benefits of this came with the publication of our written interview with *Siete Días*, which Barrozo gave up today – he had photocopied the single copy he had borrowed from the Governor. Ian was introduced as mean and suspicious, not inspiring confidence, looking like a film 'boffin', or the leader of a 'Mission Impossible' adventure; I, on the other hand, came across as pleasant, direct, etc., etc. All image-building I realize – and Ian is in reality a first class man, and much more 'solid' than I am – but in this situation it is important, I feel, to build imagery for the Argentine public. Anyway, his confidence about our peace-related or Pope-related release appeared undiminished by day's end.

FRIDAY 4 JUNE   Judy likes to think of me as writing a daily journal like Harold Nicolson, after breakfast, and this is what I think I will do – write each day's summary the next day, if you see what I mean. I have in fact written most of the above account of Thursday today, Friday, and it still seems fairly fresh. This I am writing in 'real time' as it were, simply to record – lest I forget – that there has been quite a bit of scrapping among the prisoners this morning, with blood being smeared on a cell wall, either as warning or trophy. Tony saw it all but gave a very garbled account, he finds it very difficult, for some reason, to give a direct and unembellished answer to any question. It's very odd, infuriating and it may well have been at least partly responsible for our being here – Isabel, you may recall, said the judge had formed the impression that we may not all have been telling the whole truth.

Mr Iten, from the Swiss Embassy, called, with news of a meeting today between the Foreign and the Interior Ministries, to discuss our case. I wish he would call after these meetings rather than before – the actual news, good or ill, would be preferable to the endless suspense.

During the day various sanctions were imposed on the prisoners who had taken part in the fight: the dour Chilean, Alfaro (Umbert) was put in the adjoining cell – according to Tony he went into the 'black hole' at one stage – to cool off; the others were confined to their cells, forbidden to watch TV or to heat *maté* in their rooms until next Tuesday. But by the end of the day Alfaro was back in his cell, prisoners were strolling about and – though they had lost their heating rings, and did look rather *maté*-starved,[1] and kept coming into our room for cigarette lights – most of life seemed to have come back to normal. Everyone says this is a really lenient prison, and from the extraordinary temporariness of the sanctions that are applied, it would seem everyone is right.

'Hot lips' on duty for evening *forma*, and he said everyone had to be in bed by 22.00 – but when I asked if that applied to us he winked and indicated that it didn't.

Isabel called just after 21.00, to say they were all pinning their hopes on the Pope's visit – he apparently saw the file either today or last Friday. She answered various other questions, including knocking down Anthony Whitaker's preposterous – oh God I hope it is preposterous – suggestion that it could be nine months before this case even reaches court! She said that he always sought out the worst possible scenario for anything: he even said he rather fancied there were 'one or two good points' in the prosecution case. Anyway, not to worry, she said – but I told her the wives had been very upset by his Jeremiads. Other questions she answered – about the Argentine officer from South Georgia who is wanted by the French and Swedish authorities – can there be some sort of a swap? – when Willy is coming down (post-Pope; and probably with Isabel and Hugh, if they can get permission) and other odds and ends. The press conference is at the Hilton on Sunday at 11.30, so we should hear it on the World Service later in the day. Garret Fitzgerald is indeed the chairman, and is flying over from Dublin for it.

Then she passed the phone over to Hugh who spoke to Ian for 10 minutes, and managed, as only that combination can to cast him down again. But we all recovered, and took to our beds at 23.30, reading till (in my case) 01.15. Another day passed – another day closer to freedom!

SATURDAY 5 JUNE   I'm writing this with a pen – a *bolígrafo*, in the

1 *Yerba maté*, the national drink of Patagonian gauchos. It is a powder which is put into a bowl, a hollowed-out gourd. Hot water is dribbled onto it, a silver pipe is inserted and the infusion – almost pure caffeine – is sucked out. The prisoners took pounds of *maté* every day – that and cigarettes formed, it seemed to me, their staple diet.

local patois – that Roque has used to tattoo himself with! So it will expire at any moment – it is almost totally empty, and all for one pathetic eagle, or sword or something similar to boost Roque's feelings of macho. It is such an odd phenomenon, macho – it makes total frauds of such a lot of Argentine men. I wonder if the judge's macho has anything at all to do with our imprisonment? That he is getting some actual pleasure out of appearing powerful to his friends, but forgetting that compassion and discretion are just as important ways of impressing people.

A brilliantly sunny day, clear and cold: the power station is wreathed in clouds of vapour as the warm exhaust hits the frigid air. So far – it is now 13.55 –we've not been able to hear the BBC, but my impression is that following the defeat last night of the Spanish-Panamanian Security Council resolution, there will be fighting again on the Island. General Lami Dozo has said that the battle for Port Stanley will 'not be the last', which sounds ominous. What if the Argentines simply never announced the end of the war? If they refused to accept their defeat? And did not negotiate at all? Surely there would be internal pressures on Galtieri? And the economy would just go haywire if there were still sanctions, surely? To read the memoirs of all those around Haig and Pym one day will be fascinating.

At 17.18 a great yellow moon rose out of the Chilean mountains to the south-east, a long strip of golden reflection spread across the Beagle Channel towards us. An unforgettable, blissful moment – if only it wasn't seen through the bars and the grubby windows of this ghastly place. The moon rose steadily upwards – at first its rim notched by the peaks and then, at 17.21, it cleared the mountains and floated in the darkening sky. A fishing boat, one red navigation light at its prow, chugged slowly home.

But generally, a dull, slow day. No news, no communiqués, no action – just British grumbling at the American UN vote mess-up last night. The CO on the ground, Maj-General Jeremy Moore, reported little action.

In accord with my theory that there is always one incident, even on the dullest days, Barrozo came along at about 20.00 and boomed away at us. He had a friend – the Comisario of the Border Police, based at San Sebastian (on the Rio Grande to Punta Arenas road) –

and he (since he was going to Buenos Aires tomorrow) agreed to take a letter for Hilary. Barrozo seemed to think that the Papal visit would be important for us – everyone does, building up a great deal of hope which we are not prepared to have dashed. My own private opinion is that the Pope will raise the question, will be told that our case 'will be considered' and that will be that. I'd love to think that a release would follow his visit, but I can't see it. I just hope Isabel and company will go and see the Papal Nuncio who is, presumably Italian, rather than the Cardinal of Buenos Aires who is, presumably, an Argentine.

The late night film tonight – after a dreadful thing called (I think) *Willard*, about a curiously ill-adjusted American boy who keeps scores of rats in his basement, and sends them to ruin people's parties – was *The Enemy Below* with Curt Jurgens and Robert Mitchum. It took place – I had forgotten – in *Atlántico del Sur* – and it must have been painful watching for anyone who had relations on the *Belgrano*.

One of the local 'duty-free' shops called 'London Supply' has announced that for 'patriotic reasons' it has changed its name to *Atlántico del Sur*. It will still stock Scotch, Pringle sweaters and Quality Street, though, as well as all the rest of the Hitachi-Grundig-Sony stuff.

A civilian plane today (I think) so perhaps there will be some mail on Monday. Barrozo said we have to decide about the other cell on Monday.

The new tough regime is being half-implemented: anyone (except us) who was up and watching TV tonight was told to go to bed.

SUNDAY 6 JUNE   And they were woken up at 09.00 – pretty strict, huh? We lazed on, though Ian excelled by stepping on a cup of coffee and getting it all over the floor – producing the exquisite marbling effect on this book. (If this makes it to an antiquarian bookshop in a century of two, and the catalogue says it is 'slightly foxed', blame Ian and his elephantine feet.)

Heavy rain this morning, and low, brooding skies. The promise of last night's Antarctic moonrise has hardly been fulfilled. I wonder if we'll ever see the Southern Lights? Going great guns with crosswords, though Araucaria is a so-and-so.

Watching the French Open (?) tennis championship: there is apparently some union trouble in London, and not all the signal can come through to Argentina. We get the picture – sort of – and an excited Argentine commentator talking over a very crackly telephone line. Wimbledon soon, I suppose (it was said to be 85 degrees in places yesterday – and we get this weather!).

Tony talked to Hilary, who got through early at 20.20. The Campaign was launched at the Hilton – Garret presiding, the three women were there – all saying a piece, apparently – and there were about 30 hacks present. The Sundays had pieces about the launching, and everyone expects there will be pieces tomorrow. But nothing on World Service, which is a shame. (*Noticias Argentinas* and *El Patagonico* have both been banned for 3 days for breaking the security laws!)

General Moore has been touring the troops on the Falklands today: it is confirmed that 5 Inf Bde has been landed to augment 3 Commando Bde, which was landed at San Carlos. The 5 Bde includes Welsh Guards, Scots Guards and the Gurkhas, so that should sort them out! New notices calling for a surrender have been dropped, as the Port Stanley garrison is completely surrounded, outnumbered and outgunned. Depending on that response, Moore will decide what to do.

MONDAY 7 JUNE   The television and radio are now almost totally devoid of the spirited '*Argentinos a vencer!*' types of advertisements that have dominated broadcasting for the last eight weeks. The trend began last Thursday or so – perhaps when it was realized that the Port Stanley garrison was in hopeless trouble: at first, the advertisements appeared, but the Ushuaia station cut them off after only a few seconds. Then were dropped altogether. The civil defence advertisements changed from describing 'what to do in case of air attack' to 'what to do if your child cuts himself'. Now, today, we see a new one (oh, before I mention that, I should note that about a week ago the cruellest of all advertisements showed a target in a telescope stalking a slow motion lion symbolising Britain: it finally centred on the lion's forehead – and then the words '*Argentinos a vencer*' came up). Now, today's advertisement – seen twice so far during the lunch time 'Realidad '82' shows a pair of pictures of the Pope; solemn organ music as background, and the phrases 'War is destruction', 'War is death' and 'Not to remember the past is to compromise the future'.

Now before I draw too many profound conclusions from this I should note that an Argentine short wave broadcast (at about 13.10 on 15.35 MHz) did have '*Argentinos a vencer*' playing, and was full of news about the *Invincible* limping back to London damaged by the air raids of last week. Could that have been for the benefit of the troops at Port Stanley?

The conclusion that must inevitably be drawn from the change in advertising – and yesterday there was one that simply stressed the unity of the polyglot Argentine people – is that the War is Over. Not necessarily lost (they can hardly suggest to even the densest Buenos Aires dishwasher that it has been won), but over. And that is bound to be welcomed by everyone. What follows we can't know – that seems to depend on Britain's willingness to be flexible: if she is, if there is UN stewardship of the islands then relations could get back to normal. All told the crisis has the feel of entering its final stages – its climacteric, its denouement. And it may not be a bloody one – with the message of peace being given to the Argentine people over radio and TV, it would be unsporting, to say the least, for the British to make war. But thus far today – 13.40 – we don't know. The Falklands has slipped to No. 3 in the news, with Lebanon and Chad above it! But that, I fancy, is only a function of the time of day: nothing to report so far. The BBC corr. was stressing last night, the 'extraordinarily daring operations' being undertaken which 'if successful . . . would bring Argentine surrender that much closer . . .' What can they be?

Heavy snow this morning – wet, slushy, grey lumps of it falling from a low and leaden sky. One of those few days when I'm genuinely glad to be inside – over on the Falklands it must be grim. But the weather has the look of impermanence to it, and my guess is it will improve.

Another advertisement just then – '*afiancemos nuestro futuro . . .*' – 'let us guarantee our future . . .' A long way removed from 'Argentina to victory!', and a healthy sign.

(Actually, later in the day there were a few '*vencers*' – but I think my theory holds water.)

A poor bit of behaviour on my part today. I was playing pingers with Ian and he was punishing me – either he was in brilliant form, or I was at the lowest; anyway, I accused him (or rather, told him) that he was playing too aggressively! What I really meant was – I was being a bad sport about losing! A later game showed that I had recovered much of my form, and all of my sportsmanship – I still lost, but in good grace.

No call from Isabel tonight, which was unusual. But there was a call from Iten at the Swiss Embassy, saying that St-Jean (Minister of the Interior) had been 'most receptive' to the notion that the case should be speeded up, and also advising us to be 'moderately optimistic' about the Pope's visit being useful for us. He said that another diplomat – his name is Mr Grob, I think – is going to come down this week – did we want any shopping at all from BA? I told him to bring down the stuff Willy had collected from DC, but for that he needed to get in touch with Isabel – and as I've just noted, that call never came.

Some more books today from Natalie Goodall; and a bunch of letters for Tony. But generally a low-ish day, with nothing happening, and our spirits dampened. I think we all know, secretly, that the Pope's visit is not going to produce anything for us, but none of us can get it out of our minds. So we are a complex mixture of optimism and pessimism, and dislike having to be what we should be – which is resigned to our fate.

We had a long chat before bed, and all of us realized to our surprise and dismay that we have never been asked to offer our side of the story to anyone – not even Willy. If we were guilty of a conspiracy, for example, what were we doing buying standby tickets for all of our journeys (to Comodoro from BA to Ushuaia from Comodoro and to Rio Grande from Ushuaia)? Tony thought we should start making a nuisance of ourselves by asking to see the judge – I'm not sure about that, but a meeting with Willy – a long one, with all of our story given to him in detail. Once the Pope (or Holy Father, as Lambeth Palace apparently calls him) has been and gone (without, as we must assume, any comfort for us) we will tackle Willy in a big way.

No shopping today – the absence of coffee is a real morale-depressant. No call from Isabel, either: I've suggested that I might try to call her, so that I can express to her the urgency of our seeing Willy. I think once we have seen him the urgency of the case will become apparent – in a way I'm rather looking forward to the case, because at least the situation will be moving.

Bourton on the Water, Gloucestershire

I do not know whether or not this magazine Cotswold Life *will reach you. I bought it because it seemed to be so evocative of this part of England, and because it contained an article on Edward Thomas, and his poem entitled 'Adlestrop'.*

I came across the poem some years ago and only when I came to live in the Cotswolds, and saw a sign-post bearing the name, only then did I realise Adlestrop really existed. I hesitated – should I follow the road? Would the dream be shattered?

But I took the road to Adlestrop; the reality justified the risk. Certainly the station had fallen into disrepair, but the surrounding profusion of wild flowers clothed it sympathetically, and the birds of Gloucestershire were still singing.

We hear that you are getting shoals of letters, which may help to keep you in touch.

You and your two colleagues are very much in the thoughts of many people.

Sincere wishes for a very early return to your homeland.
Harriet Walker

Swansea

I work in the Rates Department of the Guildhall in Swansea. On Wednesdays I go with my wife to St. Mary's Church, where Ann Lewis (one of the few women who are ordained in the Church of Wales) holds a lunch time service. She has given everyone in her congregation a card with the names of all those from Swansea who have gone to fight in the South Atlantic. We pray and think of them, and ask for their safe return. I have added your name to the card, and this Wednesday I shall ask Ann Lewis to remember you, and to do so every Wednesday until you are freed.

My wife and I realise that your imprisonment must be terrifying because of the unknown – and this is even worse for an innocent civilian simply reporting the news, as the Sunday Times *always has done.*

Your paper has given me so much pleasure – the very least I can do is to pray for your freedom soon.
Yours truly, James Kelly

Gt. Missenden, Bucks.

I am writing to you to add my support and prayers for your quick release from your enforced captivity. I know what agony and heartbreak you must go through and I understand the frustration of not being in a position to be able to do anything about it. I too am running a campaign to free my husband from jail, convicted of a crime he did not commit and I am fully aware of the inadequate feelings one has. My husband is in jail in Britain and I can visit him; and although he is imprisoned he is dealing with and is being dealt with by civilised people, albeit still in prison. My heart goes out to your families, because they do not have the opportunity of seeing you. Please have faith. I am sure that with all the prayers that are being offered for your safe return from all denominations you will be reunited with your families soon. I never thought that I would have the strength to run a campaign and fight British justice but I am doing just that.

God bless you all and we all pray for your early release & safety.
Lynn Saltman

TUESDAY 8 JUNE   A much more pleasant day, climatically. Cloudy when we woke, but it cleared at about 11.30. One of the detectives came and got a new shopping list – he also changed $200 for me, and got 1,460,000 pesos per hundred – a great deal more than last time. I think the devaluation was 17%, meaning that we are a lot better off, were it not for the intrinsic cost of everything here. I think I noted that the last grocery bill was about $40! (Judy wrote the other day to note that an Oxford Ball ticket was now £48 – remember how they used to be 5 gns. for an ordinary ball, and eight guineas for a Commem – as Judy said, a week's housekeeping, or more.)

I'm now watching – sort of – the lunchtime news with Ian, after quite a decent lunch of minced meat in the hollowed-out shell of a squash, with cheese on top. Not much of it, but it was tasty. Ian is having to dance around the set, literally, to get a decent picture, because the aerial is broken, and his body acts as a substitute. I had a shower this morning – the water was abundant, for once, though not exactly warm – it just had the chill taken off it. There is nothing quite so frustrating as showering under a dribble of icy water, getting totally covered with soap, and then the water stopping! It's happened to us all – we stand there like snowmen, shivering, waiting for the cold water as though it was boiling hot!

I'm reading two books: Antonia Fraser's compilation of the Kings and Queens of England and Joseph Wambaugh's *The New Centurions*, about life with the Los Angeles Police Department, which is very good indeed. (It came in a pile from Natalie Goodall, who has the most curious literary tastes – lots of odd religious books, seeking after Truth and Success and so forth.) The Antonia Fraser book is an excellent example of the kind of book I wouldn't have read if I'd not had this prison experience: it is quite easy going, and fascinating. Maybe I'll manage to get that History 'O' level yet – I see Rupert is taking history, bless him.[1] Judy should call tonight, by the way – I just hope she and Isabel don't both decide to call at the same time, and get engaged signals. Tony still a little stroppy today, promising he'll make a nuisance of himself.

New pen here – Carrot-head[2] got a bit of shopping for us today, including half a dozen *bolígrafos*. And I am very aware of the rottenness of my writing: I hope I'll be able to read it when I'm free of this place.

Judy called at 20.25 – it was a superb, long call – Sergeant Cosina spoke to Judes to say goodnight, and that helped to reassure her and guaranteed me a good half hour on the 'phone.

Apparently this Committee launch on Sunday was wonderful. She said that after the press conference and the lunch, ITN came home to Oxford and filmed the entire family in the garden, filmed the study – with the Apple computer! – and had Angus chattering away nineteen to the dozen. He was on the box that night, and is now quite impossible! Rupert was filmed, it wasn't used (because of the Lebanon invasion) – but he wasn't unduly dismayed, Judy says.

Garret and Frank Giles were wonderful too, Judes says – she bought a new dress and, according to her, looked super! Lots and lots of papers are on the Committee (and there is a poster!) including all the British editors, *Le Monde*, *La Stampa*, *El País*,

1 I had failed history 'O' Level in 1960, something that had always rankled.
2 A new guard with, inevitably, red hair.

NYT, *Boston Globe*, Ben Bradlee, Eric Sevareid, papers in Chile, Colombia, Dominica, Kenya, Jamaica. . . It is quite incredible. India, too, obviously. (But gratefully received.) The coverage was pretty good too – *Times*, *Telegraph*, *Guardian* (Anne McHardy covered it, and sent her love), the *Mirror*, *Express* (twice), World at One, *International Herald Tribune*, ITN . . . it was very clearly a *Sunday Times* operation (organized by Elaine Potter, beautifully, everyone says) with Frank Giles, Magnus, Anthony Whitaker all there – Donald Trelford was in Russia, and was represented by Tony Howard. I really feel a member of a family of the *ST* – they are all taking care of me, and it is a great, wonderful feeling.

Shirley Tomkievicz[1] had had to pull out of the Maharajahs book because I'm out of circulation, and is now offering the Moghuls. Ah well – swings and roundabouts.

Angus is in his Under Thirteen cricket at school, playing New College School on Saturday! He really is doing well – but yet my prayers and hopes are really with old Rupert, whom I see as a chip off the old block. Angus is something new – the best of Judes and me distilled into one. Rupert carries all the emotional baggage that I do – or did – and he's going to have to fight a lot harder to be loved. But Judes says he has an Indian girl friend now, with whom he is quite besotted.

The *Sunday Times* has asked readers to write to us. According to Cal over 100 letters had arrived on Tuesday morning, so I'm not too unpopular! And the Iffley Ladies Luncheon Club, too, is writing – 15 more letters! The idea is to flood the Ushuaia post office with letters to embarrass them!

Biggles got heatstroke and had to be hosed down – and in addition went berserk with the ITN microphone cables on Sunday! Alex's asthma is better, thank goodness, and he's off on a field trip to Cirencester. Pip and Juliet send their love – all were tickled by my story on TV about the police here blowing up Juliet's soap!

After the call – which put Ian in an almost euphoric mood, Barrozo came by (at midnight or even later) and talked about, among other things, the cost of prostitution in Ushuaia (Maria Correa, whose cell we move to this weekend, was apparently one

1 Editor of a series of *Time-Life* books. I had been asked to write one about the jewels of the Indian maharajahs.

such). Here, two hours with a woman who is *más o menos bonita* – ie not so handsome – is $15 for two hours. In BA, where the women are said to be 'bilingual' (meaning, I think, that they have two tongues, rather than two languages!) they are $50. Barrozo chatted without any embarrassment and went on to talk about drunk driving ($70 fine and a 3 month suspension for the first offence), and the British free school milk system, and Mrs Thatcher's abolition of it. That's why we don't like her, we said, and he laughed.

News from the Falklands is trickling back, even though Lebanon dominates everything. A frigate and 2 (or 3) landing craft were damaged in an Argentine air attack, but the British have now secured Fitzroy and Bluff Cove (they did it on Saturday, but the reports were held up, deliberately). It seems that the Brigadier found the phone system still working, rang a farmer in Fitzroy and asked 'Are there any Argies there?' 'There were some here yesterday, but they've gone' replied the farmer. 'Then I think I'll come over and join you' said the Brigadier, sounding just like the character in the old Dr Who films. 'I think that would be a good idea' the farmer said – and later that day, Five Brigade poured in! Royal Engineers got the *Monsunen* running, helped by a 19 year old girl diver who cut weeds away from the propeller. It all sounds wonderful *Boys' Own Paper* stuff. Port Stanley is now totally encircled, and the troops just await the word to go in and take it. What an incredible story!

London

Readers of the Sunday Times *have been told you would possibly like to get letters, even from complete strangers, to show you and your colleagues that we remember you, & much appreciate what a difficult time you are going through at the moment.*

First of all let me explain a little bit who I am, & why I have been so intensely interested in what goes on in the South Atlantic. My name is Elizabeth Hodson, now an old woman of 78! though may I hasten to add I feel at least 20 years younger, & am still as active & busy as I have always been. I lived mostly in Aberdeenshire, Scotland, till my wedding in 1928, and my first home as a married woman was Government House, Port Stanley, Falkland Islands!! My husband (Sir Arnold Hodson KCMG) was Governor there till 1931 when we went to West Africa. He died in

1944 – a year after his retirement.

I never got to Buenos Aires, but was quite often in Montevideo & have been to Patagonia & Bahia Blanca, where I once spent 10 days, whilst the cargo ship on which I was travelling loaded grain.

I loved every moment of my time in the Falklands – all the locals of course are of Scottish descent & I was immediately received as one of themselves & was so at home & happy with them. It is all so long ago of course I have lost touch, but I now see names in the press which recall many memories. A farmer at Teal Inlet was spoken of last week – perhaps I had better not mention names – I think it was his grandparents who were friends of mine & for some years after I left the Falklands I used to meet them in London when they came home.

In those days there were of course no aeroplanes – I travelled mostly by cargo boats, which was always fun. I once came home on one of Lord Leverhulme's whaling boats – quite a trip – as they weren't allowed to take passengers I was signed on as a stewardess, & paid the large sum of 1/- for my services! That apparently got round the regulations.

Very few ships called in – we got our mail & newspapers from home about once every 9 weeks, so you can imagine the excitement when the mail boat came in. We had no radio contact until my husband got out expert electricians from England who installed a local radio station.

Another thing my husband did was to train the local young men to become first class shots. He himself was a crack shot & won many prizes at Bisley. He brought out from Aberdeen to the Falklands a Sergeant Major Allen of the Gordon Highlanders (also a well known marksman) & they both together trained the Falklanders to such a pitch that they came to compete at Bisley 3 years running & each year won the 'Junior Kolapore' Cup – to the complete surprise and frustration of many bigger colonies, who had hardly heard of the Falklands, & certainly had no idea they could produce such a magnificent team! You are all too young to remember those days, but your grandparents would.

I must not make this letter too long – but I hope my reminiscences may amuse you – & distract you for a while from your present troubles.

May I wish you all a safe and speedy return home.

Yours sincerely, Elizabeth Hodson

P.S. The wonderful seals & penguins who love human beings must hate all the noise! I used to spend hours playing with them!

WEDNESDAY 9 JUNE   Our first encounter this morning was with one of the Chilean prisoners – a nice quiet one who works all the time – who admitted he had been arrested for cattle rustling! Apparently a cow in Argentina costs about $300, while one in Chile costs about five times as much. So he was rustling steers across a border – what a good crime, compared to the usual run-of-the-mill stuff we get here. When we suggested he might have been in for robbery he reacted, quite aghast!

Big aerial attacks by the Argentine Air Force again – three Daggers left Ushuaia, according to Tony – so it sounds like a last ditch attempt. And now there's renewed interest in the war on TV – coverage interspersed with messages of peace from the Pope (or *Santo Padre*, as he's known here). In today's action – or perhaps it was last night – the frigate HMS *Plymouth* was hit, together with two tactical landing craft loaded with ammunition. The attacking aircraft came up so fast that no one had a chance to put on protective clothing, the BBC correspondent said. And it now looks as though yesterday's reported attack on a New York based 100,000 ton supertanker, the *Hercules*, (500 m NE of the Falklands) was by Argentine aircraft (even though denied). She had already been threatened, and the plane that carried out the attack was said to be similar to a plane that attacked a British tanker last week.

20.05   Just as it began to get dark all the steam went out of poor Ian, and he became instantly very depressed, talking about never getting out of here, and of all the vengeful possibilities that this government might seek to punish us. It was a little difficult for me to answer the points, because I'd not had a word with Isabel (and she still hasn't telephoned – it is rather peculiar. I think if she's not called by 21.30 I'll try to raise her). Ian's mood tended to drag me down, too -- though I finished *The New Centurions* quite happily – Wambaugh is a very talented writer, a great find (even though the subject is rather rougher than I'd like). The upshot was that the early evening was rather gloomy for us all, not helped by the news that the attacks on *Sir Galahad* and *Sir Tristram* on Tuesday were very serious indeed, resulting in the abandonment of both ships, heavy casualties and loss of equipment; in addition a landing craft was sunk, and its crew were missing and, over at San Carlos, HMS *Plymouth* was damaged with the wounding of five seamen. Our moods do tend to rise and fall with the tide of the war.

The Pope arrives here on Friday morning we think, and leaves on Saturday afternoon. Will he ask a question about us? And will the reply be of any use to anyone? I fear much depression if he comes and – ah! at that moment Isabel called. She had had problems with circuits, she explained. And I had problems with the same policeman who gave Ian a hard time the other day – he turned the radio up and began typing. So I asked him to turn it down and he grudgingly agreed to. So-and-so – I wonder what his problem is?

Anyway – Isabel. She said we should be fairly optimistic about the Pope's mentioning us – she said the appeal was very well received in London and that the file went to Rome – so perhaps he'll pop the question. It could do Galtieri a lot of good, in image-building terms, to let us go – but the crucial question is – will the Pope ask?

London was apparently pleased with the Committee and press conference and its coverage; and Willy will come down on Monday or Wednesday or next week (Friday is the Swiss visit). So it is going to be a very tense time. I also asked again about this 9-month wait until the trial – Isabel said yes, this was an outside possibility, but most unlikely. All the responsible Ministries wanted us dealt with as soon as possible, and she thought we would be: she had seen the Foreign Ministry man who deals with our case the other day, and he was very keen that we should not be kept hanging about. She was curious to know if the *NYT* was on the list – the telexed list from London didn't include the name, but they had been very sympathetic with leaders.

But on the whole a depressing day – largely, I must confess, because Ian's moods are so infectious!

Great Missenden, Bucks.
We hope that you are well and will be home to your families soon. In the half term I went down to Selsey by the sea-side. I went with my sister and my mummy and daddy. We swam in the sea. It was cold but we enjoyed it. I made sandcastles and a sand boat. We are having lovely hot weather, all the flowers are out and the trees are in bloom. There is lovely wheat in the field and poppies and daisies. In the fields there are buttercups and cow parsley. Up our lane there is a witches tree. It has got lots of leaves on it.

You can climb it and it is much more exciting than a tree house. There is a back door and front door. And a bottom bit and top bit. I go up there with my friends and take a picknick lunch. We play witches up there as well. I looked after our next door neighbour's dog and their fishes for three days. I took Vicky the dog for walks up to the woods where the bluebells are and the green leaves on the trees. In our close there are quite a lot of children but some are moving out. Our row of houses has got children in them it is the only row that has. On one side there is Barry, Sean and Rebecca my friend. And on the other side there is Patrick and Helen who is my sister's friend and they are the people with the dog. Next door to them is Bethany and Peter, Bethany is my friend and so is Peter but he is a baby. There is Polly and Emma and Charles and Richard and Giles and Julia and Jonathan they are my friends but they are moving. We play games together and have water fights. And we play Colditz in the dark. The boys are all tough but not all the girls are. There is a green in the middle of the close which is round and then a road going round it. There are houses going round as well. This is how you play Colditz. First of all someone is it with a torch and stands in the middle of the green with the torch shining while he goes round and round. We have to start at one end of the close where a house is and go right round without a person seeing you with the torch. If they do see you you will be it in the next game.

Lots of love, Rachel Savory

BBC TV, Buenos Aires

Greetings from yet another member of the Shamrock squad. 'Spotlight' had just ended its season when I was told I'd be coming out here for 'Newsnight' and joining the other Irish citizens like David Capper who'd come out for radio. I was so glad to run into Isabel and get this opportunity of writing to you and saying that lots of people you'll remember from Belfast have been expressing great concern about you all. Even prominent Republicans who have hardly a vested interest in seeing the Task Force sail have quite properly made the distinction between Britain and British journalists and have asked me for news of you. I can't say I've much experience of writing to people in prison, but I did once send a copy of In Holy Terror into Long Kesh. It was confiscated much to the annoyance of the recipient. I don't know if the book I'm sending with this will either get to you safely or be of much interest but Isabel says you're keen on getting something to read to while away the hours. I'm also including a pocket backgammon set. The press corps in Buenos Aires have been, as you may already have heard, whiling away their spare hours playing soccer. The Shamrocks have of course produced easily the best player of the unfit lot of them. Bill Moody, BBC NI sound recordist, has staggered us all by his skill at the game. He was promptly christened Exocet and has been thus called ever since his first game on the Sheraton pitch – a tennis court with moveable goal posts which some have not scrupled to move at crucial points in the game. Air France challenged the hacks to a match last week and Paul Reynolds got a broken arm when tackled – attacked would be a better world – not by the frogs but by his own producer. So he's been shipped home. Exocet was nearly put out of action by the same maniac, but a lad who's tried out for Man Utd in his not so distant youth is not put out of action so easily. I've been going to the gym in the Sheraton in the hope of offsetting the effects of the Argentine diet. The supple young thing (male) who runs the gym classes took one look at me and said 'We'll take it very slowly'. We did. But I still feel fairly stiff. Isabel gave me a copy of the press release issued when the committee was set up on your behalf. I sincerely hope they'll be able to do something. It's certainly a very impressive list of committee members. The Irish Embassy here has told me one of the problems is that the wheels of Argentine justice grind slowly and there's a lot of bureaucratic delay. The embassy is on the 7th floor of a building full of embassies on Santa Fe not far from the Sheraton. They have taken the unusually large influx of Irish in their stride I must say. The Pope arrives the day after tomorrow and I suppose it will be bedlam. The process of getting accreditation is endless and we may all end up in any case taking it all off television. I've been off meeting priests and nuns all over Buenos Aires province – including a Dominican nun from Belfast who works out in a barrio off the Pan American Highway. The poverty was grim. And she told me hunger was now a real problem for them since most had no jobs and no social security to fall back on. One family she took me to visit had but a bed for furniture – no glass in the windows, no cooker, a cement floor, and the rain coming in through the cardboard in the windows. She was within about a day of giving birth, he had hepatitis and their two year old son had had no food in two days. Misery. Two nuns are coping with 15,000 people in the barrio many of whom live at that level. David Wickham and John Stapleton and Mickey Brennan in the next room send greetings. Mickey has been christened Baron B after a superior brand of Argentine champagne. He swears he's losing weight drinking it. I may join

him in the habit. One thought you might appreciate before I sign off –
Jorge Luis Borges was interviewed in an Argentine magazine recently and
asked his opinion of the events following April 2nd. He replied 'I think the
government looked at the situation in the country and decided to flee
forward.' The Pope's visit may provide a climate for compromise and
conciliation. We can only hope so. As a good lapsed catholic I'll put in a
few prayers on your behalf. They say the prayers of sinners and lost sheep
are more efficacious. We shall see. God bless,
    Róisín McAuley

THURSDAY 10 JUNE   I read until about 02.00 – Ian woke up and
wanted to know if it was morning! So I was able to reassure him it
was nothing of the sort. Today we are all much better and more
cheerful: it is odd the way a black mood can descend on us, for no
apparent reason. All right, on Tuesday night we were all cheerful
because Judy had so much news; but there was no cause for
Wednesday's change, nor, for that matter, for today's.

The television, as I write, is showing a film of Argentine forces
training; and today is, I think, Malvinas Day, or some such: so all
the suggestions the other day that the war-fever has disappeared
come to nothing. It's all back – there is a big demo planned in the
Plaza de Mayo tonight (I think that's where it is) and then the Pope
arrives tomorrow. So the propaganda is half-and-half, peace and
war – most peculiar. I don't quite see the sense of a major display of
bellicosity on the eve of a visit of peace – perhaps it is to ensure that
the Pope doesn't undermine the nationalistic fervour of the place.

Jorge came after lunch, looked at our new cells – which are being
painted by a slave gang of fellow prisoners, and should be ready
tomorrow – just in time for the Swiss, who will arrive in the evening,
if he catches all his connections. Jorge went away with a list of odds
and ends we need, and I gave him a million pesos to tide him over.

I asked him about our case, and his considered view was that 'the
government here simply does not know what to do with you . . .' I
hope they make up their mind soon.

No news as yet from the Falklands: as I write John Nott has
refused point blank to give any damage or casualty reports from the
Sir Galahad – Sir Tristram attacks: he said to do so would possibly
'help the enemy', but the attacks had not damaged the integrity of

our forces or their ability to assault Port Stanley. I guess any crucial equipment could be airlifted by a Hercules from Ascension – I don't know. It would have to be pretty desperately needed for an operation like that.

18.30   Well – an interesting little session down at the court. We were all hauled off there – of course, our first thought was that it might be to get some good news; but I had already prepared myself just to hear the official text of the Comodoro Court's refusal of our bail, and that is what it was. The Court's reasons were exactly the same as the judge's original ones – plus the fact that an invasion of the Falklands had now taken place, which made the national security situation that much worse. So, not bad news at all – no suggestion of new evidence, a sterner approach by the courts, vindictiveness or anything similar. But Margarita was there – with books and crossword puzzles and Spanish backgammon instructions – and she gave us what could be fairly good news. The prosecutor – whom she described as a 'special person' – told her at a party on Sunday that 'new evidence' had come to light which was making him change his view of the case, and that he was taking a more lenient approach. I asked if she was sure that was what he said, if she thought he knew she would tell us – and she said yes, she felt it was good news, and that it meant he probably wouldn't be pushing for a harsh sentence at all. Naturally I was delighted: Ian decided (probably wisely) to remain sceptical, but went round saying to himself 'the prosecutor's backing off, eh?' and wondering to himself. He's decided to say nothing to Margaret tonight, though, because she must be crossing her fingers for the Pope's visit in any case, and to burden her with optimism would be very unfair. But it is a further indication that there may be a sentiment a-building to the effect that – as Jorge said earlier – the authorities just don't know what to do with us, and in all probability want to get themselves off the hook and get rid of us. I wonder if the Pope's visit will provide the excuse – then I remember wondering that sort of thing three or four weeks ago, when the Comodoro verdict was under consideration.

Villers-sur-Mer, France
I sit here in the traditional Normandy posture, watching the rain drip off

the apple-trees. My wife Judy and I are here for four weeks. It's a small white house with black shutters, one room deep, set back from a 19th-century watering-place between Cabourg and Deauville. We bought it out of savings made on an excessive ITN salary in Washington in the late sixties, & subsequent economies: we spend all our holidays here, and it has been the means for our only child Toby – now an undergraduate at Leicester – of acquiring his one remotely academic accomplishment, a decent knowledge of spoken French. Our sense of guilt at this enviable possession we partly allay by lending it to our friends; but it breaks out in me afresh, of course, when I contemplate the present difference in the condition of the Whale family and the Winchester, which is helplessly present to my mind a good deal. It was a comfort, at any rate, to learn of the setting up of the new committee. It must do good.

I was to have been writing a short book while I was here, the kind you can do out of your head, but I've been let off. The Dean of St. Paul's is editing a series about how people would like to see the Church of England change, & he asked me to kick in; but happily my synopsis was a good deal too radical for the publishers, Mowbray's, who are chiefly in the books-to-sell-to-devout-women-at-the-back-of-the-church trade; so I've been let off. Instead I've read an excellent book, intelligible & humane, about the 1944 Normandy campaign by John Keegan, who teaches at Sandhurst and reviews for us; & I have Robert Martin and Tennyson & John Carey (Merton Prof., & another of our reviewers) on Donne to come.

We saw the Pope safely off from Cardiff last week, and he is for the moment rather nearer you than me, for all the good it will do you. It was a graceful visit, & well received; but I found myself in the odd position of being the only person to write about the visit from what you might call a Shankill rather than a Falls position, and pointing out that everything he said which indicated a new flexibility, on ethics or ecumenics, was balanced by a restatement of the old inflexibility. It's an ancient tradition in Roman Catholicism, leaving choices open for the future; but it meant that people who read the signs as indicating liberalisation were telling you more about what they themselves – entirely creditably – wanted than about what the Pope did. Leading that particular dance was The Times, where in these matters liberal Catholics – Owen Hickey, Clifford Longley – call the tune.

If I were where you are, I think the things I should most want, after freedom from fear and hunger, would be something sensible to read, something to write on, and (the thing I fear you have not got) enough *solitude or quiet to make use of both. Where you lack those things, I earnestly wish you the resolution to maintain your equanimity none the less.*

    Yours ever, John [Whale]

Rushden, Northants

I do hope that this letter finds you all well in health, and I hope also that your morale is not too down.

    I read in the Sunday Times *that I could write to you and this I am happy to do. Everyone has been watching the newspapers waiting for your long awaited release, we can only pray that before very long you will all be back home with your friends and families in dear old England.*

    What shall I write about? Well, I am a married woman, with a dear husband, who is an engineer and travels to London nearly every day from Rushden, Northamptonshire. We are just on the edge of the County of Bedfordshire, so we have all the lovely villages around to slip out to and have a drink in the village pubs. I have a daughter, Jayne, who lives in London and is nearly, but not quite, in the same profession as you gentlemen.

    In the time that you have been away from us, the Summer has started. The cherry trees have flowered for this year, the almonds and the apple trees. The currants and raspberries are now on the bushes and the tomato plants are doing well. This is partly due to the rain that we had, and then, (you won't believe it) heat! Yes, we have had about two weeks of warm hot sun. I work in a Library, and we have slowly shed our garments (not too many) during the hot humid afternoons. Stamping out 200 Mills & Boons, 50 Catherine Cookson, and 20 Barbara Cartland is not good in such weather.

    I suppose you gents live in the City? or do you commute on the tubes or by car? The area here in Northants and Beds is a rural one of course, but I was not born here, so I do know two worlds, which certainly helps in life. At the moment I am a member of the Townswomen's Guild in Rushden and a member of the Women's Institute at Wymington, Beds (just up the road) two worlds again!

    Well Gents, my husband has come in from his club and told me to tell you that, as he was in the 39/45 war in the RAF, he and some of his friends wanted to come and get you!! This certainly is a crazy world, these days; to imprison you without bail is not what all the Peace Conventions are about.

This letter has not been easy for me to write, I hope that it will at least let you know that there are people who are concerned about your welfare, how you are existing, are you having the right food, and proper medical care. Let us all hope that the three of you will see the Summer's end, the apples on the trees and every thing that you love here at home. Our thoughts are with you, Good Luck and come home quickly.

Regards and best wishes, Ivy H. Gould (and John)

Limavady, Co. Derry, N. Ireland

I see from the S. Times *that people are being encouraged to write to you, so I thought I'd drop you a line if it helps to break the monotony for you — even if it's only for a moment or two. . . .*

We think of you a lot and search the papers for news — thought you showed lots of courage and stamina when we saw you on the news clips and felt chuffed that we'd met you; you know, boasting to our friends and putting the Wedgwood plaque on the house 'Simon Winchester slept here' — nothing too obvious.

There are many questions I'd like to ask you but I suppose you can't write back. Can I send food parcels? Stupid question! Game pie from Fortnum & Masons? Do you get outside at all. I just can't imagine the boredom and strain — grim. However, Nil Desperandum (or something) we're all rooting for you — even the Irish it seems! I pulled a tendon while on the slopes this year and was confined to the hotel bedroom for one day only & that was too much. I was extremely glad to hobble downstairs as soon as I could next morning to breathe different air and touch civilization. Mind you — it was some place. It was an unbelievable hotel in Courchevel, French Alps — custom built right on the side of the piste and full of trendy French with too much money to spend. One lady wore a different fur coat to dinner every night, wearing it from her centrally heated bedroom to the centrally heated dining-room where the waiter took it with a great flourish, to the cloak room, which she had passed on her way in. Two plump ladies of 50+ had obviously been to Rent-a-Gigolo on their way, and had collected two young men who wore grey flannel trousers and cravats, like a uniform and leaped forward with lighters at the ready whenever required. The plump ladies had punk hair-dos, wrapped in foil, and they wore white, tight-fitting space-suits — at night that is, NOT on the piste. In fact, I don't think they did any ski-ing. The young men were

always in & out of the sauna though the ski-ing was really good too – lots
of varied runs so even timorous skiers like me could whizz about for miles
with some confidence and get the adrenalin going. The food was real
gourmet stuff too, though I stuck a bit one night on the goat's cheese with
crab sauce.

Love and good luck from Valerie Smyth

FRIDAY 11 JUNE   The big weekend starts – Pope, Swiss, Willy –
all potentials for some excitement. But before that there are two
things to mention. First of all, Ian didn't get his call from Margaret
last night – poor chap waited until 22.00 – 02.00 in London –
hoping she would. I wondered if the unpleasant guard had put
down the 'phone on her, as someone did to Hilary a fortnight ago.
(His name, by the way, is   – damn; I've just forgotten it!) But
according to Cosina, he wasn't on duty last night, so we assume it
must be circuit problems.

Then, at 14.30, we moved to our new cells: here is an approx-
imate plan of them:

If I have it right, our windows point 70° – I deduce this because
the runway is 340°, and we faced that directly from the windows of
our old cells – so they must have had a bearing of 160°. Since we are
now at 90° to those cells, our bearing, from our windows, must be
70° – but 2½° more than ENE, 9 degrees or so less than ENE by E.
So we should get a bit of sun in the morning, if Monte Olivia
doesn't block it off completely. This is the first time I've seen it – a
great, four pronged pyramid – very spectacular, and dramatically
different from the rounded mountain to the south of it. It is almost
as though Mount Kenya and Mount Kilimanjaro were next to each
other, or as though Sgurr Alasdair was next to the Red Hills (which
it is).

Later on, the Swiss Embassy Vice-Consul – a Mr Grob – arrived,
to the admiration of a police station staff all of whom were falling
over each other trying to be nice to us. Grob is a thin, pale, tall,
dark-haired man of about 28 – nice enough, but without the style –
and the enchanting smile – of Werner. We had whisky with him and
with Barrozo, during which he told us he'd be back at 09.30 to take
our shopping list and give us some of the great collection of letters
and odds and ends which came down from Washington, and from

Isabel. Not all – more will come down with Willy on Wednesday or so. It was good to see a Swiss again, though – the way the staff jump about to impress him is quite astonishing: it might make a more sceptical person than me dubious in the extreme! He was given a tour of our cells, and then for purposes of comparison, a tour of the old cells – he reacted with depressing (to us) enthusiasm to the better conditions.

Then dinner – knives again (though oddly we didn't use them at all!) – which was served by Abundano, the waiter. Chicken soup, then pasta and meat – we had cheese and coffee – not bad! People kept coming in to offer us various comforts – the nice little guard, Piedrabuena (Charlie Chaplin, or Tom Thumb) lent me a pop music tape; another, Porky, had the World Cup running order xeroxed for us; and then Grieco came in, telling us we could have a drink with him tomorrow. He's very happy because his oldest daughter – the medical student, who has been very unhappy in Buenos Aires – is home for the weekend. He said journalists were starting to call, asking for interviews; a South African (he said Anton – that was the name of the Surinamese from right back at the beginning of all this, wasn't it?) called, and Grieco said no problem, why not. One does get the persistent feeling that there is either a lot going on, or some frantic PR work on our behalf during the Pope's visit – which began today, in pouring rain.

Margaret managed to get through today at 20.25 – she had run up against busy circuits all last night. She said that Hugh had called from BA yesterday to tell her that the Papal Nuncio (in BA) had replied, in answer to a question about whether the Pope would raise the matter of our imprisonment with Galtieri, 'It is quite inconceivable that he would not'. Good.

The heating engineer has just been, and lo! the radiators now work! What a Swiss diplomat can do! And best of all – though I'm sure it is temporary – the door is open! We could walk out of the prison at this very instant if we chose to. Perhaps that's what they want! It would certainly get rid of a problem for the country.

This move seems, at first blush, to have been a good thing. Our circumstances have improved hugely, but we can still go next door to our old cells for visits. To think that poor Ian fretted so about it all. He is such a terrible worrier. He's as happy as a sandboy now, and as I write is playing with the hot water system, like a child with a Christmas toy. What a change!

SATURDAY 12 JUNE A long and interesting day – really a delightful Saturday. We were up at 09.15 to await Señor Grob, who came at 09.45 to take a shopping list and, incidentally, left behind what we had all been waiting for – the package of letters from home. It was just like Christmas: books, Scrabble, backgammon, and, best of all, piles of letters. Lovely pictures of Judy, the children and the dogs – taken, possibly, by the *Oxford Mail* photographer. There are three shots, all excellent, and I've been showing them to everyone in sight. I am blessed with such a handsome family – I'm the only blemish! Then there was a drawing, 'A seen from the crisis' (*sic*) by Alex; letters from Judy and all the children, including a splendid joke from Rupert (about making a cat go 'woof'[1]), letters from Father, Rev. Crusha, Liz Kabbara and a host of others. Also a long one from Isabel, as interesting and informative as usual. She says George de'Ath told her I'm the one that's keeping the others sane, which I'm not sure is right, but it is nice to give that impression. Ian was very odd today – he clearly wanted to take the lead in the talks with Grob, feeling (I guess after that *Siete Días* article and other things) he was slightly in the shadows. But he came across rather nervous and uneasy, I thought. Is this bitchiness on my part? Judy's letters were surprisingly tender – in a way so very different from usual affectionate tenderness. They were rather like love letters, in parts, and rather took my breath away. This experience will change things in some way, I expect. Looking at Judy's picture, which is before me as I write, I'm struck by the very unoriginal thought that there are families just as lovely, hoping for just the same things, filled with just the same feelings, in Argentina too – everywhere, in fact. Oh Pacifism – why don't you win? How horrible that families like this have to suffer so. There was a *Sunday Times* picture – or half of one – of 'The Widow of Stubbington': a girl obviously widowed by the war, reading mail, or looking at pictures of her and her dead husband. She's wearing a tartan skirt – she could be Margarita Vásquez, or perhaps one of the pretty girls at the court here.

1 'You douse it in petrol and throw it on the fire.' Horrible child!

I'm listening to 'Let it Be' on the Walkman – the tape Piedra-buena made for us. 'And when the broken hearted people living in the world agree, There will be an answer, let it be.' It's difficult to be flip at a moment like this – heavy snow falling outside, war raging over Port Stanley (the British advanced five miles in an early morning raid – 'Give 'em Hell Jeremy', the worst side of me says!), the pictures of Judy and the Stubbington widow, and 'Let it Be' on the tape.

Anyway, a few minutes after noon, Grob was back saying that all the shops were closed because of the Pope's visit, which was going great guns up north[1] (and in brilliant weather, too, in contrast to yesterday's rain and wind). He managed to get only a few odds and ends – but one of them was the colour TV, a Toshiba – under licence called a 'semp': it works beautifully.

At 17.00 Captain Grieco and his oldest daughter, newly arrived from BA – she's a medical student there, and very unhappy about the war – asked us to come in for a drink (the Swiss and Barrozo were buying the TV and seeing Sagstume) and we chatted for a while – I gave him Alex's picture and the excellent *ST* story about us (including a quite brilliant sketch – from Cal's memory – of our first cell) and the picture of the family, all of which he had xeroxed. Then the reason for his niceness – Venezuelan TV were downstairs, wanting an interview which Grieco wanted us to give. Ian not so keen, but we did, and it worked very well, they were a little hostile to the British view, but were extremely professional, with a fine interpreter.

After that excitement – and the mess was full of police and many people all of whom seemed very friendly indeed, not at all hostile – we had a brief final chat with Grob, who told us that Sagastume was looking at the evidence once again to see how overwhelming it was. Ten days more and there may be some sort of decision, he said. Is it a sign? I wrote to Frank Giles saying there seemed unmistakable signs that this was all winding down – not that I was becoming unrealistically optimistic, but things were being said that sounded as though this may all be coming to an end. But if not – well, as long as Judy's letters keep coming, I'll be fine, I know. But if I am keeping

1 And what a long way North – it was sometimes difficult to remember that the Argentine capital was 2,000 miles away.

Ian going, it's not all that easy at times.

I'm writing this standing up in the bedroom: I've spent a lot of time here, away from the others. It is probably not a good thing, but I like it – cold though it may be. Today I'm trying to diet a little, as the old tummy is thickening! We've said that on our release we'll starve ourselves so we look suitably haggard – it won't look too well! Funny – if people ask were we well treated and, on our saying yes, ask about the horrors of the post-*Belgrano* period, I'll have to say that one's memory of prison nastiness is very short – one is conditioned (at least I am) by the last act of kindness, not a distant act of unpleasantness.

The *Private Eye* material came: and a brutal piece it was, too – some enemies out there. But SH and SG (Gloucestershire)[1] wrote nice letters, which Ingrams published – Susan's was extraordinarily written, full of spelling mistakes and grammatical errors, and yet the overall impression was curiously powerful and right, like someone spluttering with rage and fury, and conveying the mood perfectly. Then Mike Leapman set the record straight in William Hickey, thank him, bless him.

SUNDAY 13 JUNE   I woke at 07.20 to lie in wait for Grob, who picked up a bunch of letters to take up to BA – he'll hand them to Isabel tonight or tomorrow, and let's hope the London ones (Judy and Frank, for me) are pigeoned out, so they get them soon. It is snowing hard as I write this: all from the north, great sweeping gusts of tiny flakes, so it should drift. The sky is leaden, full of snow. The World Cup begins today – with the Argentina vs. Belgium game which we'll see in Glorious Living Colour. (We've dubbed the Pope – à la Bruce Loudon[2] – the LOG – Lamb of God). I finished the *Observer* x-word last night at 02.45! Is there really such a thing as a 'Trembling Poplar'?

19.00.   Listening now to the BBC – the best reception ever here, I think – 15.24 MHz – it's a crisp, cold, quite clear evening – dark of course. I can almost hear Roger Collinge turning the pages over.

1 Simon Hoggart and Susan Hillmore.
2 Bruce was a friend from New Delhi who liked to speak in initials – things were 'TW for W' – 'too wonderful for words'. The 'AB of C' was the Archbishop of Canterbury.

The BBC's broadcast quality – and I don't mean the quality of reception, but of its output – is really superb. Collinge is still my favourite news reader: Michael Birley, though he sounds so stern, is also excellent. All of them seem friends to us now.

The news from the Falklands continues to be good for the British – and it turns out only 50 died in last Tuesday's tragic attacks on the *Sir Galahad* and *Sir Tristram.* Nott gave a press conference – HMS *Glamorgan* was hit – 9 died, but it is still 'operational'. The news of last Tuesday's casualties was deliberately withheld to confuse the Argentines: and it seemed to have been successful, in that they seemed to overestimate British casualties massively.

'There is still some way to go', John Nott said, in reference to the recapture of Stanley, 'but the result is not in doubt'. The Red Cross has suggested the 600 civilians currently in Stanley be placed in a safe zone of concrete buildings. Britain has agreed, but has said it must be done quickly. Argentina is 'considering the matter' – meaning they could hold the civilians as hostages, as we've always feared.

Later on – 01.00 local – it was announced that both sides had agreed that all the local civilians would be placed in a neutral zone in and around the Cathedral, and that this would be untouched, if possible, by shell fire. Let's hope that in their desperation the Argentine Army doesn't take refuge there. We finally got into bed at about 02.00, with Ian belly-aching about our being so late. We watched a film on TV till 01.30 or so – it was an escape film about Alcatraz, which made us all think!

MONDAY 14 JUNE   Although I woke briefly at 07.30 and again when the guard came and looked in – very quickly – at 09.30 – we all slept until way past 11.00, and I had a steaming hot shower. (Ian had forgotten to turn the tap on;[1] and by the time Tony got up the water had cooled down! Such justice.) Now it's lunch time, and the day begins. It snowed quite hard in the night, and Mount Olivia is all white, glistening like a fortress.

A World Cup match this afternoon – Poland and Italy. I'm afraid

1 A complicated arrangement for getting hot water – it involved turning a tap on until water began to cascade from an overflow onto the prison's flat roof – then, ten minutes later we would get a few gallons of hot water, if we were lucky. We never understood why.

it really doesn't interest me very much, so I crept into the bedroom and tried (not terribly successfully) to do the crossword. I listened to the Brandenburg Concertos, one after the other – a great cultural afternoon. (Yesterday Ian and I played Scrabble – I won, I won!) with a score described in the Rule Book as excellent. No call from Isabel last night, by the way – possibly she'll get through today, although with the Pope having gone now I wouldn't blame her for taking a well earned long weekend rest.

Things are rather tense between the three of us this afternoon, and I'm not sure why. I suspect my not having watched the football and our very slight argument about reading in bed contributed to our mood.

16.07   A Communiqué, saying there had been a 'conference' between General Menendez and Maj-General Jeremy Moore. No word what it is – the initial Argentine Communiqué, No. 161, broke into another prison film (!) this time a comedy.

17.05   I'm shaking a bit: the Joint Chiefs of Staff in Buenos Aires have just announced officially that there is to be a cease fire between the two armies on the island. General Menendez is flying back to BA; it is assumed he will discuss, with the Junta, the terms of surrender. David Capper, talking live from BA, suggested that the Argentines have been prepared for this kind of an end – even the football result yesterday (the Argentine team lost to Belgium, 1–0) dampened the bellicose mood, as did the surprise return yesterday of more than 1000 soldiers captured in Goose Green and Darwin.

We drank the last of Cal's brandy – 'To peace – peace and freedom' – at 17.20. Outside it is snowing hard, and the grey and gathering gloom reflects the grim mood of this poor country. I feel genuinely sorry for the good people – for Grieco and Barrozo and people like them, led on to this brink by the ass, Galtieri. He must bear an enormous responsibility on his shoulders – a terrible crime, I believe. I wonder whether he sleeps well at night.

So – what now? I feel sure it can only be a matter of time before an honourable end to this business is announced, and the ships and the hacks can go home. Perhaps us, too, although we come under the heading of 'mopping up', or 'crossing the t's and dotting the i's'. But unless the Menendez meeting goes very badly, unless Galtieri announces that the war goes on – and he is perfectly capable of doing such a thing – I would have thought we were on the home stretch. Let's hope this diary never reaches page 300 – although if it does I'll stay strong and resolute. I know I've got it in me now – I'm a lot stronger a person than I thought.

For the record, Communiqué No. 161 came shortly before 16.50.

19.00 Mrs Thatcher has apparently told 'cheering MPs' that the two commanders are now discussing surrender terms. White flags have broken out in the capital, and Argentine troops are throwing down their arms. The cease fire took effect, officially, at 16.00 local, but may have been observed some hours before that. The British troops have been told they can only open fire in self-defence.

The toll thus far is approximately:—

Argentina: 750 dead
            100 aircraft lost
            General *Belgrano* sunk
            16,500 p.o.w.s
Britain: 250 dead
            several aircraft lost
            HMS *Sheffield* sunk
            HMS *Antelope* sunk
            HMS *Ardent* sunk
            HMS *Coventry* sunk
                Sir Galahad abandoned
                Sir Tristram abandoned
                Atlantic Conveyer sunk
            1 p.o.w.

What a terrible waste!

TUESDAY 15 JUNE Our ninth week here ends at 11.20 a.m. I got up quite early – for me – put on the water for coffee, and the wireless. When Hot-lips and Tom Thumb came by at 09.40 I was awake, and bellowed 'La Paz!' to them; they smiled their agreement, and said that we'd be out soon now that the trouble was over.

A grey old day, but a lot warmer than yesterday: the snow is melting, and the constant drip on the corrugated iron roof is presumably one of the familiar sounds of an Ushuaia winter's day.

The first words of the BBC 16.00 news I heard – the signal was very weak – were 'arrangements for the rapid evacuation of the Argentine troops on the islands . . .' so presumably (there are no 'obviouslys' in this situation) the surrender has been accepted. Yesterday Brigadier-General Lami Dozo, the Air Force Chief, was talking of a 'new basis' for politics and economics in his country in the wake of the defeat in the Falklands: could that be a signal for the removal of General Galtieri? I rather think so, but Ian didn't read anything like that into it. We are wondering what we would do if we are offered bail – I think it might slow the court's progress down if we were set free on bail, and quite frankly I'd rather have a month more in gaol, rather than six months in an hotel in Ushuaia. A tricky one, that would be.

I was trying to work out the costs of all this to the *ST*, and came to the conclusion that in fact had I been at the Sheraton all the time, I would have set them back a good £800 p.w. – I can't have cost them that much more down here, and they get all the publicity. So I'm stopping feeling guilty about the money. Except, of course, they've had to pay Isabel's hotel! Oh, why did I think of that!?

21.30 Judy rang – pretty optimistic, now that the surrender – of 15,000 Argentine soldiers – is official. I spoke for 25 minutes – all well. She had heard from Willy/Isabel that Sagastume was going to Rio Grande to re-interview the man who arrested us – I wonder why? I still get the persistent feeling we are going to be written out of this story fairly quickly, and I conveyed that impression to her. I passed on messages about my wanting to contribute to the Paul Eddy book; and she, in return, had the very good news for me that *Their Noble Lordships* is to be published on the 23 June as a Book of the Month Club Alternate, which could mean quite a decent sale. So possibly our financial situation will seem less bleak soon.

Galtieri has just addressed the nation – very sombre and sober – nothing like the bombast of a month ago when, with three zombie-like officials behind him, he hectored the nation on the right of armed aggression. But (though I'll wait for the official translation, via Harold Briley) it didn't sound a very bellicose speech. He's told the people that the Falklands have been lost; there have already been big demonstrations – hostile to Galtieri, and the Junta Militar

– outside the Casa Rosada. So what now?

Willy called, and sounded more optimistic; he was going to speak to the judge today or tomorrow to try to get a steer on what our fate will be. My main impression is that we ought to get out of here in a matter of weeks. I cannot see them holding on to us; no one seems to be in a vindictive mood at all – certainly all the guards seemed friendly enough (at least – they did before the Galtieri speech!).

Reading, Berks

I hope you are well and I hope you aren't too sad. It is summer here and all the lovely flowers are out and the butterflies have come out as well. We have drawn a picture of the HMS Glasgow which Dawns uncle was on. We wrot a letter to him and then Dawn went to Italy and the day before she came back to school we had a letter from Dawn's uncle. We got it that day. He also sent us some photographs of the HMS Glasgow. I hope you will be out of prison very soon. Lots of love.

Love from Catherine

WEDNESDAY 16 JUNE   Letters this morning from Juliet, and from John Peter at the *ST* – both letters long and interesting: they are dears!

Woodward talks of the terrible plight of 15,000 Argentine prisoners on the Falklands – a 'major disaster relief problem' he says, which can only be alleviated by a pledge from BA that the fighting is over. This pledge is not forthcoming, thus far. At the moment I'm listening to Hugh O'Shaughnessy talking on The World Today – very fractured broadcast; he was a slightly awkward customer.

I sent a note to Barrozo about the prisoners – it occurred to me (perhaps rather rashly) that since Buenos Aires was in such a shambles, it might not be a bad idea if the naval hierarchy in Tierra del Fuego knew the situation. But even if it was incautious of me to have written it, it a) showed the police I have humanitarian concern for Argentines and b) it helped me practise my *castellano*. No reaction, anyway, so perhaps it was simply ignored!

At about 22.00 the final communiqué, it seems – a long, ten point explanation for the loss of the military action, and – from what we can gather – the formal announcement of the end of hostilities in the South Atlantic. Perhaps this is what Pym and Fieldhouse and Woodward wanted. I'll listen to the 02.00 BBC news and see if there's any sort of announcement.

Ian very worried about the exact translation of the communiqué, but we managed to get through the evening. He is, I am afraid to say, quite impossibly trying at times.

Buenos Aires

I hope all this material will keep spirits up for a while – some of it is the stuff that Magnus sent via Whitaker to Washington and I had hoped to pigeon down last week, but the phantom BBC man let me down – I got the message about exercise machinery, but haven't located any yet – I'm getting slightly swamped with impending Popery & have to file tomorrow, so I thought I would renew the search on Monday & Willie can bring it when he goes.

Do you know, I had hoped I might be able to travel with the Swiss, but partly because they elected to go the day the Pope arrives & partly because they jumped the gun over the request before I had had time to soften up contacts, this trip is impossible – I shall keep trying, though, once the air clears a bit. I have given the Swiss 10 million pesos for you – I suggest you buy a tv there – apart from problems of transport, they should be cheaper in Ushuaia – if that doesn't work, let me know & I shall ask Willie if he could take one down. Also, if it consumes too much of your money, I can give him some more for you. We haven't fixed a date for his visit, but we are talking about early next week – I'll let you know by phone – sorry about the interruption in communications – I went up to Mendoza on Monday & was to take a flight back which would get me in at 8.00, but the military commandeered the plane, so we were stuck until 10.30 p.m. Monday they told me the phone was out of order – I now gather Judy got through so perhaps it was just a fumble fingered BA operator who didn't want to break off his knitting. I hope by the time you get this I shall have succeeded in calling.

Life continues at the Sheraton – lots of the first wave of hacks have left – except for the British who can't – no renewals of visas and no more new ones, so if we leave the country we can't get back – the hard core are all rather ground down with waiting for the resolution of the conflict – it's all taking so much longer than anyone imagined and has taken on the aspect of a slow slide into a much worse mess. I find it quite appalling that all this should actually increase La Thatcher's popularity, but that's what seems to be happening.

Everyone is diverted at the moment by the Pope and then comes the World Cup – in BA people seem almost bored by the war now – people don't talk about it as they used to – if anything they worry about what follows – everybody is jockeying for position, but so much depends on the military outcome that nobody can be sure what will happen.

I'm rather dreading the Pope's visit professionally – most inconsiderate of him to arrive on a Friday & the thought of battling through millions of people appals me – everyone but the networks have given up the idea of going to Lujan – not enough phone lines or helicopters for the hacks. I've also had to grapple with Catholic politics – a subject for which I discover in myself very little aptitude or sympathy – perhaps my atheist mother had a stronger influence than I thought (she was, after all, a Southern Irish Protestant atheist).

I had a long talk with George de'Ath who was in culture shock having come up from Ushuaia to BA: its rather like crossing from the PRC into Hong Kong – you can't believe the abundance & frivolity – you are going to have a terrible case of it when you get out, I imagine. I have been reading Bruce Chatwin's In Patagonia *– lots of mentions of Ushuaia & the jail – though a predecessor, I think, of yours – if you haven't read it, you might enjoy it – he is quite bleak about Patagonia though; for him it seems populated almost entirely by the mad & the sad. Perhaps, on second thoughts, that's not what you need.*

There have been a couple of initiatives here on your behalf – letters circulating for mass colleagues' signatures and sent to the powers & the press. The rest, I think, you know about – I enclose a copy of the telegram from the committee to Galtieri – the letters were similar.

I'm not bored exactly, in BA, in spite of how I looked at the Press Conference – that was a result of having to wait for an hour for it to begin. I miss some of the hacks from the first wave who became good friends, but have been replaced for humanitarian reasons or other wars – and I am sad that I missed the spring in my cottage garden at home – but these are very small things – on the whole I enjoy it here – the Sheraton apart – I like the Argentinians & tho' exasperating at times, I find the story endlessly interesting – I get frustrated about you three – and about how complicated your situation has become – and feel great pangs of guilt & failure that you are still there – it's sometimes rather daunting that outside events have played such a malevolent role at every turn and I am very impatient for it to finish so that we are not constantly shouting against the wind – but then I tell myself that there are quite a lot of plusses for the efforts of the last two months – there is a great body of international opinion rooting for you – both press people, of course, but also statesmen, international organisations, Foreign Secretaries etc – and, indeed, though you may have less sense of this, in Argentina too many very influential people are watching very closely, lest anything go wrong. I do believe that when the gale dies down a bit, all those voices will sound a little louder than they can right now.

You must be tired of all these reassurances and no progress – George says you are the one who is keeping the three of you sane, which can't be easy. Everyone admires all this strength of character enormously, though, and perhaps you might feel in the end that the experience isn't wasted, however dreadful at the time. I think about you all, trying to imagine what your days feel like – and the rage & frustration you must be feeling – I find it's like the war – it started as such a small thing and I constantly think I'm dreaming that it should have gone on so long and grown so bleak . . .

– Thursday – time catching up with me – take care,
love, Isabel [Hilton]

Buenos Aires

Just a brief note to let you know that your Irish friends haven't forgotten. A lot of people from the Taoiseach down having been trying as best they can to help things along. It's extraordinary to find so many good things there and then these dreadful flaws which help destroy the outside world's faith. When I arrived one of the first things I had planned to do was thank you for the long piece you did for RTE on your arrival in BA from the South Altantic. Having come 8000 miles this seems a strange way of doing it, but everyone back home had been saying what a terrific programme it made. Trust it won't be very long now before once again you resume your relationship with the radio audience in Ireland. Haven't ever had the pleasure of meeting either of your journalistic colleagues but we're all thinking of them too and, in our Irish way saying a prayer for all of you and your speedy release back to family and friends. Having seen the film from the South I know the spirit is intact and the sense of humour, despite it all, undimmed so keep it up until we can soon crack the bottle of Jameson 15 year old and raise a glass to good times past and better to come.

Slainte, Gerald Barry, RTE News

THURSDAY 17 JUNE   He was still worried this morning, too. But after some World Cup (on TV) and table tennis (in the other cells) has perked up.

A confusing day – though a brilliant one, in terms of the weather – clean, crisp, cold – with the news breaking very curiously. Let me chronicle it: at noon, the first news we get here, the BBC was still saying that there had been no agreement on the repatriation of the 10,660 Argentine prisoners on the Falklands. But Briley reporting from BA said that the most senior army officers met late into last night and that most of the 14 there were in favour of a negotiated settlement with Britain – Galtieri wanted to disassociate himself from the ceasefire and was blaming General Menendez for what happened.

Mrs Thatcher said that *Canberra* would go to Montevideo with 5000 prisoners; officers would be kept, and possibly sent back to Britain unless the British get a clear understanding that all hostilities in the South Atlantic had come to an end.

Then at 15.26, during the 18.15 edition of Radio Newsreel it was reported that *Canberra* would be allowed to an Argentine port, after all: this sounded like good news. (Also it was said that our plight would be discussed in the 19.00 edition of Outlook.)

But then, at the very end of the Reel there was an announcement that the latest news from BA was that Galtieri had been removed from office and that his successor was a hard liner who was against a negotiated peace with the British. We have a tense few minutes now (while Robert Robinson is on with Brain of Britain) waiting for the 19.00 Outlook headlines – if a harder liner is in power, what is to become of us? And what is to become of the country? The BBC said yesterday that jamming of the Spanish-language services had stopped; that, taken with the news of the *Canberra*'s acceptance at Comodoro Rivadavia (possibly) did look encouraging for the peace. This new development sounds stunning, and I hope it's not true, for all concerned.

19.04   It was announced that Galtieri has resigned; Saint-Jean is the new interim President, and it is possible that a civilian, like Costa-Méndez, will be the new President; and a General Nicolaides has taken over as Chief of Army Staff and (presumably) head of the Junta.

As I write this – at 00.05 – Comisario Barrozo is here, greatly excited at having received a letter from Cal (though it was in English: I thought the Spanish scholars on the desk would have come to his aid!). He sat and discussed the situation in Buenos Aires and the South Atlantic for over an hour, then demanded that whiskies be brought to our cells and we are just now waiting for them to be brought. I'm beginning to wonder how on earth we'll get him out!

Lots and lots of letters today; 3 from Judy alone; and lots from friends in the US. It was a field day.

FRIDAY 18 JUNE   I made a list this morning of the people who – though not relations – have written to me. Thus far it is 58, plus some strangers who didn't give their names. An extraordinary display of affection; it has made my self-esteem soar, quite seriously.

The first news today is that Argentine has informed the International Red Cross that it will give safe conduct to the *Canberra* and the *Norland* to transport prisoners from the Falklands; they will go to Puerto Madryn which, if I remember correctly, is where the first Welsh settlers arrived in Argentina earlier this century (or was it late last?). Thus far the Argentine government has said nothing about a total end to hostilities in the South Atlantic, and until that happens the British will hang on to about 1000 prisoners – officers and other commanders.

On the radio yesterday Pym talked about the three of us, and Mrs Thatcher raised us in the House of Commons – Ian believes we are now being linked to the release of the Argentine prisoners. Perhaps we'll find ourselves on the *Canberra*! There is one British prisoner, a Harrier pilot, who Barrozo says is in hospital in Comodoro Rivadavia.

Barrozo – who waited in our room, giving us whisky, until 00.30 – said he understood the South of Argentina would get normal flights as from today – so perhaps it will no longer be an operational zone, forbidden to journalists. That will make everything – mail, visitors, etc., – much more available.

Barroza also said that General Nicolaides was a man of '*línea dura*' – hard line – but VOA said he was in favour of a negotiated peace with Britain. There are to be ceremonies today in which power will be formally handed over by Galtieri to Saint-Jean (the Presidency) and Nicolaides (the Army) . . . The BBC says that Admiral Anajar may go, too, and Lami Dozo this morning was talking about the need for a new governmental structure. I was right when I interpreted Lami Dozo's remarks the other day about 'a new basis for politics and economics . . .' as a hint that there was to be a purge, and perhaps a return to civilian rule. Ian didn't agree – so I'm personally pleased that my judgement – or reading of the tea-leaves – was so much better!

The BBC later reported that the Foreign Office Junior Minister – Cranley Onslow (?) – told the Commons that he had asked the Swiss to try and secure our release 'in the context of the repatriation of the prisoners . . .' Then Mr Grob telephoned, to say first of all, that Isabel had got permission to come down, and would be here with Willy on Monday afternoon. I asked Grob about what I had just heard on the BBC – he replied that he didn't want to raise any false hopes, but that 'things were going on' and there was some reason for hope. So it is good to know that we are caught up in a diplomatic effort, too – even though I am a little discomfited by the linking of us to a) the prisoners of war and b) the British government. But beggars can't be choosers, I suppose. The first prisoners arrive at Puerto Madryn tomorrow.

Argentina has told the UN it will end the state of hostilities if a) British troops are withdrawn b) the blockade ends and c) economic sanctions are ended. That all sounds reasonable and negotiable, so we're all quite optimistic. There's clearly no need for British troops in any numbers on the Falklands if there's no state of war, so it ought to happen, though slowly.

Tonight a remarkable ceremony took place, the installation of General Nicolaides to Chief of the Army Staff and member of the ruling Junta, and the removal of Galtieri. Admiral Anajar made a speech thanking Galtieri, who looked sober and sad – I even thought his granite face had a trace of tears in the eyes, and that there was some remorse for taking Argentina down what turned out to be a disastrous road. But I couldn't be certain. Nicolaides looks a miserable so-and-so, and there were no smiles or back-slapping between any of the four: a very sober ceremony, with a huge blue and white and gold Argentine flag behind the men, and rank upon rank of generals and admirals and cardinals in attendance. But it was a dignified ceremony – not at all like the supposedly traditional 'hand-over' in lesser republics – usually a bullet in the head is the necessary persuasion! But this ceremony only involved the Junta and the C-in-C's job: there is still some confusion over whether Saint-Jean becomes Acting President and whether Galtieri gives it up. Briley doubts there will be many complications over that.

SATURDAY 19 JUNE   Barrozo arrived at 11 a.m. today, with his two children and three bottles (well, half bottles, actually) of red wine. We had one for lunch, and it was superbly reminiscent. Then tons more mail – for me – and, later, two telegrams for Ian (it being Father's Day). I really think I'd like to do a prison diary with the text of all the letters sent to me, as an illustration of the English as a compassionate and caring people. Two of the letters were from my bank managers! And a fascinating one from a lady who used to live in BA and knows of Ushuaia. Mrs Theobald, her name was – with her, I shall get in touch. David Blundy also wrote a lovely letter – he is so nice. The Jefferson Hotel thinks of me – Sally, especially! It's incredible to know that so many people care. As I've said before, I'm really humbled.

The situation really is coming back to normal – on television tonight there was what one might call 'normal' Saturday night's programming – pop music, women's soap-operas and such like. And a horror film, to boot. Absolutely no propaganda advertisements – no 'The Reoccupation of the Malvinas was an act of a strong and united people . . .' or 'Argentina to victory . . .' or anything remotely similar. Just advertisements for local shops and the tourist industry. Possibly with the region opening up again we shall see tourists once more, although ironically there's a shortage of hotel accommodation now that the Albatross Hotel has burned down.

The Argentines have complained (actually the communiqué went out last night, but the BBC picked it up only today) that the British have occupied the island of (I think – I must assume) Southern Thule, in the South Sandwich group. If so that'll be a welcome reversal of a situation that's existed since 1977 or so, when the Argentines occupied the rock and put a 'scientific station' so-called, on it. That was the incident for which the FO should be blamed most of all – the fact they did nothing about it, that is.

At home today the TV news was extended to take film received back from the Falklands – the first news film transmitted. Brian Hanrahan was grumbling a little about the total lack of TV pictures for 10 weeks. HMS *Glasgow* arrived back at Portsmouth today – a Type 42 Destroyer, with a gaping hole just above the waterline. 'The luckiest ship afloat', her Captain said. Ironically, HMS *Canberra* was escorted into Puerto Madryn today by ARA *Trinidad*, also a Type 42 ship, probably also built at Barrow in Furness. HMS *Illustrious* – sister ship to HMS *Invincible* – left Walker ship yards of Swan Hunter for six weeks of trials yesterday. The work on her was finished 3 months ahead of schedule – which might well help the future of dear old Wallsend![1]

Another ferry left for Port Stanley today – with engineers, air traffic-controllers, bomb disposal squads and 20 nurses. Life is getting fast back to normal on the Falklands too.

Tomorrow dear, blessed Isabel comes. With Willy, whose talks with Sagastume may be critical for our immediate future. But it's Isabel who I'm really longing to see.

Two phone calls today: Bob Schieffer of CBS, and James Brooke (or Baker?) of the *Miami Herald*. It was nice to hear from them: I asked Bob to call and thank Walter Cronkite.

Tapes from Jane Scotti today – Joan Baez, Bob Dylan, exactly as I asked a very doubtful Margarita[2] last week. She – both of them – have been absolutely marvellous. I only hope we're not whisked away so rapidly we won't be able to speak to them. Joan Baez has just sung 'Love is a Pain in the Ass' to a cheering audience. What's wrong with them all?

1 I had worked for three years in Newcastle upon Tyne, and loved the shipbuilding towns downriver – of which Wallsend was the best-known.
2 She had doubted that she could ever find Bob Dylan songs in Ushuaia.

First of all many apologies for not writing earlier. Most of us only knew we could get letters through to you a few weeks ago. As a one-man band there has been very little time to put pen to paper.

Despite the lack of correspondence we have all been thinking of you. As you probably know we wrote a letter to the Interior Minister General Saint-Jean and the Pope recently asking for their intervention. Now Saint-Jean has become interim president we are hoping to renew our efforts and send another note to him.

Life here is as routine and methodical as it must have become for you. We all watch the seasons pass by from the same hotel room we moved into months ago. A rather weird sense of humour has developed. Most of the hacks now call each other Bill for some unknown reason. I'm Bursting Bill because I've put on so much weight since I've been here. I argue that my shirts have shrunk so much in the hotel laundry but it makes no difference. It looks like I'll be Bursting for ever more. . . .

Our colleagues with our troops on the Falklands have distinguished themselves throughout with often brilliant despatches from the front. Max Hastings in particular did remarkably well and became the first Brit to set foot again in Port Stanley since the Argentine invasion. He was with the leading paratroopers when they were ordered to halt just outside the town before the Argentine surrender. Stripping off his army gear to his civvies he walked in past the bemused Argentines past Government House holding his arms in the air and a white handkerchief. He went straight to the Upland Goose Hotel (remember the food, Simon) for a drink. Des King was already holding a party. No doubt he would want to know if his cheques had been sent to his bank or not! Max certainly became the hero of the hour and there seems no point in entering the Journalist of the Year competition . . .

Best regards,
David Graves

It's some years now since we met in a hospitality room of the BBC in Belfast, where the future of Ireland and its relations with Britain had been solved many times by opposing politicians made sentimental by drink. I think you had just come back from a notable trek down the Rockies – or my memory may be playing me tricks – you may have been visiting Belfast fresh from India.

I'm here because I have an Irish passport and can operate easier than the Brits. After two years on BBC-2's Newsnight programme I returned to Belfast, first to 'run' Television Current Affairs and then – shortly – to succeed the amazing W. D. Flackes as Political Correspondent. He retires in a couple of weeks and is leaving to a resounding series of farewells. He is a man who kept his balance without ever greatly risking his neck, I feel. Another kind of journalist, he reflected on his BBC career after 15 years with the Press Association in Westminster: a stickler for accuracy, a passionate filer, but with the considerable black humour that sustained him, kept well under the surface.

I hope to stay in the job for a short enough time to avoid the award of an OBE.

Northern Ireland has been good to many journalists, yourself included of course, as your warm hearted pieces so often acknowledged. I remember a fairly recent piece of yours in which you sang the praises of a little piece of mellow civilisation – the Linen Hall Library. A new librarian, John Gray, has started to rattle the tin for it. Somehow it will survive, I'm sure of that, and the old leather chairs will creak to my weight – and yours – for as long as we're around.

In the past few years, quite a lot has inevitably happened to me. You might just remember my wife. She's Helen Madden, who presented the kids' programme 'Romper Room' on UTV, in between the racing and the news summary every afternoon. She gave it up when the UDA coopted the programme title for their own appalling purposes. We've 2 children, Simon, who's almost 3, and Rebecca, just three months. Simon is old enough to say, when he sees my reports from here on TV – 'Daddy's not coming home' – and then runs away.

I left Northern Ireland in 1979 to go to 'Newsnight' – a peculiarly ineffective programme, often, but which carries a fair proportion of BBC TV's journalism. Best trip was Poland, August 1980. We were lucky enough to get visas at a time the Polish government thought they could handle a wave of strikes and a lock-in at the Gdansk shipyard. We drove from Warsaw in a fleet of cars 300 miles to Gdansk, and straight into the shipyard past the blank faces of the Militia. The men surrounded and cheered us, shouting 'BBC'. I hope it doesn't make me sound too much of a company man if I say I was – well – quite proud.

My son was a couple of months old when I made the Polish trip (which went on for a couple of months) – and my daughter was the same age when I came here. I have to tell you that you played a part in the latter pregnancy. One of the subjects least dear to my wife's heart is the subject of the peerage. But she greatly took to your book, and even brought it to maternity ward. Nicely written, of course, and quite different from Enoch Powell's more sombre study. It also has the merit of being a lot easier to hold than the book of her first delivery, J. K. Galbraith's memoir of his early life in Ontario – a really unpromising subject which he managed to make sound scintillating.

Having been out of 'News' and into 'Current Affairs' so long (you'll recall that curious BBC distinction), it's odd to have returned to News here in Buenos Aires. The BBC have ridden out one of the storms that threaten to sink it because of our fairly even-handed coverage. Mrs T regarded our reporters' habit of referring to 'the British' instead of her word 'we' to be evidence of BBC sedition. Imagine if reporters called the Brits 'we' in Northern Ireland!

One big difference between News and Current Affairs is the obsession News have with the politics of feeding (satellite feeding from the local TV station, to headquarters). They are quite Byzantine and deserve a footnote in the main narrative. Alas it might be risky to say too much here, but, basically we manage. There's little debate about story content: all energy is consumed by the bloody television process. I recall that after 9 years reporting on N. Ireland, there was hardly one editorial post mortem, but endless agonising about the production process. Its just the same in the field.

The ENG gear of the camera people is a wonder, but its disadvantage was proved last Tuesday. We all trooped up to the Casa Rosada to obey the injunction of El Jefe to hear the word from the Malvinas. A young Peronist crowd began chanting, then pushing and finally rushing in the direction of the Casa's entrance. In the time-honoured way, the police did their duty. Just as familiarly, we filmed from behind their lines – when suddenly, the line turned about and attacked us. Print journalists were fairly OK, but the cameras bore the brunt of tear gas grenades, rubber bullets – (a couple of pellets had to be dug out of one cameraman's leg) – and batons. Every one of our 4 cameramen was hurt, but thankfully not badly.

The moment of outright hostility has passed, I think, and we must record our genuine amazement, under the circumstances, of the friendly treatment we've received from Argentines, both officially and in the streets.

When this war is over – and it must be soon – I wonder what you'll want to do, after your return to life? Have you ambitions for editorial power, or is the pen still mightier than the unions? I'm glad that in recent years you've returned to graze on the southern slopes of our more expensive papers after your time with the Mail. You will have to write about all this, of course – if you can.

In this stream of consciousness, written after a fagging day trying to sort out the direction of Argentine policies – I've recalled something of the times our paths have crossed – or rather my narrow track has met your motorway.

Simon, your work has been so good, it's almost been embarrassing when I've compared what I broadcast to what you wrote. You must know that, as they say, our thoughts are with you. It's a poor phrase, but is literally true. Journalists have ephemeral concerns, and they're sentimental too. But we all share your frustration just a little, it doesn't go away, nor does our feeling for you subside with the next morning's hangover.

God bless, & love – with many regards to the others,
Brian Walker

SUNDAY 20 JUNE Today is Flag Day ('*Día de la Bandera*' – I suppose it is) and I was woken to the sound of the Navy Band playing the most unattractive National Anthem, which sounds like a scene from one of the more tedious Busby Berkeley movies! Ian's ear is painful, so he is a little grouchy. The strain really is showing on him, poor lad – I fancy he's aged five years since we began this, but a good holiday and he should bounce back. For me – I can honestly say I've learned things – about others, about prison, about me, about Spanish (!) and, just as long as this doesn't go on for too much longer, I'll think of it as an interesting journalistic experience. But for Ian it has passed that stage, I think.

The Buenos Aires PR team is getting angry about the British having retaken the South Sandwich Islands – but the surrender is supposed to have included all the islands claimed by the British in the South Atlantic – that includes the Falklands, South Georgia, South Orkneys and South Sandwich. Still, it's a further blow to

Argentine pride because the only people on South Sandwich were scientists (plus a small Naval detachment): the British said the people were there illegally, and took them off after a helicopter raid (so say the BA people) with machine guns being fixed. What do they expect?

Later we heard that the EEC Foreign Ministers had agreed to lift economic sanctions against Argentina provided there was no resumption of hostilities between the two countries: that's another good sign, I guess. The arguments in favour were advanced by West Germany and (?) France, and a detailed statement will be published tomorrow. But there are no yelps of disapproval from Britain – either that means there are none, or Gordon Martin (the BBC Diplomatic Corr.) is off for the weekend!

I've found a new song to like. It's an old Bob Dylan song, sung now by Joan Baez: it's called *Lily, Rosemary and the Jack of Hearts*, and I spent a good part of this afternoon standing on the bed rail gazing east down the Beagle Channel listening to it. I spent some time wondering about the phenomenon of womanizing. Almost every journalist seems afflicted. But not Ian – perhaps it's Ian's ability to say 'You fellows live such complicated lives' that marks him out as so different. Is he happier? He certainly doesn't seem so. There's something to be said, then, for 'a complicated life'. It means lots of love, a mosaic of a satisfactory existence, if not a perfect image of satisfaction.

MONDAY 21 JUNE The shortest day of the year – here (and the longest day, and the shortest night at home). Last night when Hilary called Tony – she got through at 20.24, which was about par for the course – she said that Willy and Isabel's plane had been commandeered – '*expropria par la usa militar* . . .' – and so they would come today instead. I hope they do, although I'm fully prepared for them not to. Ian, as usual, finds their non-arrival a reason for more introspection and depression.

One note about pingers games: whenever I win a point it's a delight; whenever Ian loses one it's a disaster. He is a much better player than I am, but takes a loss terribly badly – though not outwardly. Tony simply won't come over and see the other lads, and I don't blame him. They're a pretty uninspiring bunch, and I'm afraid my liberal opinions of them as people have broadened somewhat. Yes, they're pleasant enough, kind in a rough way, but dull as ditchwater! But now there's a 20-year-old girl named Noelia in the cell we used to have – a pretty lass with bushy reddish hair and very tight jeans. She's Uruguayan, I think, and is here on the inevitable '*documento*'[1] problem. She wrote a note to Pinto, signing it with '*besos a mis amigos* . . .', but he didn't seem as outwardly excited by that as he might have done. I feel that prisoners, like so many Latin men, are full of themselves when they're presented with a woman at a distance – they'll make sexually unpleasant noises and so on – but when actually confronted by the real thing, they quail a little. A lot, in fact – not one of them yesterday seemed particularly keen to engage Noelia in conversation, though it is quite possible they had been warned not to.

I washed my hair this morning in preparation for Isabel's visit! Lunch was meat in some terrible crinkled old batter – I christened it 'Grandma's Feet'; it tastes nearly as bad as it sounds. Very greasy, too. The inevitable soccer on TV – even Tony is beginning to grumble about it!

18.00 Tony has just told Ian that he is getting him down with his constant depressing analysis of the situation. I don't know. Am I dying intellectually? I just think nice thoughts all the time. I read. I write this log. I'm quite content because I know it's all going to be all right. But Ian – he's impossible.

22.00 Isabel and Willy appeared. The judge is now, it seems, willing to grant us bail. We should have been delighted, but curiously (at least to Willy and Isabel, no doubt) weren't. We don't want to hang about in BA for weeks and weeks, letting the Judge off the hook, allowing him to make no decision at all. We each had two very large whiskies, which, I am sorry to say, put us in an argumentative mood. I snapped at Ian for suggesting out loud that my worm pills had been tranquillizers; Tony said he would take bail whatever, no discussion (or changing his mind). But then we all calmed down. Tony went to sleep and woke up at 01.00 and we had a cup of coffee and then chatted amiably – the other two having wild hysterics over the other prisoners' antics. I felt odd: slightly shamed at my behaviour, but slightly pleased that I had got my point over,

1 Problems over not having the right papers kept many people in prison, it seemed.

retained a position of authority in this business. But we are getting on each other's nerves, no doubt at all. But one important thing is an ability to count to ten before saying anything wounding: no one, so far, has said anything cutting to anyone else. We've each formed alliances – Tony and I talk about Ian's nervousness; Ian and I talk about Tony's aggressions; and I'd be a fool to suppose that Ian and Tony don't talk about me too. What about, I wonder?

Anyway the plan seems to be that we'll get Willy and Isabel to try to bring pressure to bear on the judge – to ask the Swiss to ask the fate of the ten-day review of our case; to ask for bail to leave the country; to ask to be able to go to BA via land (with inevitable crossing of Chile midway); to demand to know when a final decision is going to be made.

Barrozo looked very sad when we were all talking tonight. He came in, rather sheepishly, once Isabel had gone. He wanted an English newspaper. I think he knows he won't get too far unless he learns English.

Lots of stuff from home: shirts, cravats, soap, tea, powdered soup, chest expanders (!), tapes and other things. Also letters from the lads in BA – particularly fond one from Brian Walker.[1]

TUESDAY 22 JUNE   I woke early – well, 09.00 – and pottered around making coffee and showering and then talking to Ian and making notes about what to say to Willy when they arrived. They did, at noon (having been until 02.30 with some people at the court) and our impression, after a chat of about an hour with them, is that Isabel too has become afflicted with this infuriating vagueness that appears to be characteristic of the Argentine Judicial system. It was so difficult to get an accurate and believable answer about anything.

But this seems to be clear: final application for bail, which will be granted, will be made tomorrow. The money – $100,000,000 each (about £4000) will be sent from NYC (indeed I think Phil Knightley will be doing that today) and we will be allowed to go. Then Willy will apply for permission for us to visit our families in England – if that is granted, that's what we'll do. The thought of turning up in BA and being allowed no further is indescribable, though. I want

1 The BBC's Northern Ireland Political Correspondent, an old friend, a splendid journalist.

nothing said to the press, though, and I pray that Hugh – who has this habit of filing stories to Reuters all the time at the drop of a hat – will keep his mouth shut. Willy was going to see the Fiscal today, so maybe more news later. I'm feeling very taut and nervous about it all.

A hospital ship with what Grieco said were hundreds of prisoners came into port at 12.00. Grieco and the judge both blame the army for what happened on the Falklands, and are deeply angry, one reason the judge now feels like letting us go.

Isabel and Willy came back at 21.00, just after I had talked to Judy – and, sure, the message that I was 'institutionalized' had been passed on! But the new message is that bail will be granted – we sign the papers tomorrow, Willy brings the money on Monday, and we'll be free on Monday night. So – five more days in here, and then that's it!

Barrozo came to our cell at 23.00 – '*Me alegro por ustedes*!' he said. We can go for trips in town in a police car, and generally have the run of the place 'so you have no bad memories of Ushuaia'. I look forward to it immensely.

Isabel is a treasure. And Judy, too!

Mail today – Christopher Sykes, Cameron Davis (from school), and Amanda Holden.

WEDNESDAY 23 JUNE   Publication Day in New York. Freedom Day in Ushuaia. I hope. This is written the night before.

But this is being written on The Day itself. Ian got up complaining of feeling a let-down. I don't share that, I'm afraid. I'm just looking forward to being able to be imperious and tyrannical again! But 'strong with the weak, weak with the strong' – never. That will be a watchword of mine from now on.

Woken by three blasts on the foghorn of the hospital ship, leaving. It turned into the mist of the Channel and headed east, for the open sea again. Yesterday it was busily disgorging soldiers home from the war – looking quite victorious and cheerful.

We are busily deciding what to do with all our stuff – I favour giving it all to Jane Scotti, to be used in case we have to come back, but disposed of if not.

A new and ghastly advert heard during the coverage of the World

Cup. 'Footballísticamente.'

18.00 It's official! We can go back home! Freedom. At last.

(17.05 BBC said 'Bail for the Ushuaia Three'.)

23.05 Well, after all that hysteria, it really is true. The judge called us into his office to let us sign our bail agreements, in which he said that since there was no longer a war there was no need to hang onto us. Then, looking nervous and stern, he said: 'Well, I suppose you will never have to come back to complete this case. . . ' 'Never?' I asked. 'No – never.' We can go home, in other words. We get our passports, permission to travel out of the country 'for resume of work' and can – with a wink and a nod – go, for ever. He said he had prepared a discourse for delivery at this moment, but wasn't going to give it. But after leaving, he returned to say – 'I want you to know the Argentines are not bad losers when it comes to the treatment of non-combatants'. He was obviously angry and hurt about the losses, and struggling with his having had to make this decision.

Then – whisky with Grieco, who was truly astonished at the decision, and then champagne with Willy and Isabel. We will leave on Tuesday for San Sebastian, Porvenir, Punta Arenas and Santiago. We ought to be home – with luck – on Thursday next, one week and one day from today – the 1st of July. I just hope we don't have to write a piece for that week's paper!

I'm feeling relief, of course, glad that it's over, grateful beyond words for all the hundreds who have been involved in all of this. I have my doubts about the judicial system here. I've found out I am a patient and resourceful person, able to think, and function clearly under extraordinary circumstances. I've learned ping-pong and *castellano*. I don't look upon this as a waste of time at all. I like Grieco and Barrozo. I've learned a great deal about the Argentines – for whom I feel great sympathy – 'the whole world is laughing at us', said Grieco – we've never had to say that, and it's difficult to imagine what it must be like to have to. But I am sooooo glad to be getting out. It will have been 77 days without liberty, if we are released next Tuesday morning: and that's a long, long time. But both the *Listener* and the *NY Review of Books* have accounts of prisoners who – in Wakefield and in China – have spent a great deal longer. This was a small view of suffering, a vision of nightmares. It could have been so much worse. Thank God, though, for friends and colleagues like I've been lucky enough to have. I will never, never forget them.

THURSDAY 24 JUNE   Dozens and dozens of letters today, and a copy of my book, which looks most handsome. But a slow day, with guards (some of them, at least) coming and congratulating us on our news. A cable from Judy, sent at 09.53 her time – expressing 'Ground Control's' delight, arrived at 11.00 our time, and one from the *Observer* took only five hours.

All the other prisoners heard about our freedom during the day and congratulated us. 'Jack Nicholson' insisted that I write a piece – with big headlines – about the inhuman conditions in the prison, and send it to his house in Bahía Blanca. Maybe. They had a bit of trouble in their wing today, it seems: the police wanted them to have their hair cut, and the prisoners didn't – Salis said it was a violation of '*los derechos humanos*'.

We went down to the judge's office tonight to be given back our documents – passports included! It was good to see them again. And the piece of paper that was supposed to be in Ian's contact book which caused us hours of agony at the beginning of all this[1] – it wasn't there. As far as I am concerned it never has been! All that fuss! But I shouldn't laugh: I would have felt just as bad in similar circumstances.

It looks now as though we'll head for Chile the very moment we are released: Ushuaia to Porvenir via Rio Grande, San Sebastian (Argentina), San Sebastian (Chile) and Porvenir ferry to Punta Arenas, and then by air to Santiago. There may well be some BBC chaps in PA, which would be splendid.

A small cloud on *Noticias y Algo Más*, with an interview with Sagastume – he said (for public consumption) that we were being released into Tierra del Fuegian jurisdiction. But all the indications are that we can go home: he is simply not saying so on record. Also when Margaret talked to Ian tonight, she said she had been told of

1 Ian had been sure a scrap of paper giving the address and telephone number of MI5 – which he had copied from a London newspaper – had been tucked into his contact book. He had worried about it for days and nights during the interrogation period – and clearly I had, too, as nowhere in the diary do I mention it, in case, I suppose, the diary was ever read.

our impending release and return to Britain yesterday afternoon – before we were told, even. I think Willy and Isabel knew full well what the judge had decided – after all, how did they know to bring the champagne? Of course they had been told.

A gastronomic discovery: peanut butter and Dundee marmalade!

Shall I buy a fur coat for Judy? I think that the fur of the Fuegian fox is greatly prized: if it makes financial sense I might do just that. But I've a horrid feeling everything that's for sale here is pretty tacky: I'd rather spend the money on a holiday.

The St. David's piece is in *In Britain*[1]: I will do another as soon as I get back.

Returning to Britain on a Thursday, incidentally, means that I will have to write a piece! Oh what timing!

FRIDAY 25 JUNE   Sorry – nothing special about the date – I'm simply losing my mind, concentrating only on how to get home, and what to do when I get there. A Swiss diplomat – a Mr Dyer, or something like that – phoned at 09.15, when we were all fast asleep. He wanted to make arrangements for our safe passage out of the country, and agreed totally with our plan to get out into Chile direct from Tierra del Fuego. So he is getting Isabel to call later in the day with details of our journey home.

Then, another classically Argentine Event! Barrozo had promised to take us on a 'special police lunch' at the border station of Lapataia. The drive was spectacular, and Lapataia itself was stunningly beautiful – a lovely, still, deep, green lake (Lago Roca), with huge and very sharp peaks. Rabbits, ducks, buzzards – guanaco skin on the wall of the police hut. The road was very treacherous with the snow, and as we didn't have chains on the tyres we had to rely on Barrozo's (admittedly expert) driving. But why was it classically Argentine? Because, although we loaded the boot of the car with wine and bread and meat, it was decided – for some reason or other, possibly the cold – not to have lunch at all. So we turned round after half an hour or so and came back, to be locked into our cell once more!

1 The first of a series of articles I was writing for the monthly magazine of the British Tourist Authority, about the far-flung peninsulas of the British Isles. The somewhat unfortunate headline over this first piece was 'On a clear day you can see all the way down to South America . . .'

Barrozo said that between Ushuaia and Rio Grande there are 8 police checkpoints, all linked by radio – our progress can be monitored all the way to the border, and our security can be more or less guaranteed. As Barrozo said – 'If you are hurt, I will be –' and he drew a finger across his throat.

Al Haig has resigned – the only decent story out of Washington for a long time.

Letters from Amanda[1] – with pix from Joe and Ben – and from Judy. How nice to be loved!

After Hilary called at 20.40, Judy rang and we spoke for 15 minutes or so – she said that they were all a little pole-axed to hear Pérez de Cuellar announce that we would be reunited with our families on Monday! Pole-axed because they had done their best to keep it quiet. But the paper is not annoyed at all – in fact thinks the publicity can do nothing but good now. Judy says all is well and everyone is very excited at the prospect of seeing us again – as we are all of seeing them I might add! Judy has baked a cake, so I have to get out!

Isabel called a little later on, and we discussed practicalities – the paper will try and call me tomorrow at 09.30 or so, so I'd better be awake! We are getting into a very tense period – lots of nail-biting, Isabel said – hoping all goes well. Willy sounded a little miffed that escape from Argentina was our very first priority, but I'm afraid there's not a lot of room for sentiment in matters like this, with moods like we hear about and read about. Hugh may meet us in Porvenir, or somewhere similar – that'll be pleasant! Apparently the money is all here – the *Observer*'s a) went to NYC instead of Washington, b) was late arriving in BA as a consequence and c) was less than the amount required! Isabel said we'd toss for it! Why can't Willy come down on Sunday – that I must ask someone tomorrow as a matter of urgency. We don't want to hang about any more than we have to.

SATURDAY 26 JUNE   Woken at 09.30 by Magnus calling – except the line was cut twice before, and I got to speak to him at about 10.15. It was splendid to hear him, and he seemed genuinely pleased to hear me. The plans for our departure seem well laid, and

1 Amanda Holden, married to Tony – great friends from Washington days.

it looks entirely possible that Hugh will meet us in either Punta Arenas, Porvenir or San Sebastian, Chile. We expect to get out on Monday night, and up to Santiago immediately thereafter. Possibly we'll go via Lufthansa to Frankfurt, or via (my suggestion) Miami to pick up a London flight direct. Magnus took a quote from me saying that the pressure from the Committee had undoubtedly done the trick, and I hope they'll use it.

The 'Special Argentine Shopping Expedition' seems to be going much like the 'Special Argentine Lunch' – i.e., it hasn't happened yet, and may not until the shops have closed! We wonder if the Argentine army takes its orders literally, or does the reverse! If advance is ordered, do they go back, or stand still? It seems axiomatic, anyway, that either the reverse of an arrangement happens, or something tangentially different.

Actually, having said that, Barjela has just been in to say we can go shopping at 15.00, which is when the shops open after their lunchtime siesta.

Well, we didn't go shopping: Bordon[1] came by and gave us all our money back, but said the shops were closed – classic! Late night horror film, bed at 01.30.

SUNDAY 27 JUNE   A grey day, and it – like yesterday – promises to be long, dull and tense – though Judy may well call. (Ian arranged for Judy to call after Margaret echoed his exasperation at the total lack of news and information when Tony and Hilary talk. This was amply illustrated by the calls Tony and I had on Friday; there was nothing at all in Tony's call – almost as though nothing had happened, while Judy, 20 minutes later, was full of information about Pérez de Cuellar having announced our freedom, etc., etc. It has been irritating for Ian and I, having a Thursday to Tuesday 'information gap' each week; now we know that our exasperation merely mirrors Judy's and Margaret's. What on earth do Tony and Hilary talk about?

Hot-lips bought us a bottle of white wine for lunch – out of his own money, and to say farewell to us (he goes off duty tonight, and when he returns tomorrow, we'll be gone, we hope.) It was very kind

1 One of the most pleasant guards, in the national prison service (not just a locally-hired 'goon', like most of the others).

of him – he didn't have a corkscrew, so he pushed the cork in with one of his cell keys!

No news at all about Argentine (not on the World News, anyway – possibly there will be on News About Britain at 18.09 – now it's 17.15 GMT – 14.15 here). Is it that the story's dead, or has everyone gone home?

'Home' sounds typical. A national rail strike. A tube strike. Possibly a bus strike – NHS workers on strike. Thunder storms. Floods. Test rained off at Old Trafford. Wimbledon 100 matches behind schedule. But in spite of – or in fact, perhaps partly because of – all this idiocy, I do so want to see dear old England again.

I was reading a fascinating article in *Atlantic* about millennialists, those who believe Christ is coming again, and that the foundation of the State of Israel in 1948 and the occupation of Jerusalem in 1967 are the predicted precursors of that event, with all the turmoil on earth today being part of a preordained pattern, not bad at all, but Good. The 'mark of the devil' – 666 – is the key to it all: if Kissinger (whose name is an A = 6, B = 12, C = 18 code = 666) and Reagan (whose 3 names have 6 letters each) go on TV and tell us to write 666 on our foreheads, then we'll know the world is ending.

Another Argentine phenomenon: we've all had our showers – so the water has suddenly become hot! And Tony washed his clean socks – obviously what Argies do! (Crack army battalions are presumably those that showered first:– inspectors award marks for the crispness and cleanliness of white flags.)

19.30 A lovely afternoon, spent with Grieco and Natalie Goodall, her daughter Annie and, later, Jane Scotti, who cried with pleasure at the news we were likely to be freed! She is a wonderful girl – from Birmingham, she hitch-hiked around here and helped Natalie with her huge collection of dolphin skeletons. Annie is off to study computing science at Oberlin College – and I realized to my horror I couldn't remember the name of the college I taught at in New Concord, Ohio, in the first of the Woodrow Wilson Fellowships, when I met Marji Bayers.

We had tea, chocolate cake and croissants – called '*media lunas*' here, they are glazed and sweet and pretty good. Tea came with a jug of milk, the first milk for nearly three months!

Natalie is a remarkable, cheerful, highly organized woman who has made Fuegian wild life a speciality of hers; she's married to Tony Goodall, one of the descendants of the first settlers of the territory. She has a great collection of books about Cape Horn, and thinks *Blind Horn's Hate* by Richard Hough (I think) rather less good than Matthew thinks. Her favourite is *The Uttermost Part of the Earth* by Thomas Bridges (Hodder, 1948).

Natalie sold us T-shirts, maps and other odds and ends, so there's no need to go souvenir shopping. She also gave us lots of advice about how to get out of here – the fact that Captain Grieco was there prompted him to help. So, tomorrow, we get a police driver who will take us to Rio Grande just as soon as the paperwork is complete; Grieco will be in Rio Grande (since Admiral Anajar is going to be there on a formal visit), and he will book us into a secure hotel. Then the taxi will take us to the frontier and – if the papers are all arranged – to Porvenir itself. The organization sounds fair.

I had to give Grieco my only copy of *Their Noble Lordships*! 'That looks interesting!' he said. 'Can I have it?' So I had to sign it. 'In memory of 76 very interesting days' I wrote, to his great amusement.

MONDAY 28 JUNE   Well – this is it! A very brief note only. Up at 09.30, off to the Chilean consulate to find, as we expected, no problems about visas or car papers for the Ushuaia–RG–SS–Porvenir trip. The Swiss Consul rang to say Willy had left BA, and that a British diplomat was waiting for us in Punta Arenas. Then, shopping for a cheap suitcase for me. (Ian bought an awful nylon skiing jacket for more than it would have cost in London.)

After that we took the TV to a home for poor children, run by nuns; then said farewell to the others and at 16.30, surprise! – Isabel arrived. Willy had deposited the 300,000,000 pesos, we were free to go.

A snag. The judge, in his infinite wisdom, said no to the Chilean plans.[1] So hurried calls to Magnus to alert the Swiss (poor Hugh

1 When the judge heard of our plan to go to Chile he was livid. 'I will not let you go from here to a country which is as much an enemy of ours as is Britain,' he said. First he said we could not go at all. Then he relented, if the bail was doubled. When Willy said he had no more money he said he would let us go only if we halved the time which we would spend outside the country. Naturally we agreed – knowing that it made little difference whether we were allowed out of Argentina for two months, or

and Connors of FCO, in Punta Arenas) that we would go to BA.

Drove to Rio Grande – through the incredibly spectacular (and very icy) Martial Range, the last hurrah of the Andes, then onto the Patagonian Plain (though still in Tierra del Fuego.)

The freedom – to sit in a restaurant, eat what you want, when you want! Proper loos!

We got to Rio Grande at 01.30, in easy time to catch the 02.45 plane to BA.

And in fact I'm sitting in the plane now, at the very airport where we were arrested – eleven weeks all but nine hours later!

Captain Grieco, smart in his formal Navy greatcoat and white silk scarf, came on the plane to say his goodbyes. He was holding – very proudly – a note from Cal thanking him for all he had done. And he made a little speech:

'I hope you will forget the bad things about Ushuaia, and remember the good things and people you met. I know you are good fellows, but please write in your papers that we feel very, very deeply about the Malvinas. And we will be back. They will be ours. But let us meet in the future, and have a drink – to peace.'

He looked strained, and dignified, and very sad. I watched his proud, erect figure leave the plane. I could feel his sadness, and his envy. Look what he was going back to,[2] and compare it with what we were looking forward to. I like him – he's a clot in many ways – but he's a decent human being, and I feel sympathy for all he's gone through – far more, in fact, than we have. Because for us it had to end happily. For him, the tragedy goes on. I hope he leaves one day: he's too good for Argentina.

And so it ends – or it will later today, when we get out of here. As I write this the plane is still on the ground, but it'll be wheels up and off 'the Uttermost Part of the Earth' and back to the real world

---

one. The important thing was to get out. But the snag was a tense moment for us – for a while we really thought we might not get out of Ushuaia at all, and cursed ourselves for having dreamed up the 'sophisticated' plan to get out safely. Poor Hugh O'Shaughnessy and a British embassy official went down to Southern Chile to wait for us.

2 Sadly for the good Captain he was arrested some months later. The latest information is that he is still in prison somewhere in Patagonia, charged with not carrying out his duties properly. So far as we were concerned he carried out his duties admirably.

again, after a quite extraordinary and fascinating interlude.

TUESDAY 29 JUNE   Arrived BA *Aeroparqué* at 07.00 – when I got
out of the aircraft a tall man stepped out of the shadows. 'Are you
Simon Winchester? I am Peter West, British Interests Section,
Swiss Embassy . . .'. It was a great moment. Daniel Dyer from
the Swiss Embassy itself was there too, and we were hurried
through the VIP suites to a waiting Mercedes and rushed – doing
U-turns and jumping red lights to avoid the waiting press – to the
British Ambassador's Residence. David Joy and his Spanish wife
Montserrat were there – and we had breakfast. Warm toast and
butter and good coffee: it was lovely.

Bob Friend of the BBC called – he had been one of those
reporters we avoided at the airport earlier – and said he'd be at a
press conference at 15.00 which Isabel had organized. So then I
called Judy and told her we were nearly out. All that had to be done
was to get Foreign Ministry clearance, and that was that. Willy and
Dyer said it would be no problem. Huh!

A shower. A proper shave. A proper loo. A lie in a soft bed. The
Swiss Ambassador – Mr Badmer – called; he is being posted to
Rome, and I hope to see him there. Then lunch – soup, beef,
meringues and The Champagne from Moody Brook. I toasted
Isabel and, when he arrived, Willy.

Then the press conference at 15.00, with lots of lovely people
(Róisín McAuley, bless her) asking gentle questions. And then it
was time to go. We were taken in two Swiss Embassy cars – Willy,
Isabel, a Swiss diplomat and I in one, Ian and Tony and Peter West
in the other – and got to Ezeiza at 17.30. Magnus had booked 1st
class seats on Iberia 998 to Las Palmas and Madrid, and then on a
British Airways flight to Gatwick. First Class – good old Magnus!

The Argentine Tar Baby almost didn't loosen its grip. For a
while we were held in the VIP lounge, panelled, unbearably hot,
mindless Muzak, while a girl and some dreadful goon prevented us
getting out, or Isabel (who screamed and yelled!) getting in. Finally
we were all together, and just after Iberia announced the last call,
and we were all getting nervous, we were led out to the beautiful big
plane. We said our fond goodbyes to Isabel and Willy and everyone
– and, at 18.30, 24 hours and 15 minutes after being declared

legally free – on bail – at Ushuaia, it was Wheels Up and off into the sunset.

Ten minutes later we were safely out over the River Plate and into Uruguayan air space, and duty-free goods went on sale, we were out of Argentina at last, and free! It really is, as Isabel said, a very nasty country housing some very pleasant people. But oh, those last few moments were nasty. You could disappear for ever in a place like that.

Anyway this is being written at 03.15 Argentine time – 07.15 in London – and we are beginning our descent into Las Palmas. So as someone remarked yesterday, quoting *The Doors*, ironically the song which opens the film *Apocalypse Now*, 'This is the End.'

Epilogue.....

The flight took nine hours; the film Iberia had chosen, *On Golden Pond*, was suitably sentimental. Judy and the children and I had once spent an idyllic August in a cottage by Lake Conway in New Hampshire, and this brought the memories flooding back. I had to blink back the tears more than once.

We touched down, briefly, at Las Palmas, and arrived in Madrid at noon. There was a reporter from the London *Standard* there – a taste of things to come, I imagined, since Magnus had asked solicitously whether we minded giving a press conference at Gatwick. We had a few moments to spare: I called Richard Wigg, to give a certain symmetry to events. I had, after all, dined with him at Barjela airport on my way out to the Falklands, and it seemed fitting to at least thank him for his letters while I was on my way back.

The British Airways jet was waiting: it had been held specially for us, and when we boarded there was a ripple of applause. A distinguished-looking figure stepped forward and welcomed us 'back to British territory', adding that he did so on behalf of Her Majesty's Government. I confessed that he had the advantage of me, but he appeared not to mind at all. 'Neil MacFarlane', he said, cheerily. 'Minister for Sport.' He had been attending a World Cup game in Madrid, and his choice of our plane for his return to London was simply happy coincidence.

Thanks to a stewardess with the delightful name of Deirdre O'Hagan Brown, Tony and I managed to get very pleasantly drunk on the way home, finishing rather more quarter bottles of Moët than was perhaps sensible. But I was sober enough to take good care to watch for the moment we made our English landfall, and the hedgerows, and the tiny fields, and the magnificent greens of the Sussex countryside were as I had imagined in all those days away.

When we landed, and passengers muttered their farewells, the crew asked us to stay on board for a while: customs and immigration would come to us, they said, as there was 'a little excitement' outside. Two men in uniform did indeed arrive. They told us there was no need to show passports as we were quite recognizable enough, and they were sure we had no contraband. They could have examined my Globetrotter; a couple of old shirts, stained from eleven weeks of rather unsatisfactory washing in the icy Ushuaia water, and that was about all.

Deirdre O'Hagan Brown gave me a farewell kiss, thrust five or six more bottles of champagne into my pockets, gave me a red carnation and then, with Ian and Tony, propelled me to the aft door. We looked down the steps to see a sight for which we had never bargained.

There, in serried ranks below us, were fifty photographers and TV men, all waving and cheering, and clicking madly away. I recognised a man from the *Mail* with whom I had worked some years before; Tony kept seeing chums of his, lads of his own trade; and soon I spotted Sally Soames, the enchanting photographer from the *Sunday Times*, the one photographer I would have chosen had I been asked.

Five minutes later and a policeman – how good to see a British policeman once more! I thought – led us into the terminal building, an official explaining that we would be taken into a room for 'ten private minutes' with our families. We went through a series of unmarked doors, and then suddenly, there they all were – wives, children, all hugging us, shaking hands, slapping backs, patting heads . . . we all knew so much about each other's families we wanted, of course, to meet them and find out how they had survived the last three months. Judy looked splendid – happier than I had seen her for years; the children, too – and yes, how they had grown!

I cannot in all honesty pretend that the press conference was a particularly illuminating event – many of the questions were those that had been asked at the British ambassador's residence in Buenos Aires the night before, and our papers – who were, of course, heavily represented (the Editor himself, Frank Giles, had come down to Gatwick, though Ian and Tony had to make do with an *Observer* deputy, since Donald Trelford was on holiday) – reasonably enough wanted to make sure we kept the better nuggets to ourselves, so we had something to write for the following Sunday.

It was over in an hour, and then, with a *Sunday Times* driver at the wheel, we took off for Oxford. He would have driven us the whole way, but for the chance of saving time – it was rush hour in London – we asked him to go to Paddington, and we caught a train home, and then a taxi to Iffley.

At home, someone had hung a giant Union Jack from a window, and there were telegrams and letters welcoming me. The garden – where I had been working on the bonfire when Cal's call first came all those weeks before – was alive with all the flowers and fruits of high summer. The roses were out, the apples and the greengages. The lawn was neatly trimmed, the field leading down to the Thames was alive with wild flowers, and cattle lay peacefully in the evening sun. Biggles and Tusker went into paroxysms of crazed delight when I went through the front door – all that I had imagined about this homecoming was true, and more.

The next few days were spent reading – some of the hundreds of letters Judy had received from wellwishers while I was away – and writing – the 3,000 words Eric Jacobs wanted for the Review Front page he edited. It duly appeared, together with a splendid family photograph Sally Soames had arrived to take, and on the same day, of course, as an equally long article by Ian in the *Observer*, illustrated with some of Tony's pencil sketches.

The next morning PHS in *The Times* wrote that he had preferred Ian's piece to mine – my writing was tinged with 'braggadocio', he said. Ah well, I sighed – good old Fleet Street. Everything just as normal!

The following week Magnus – working on the principle that you should remount a horse immediately after falling off – asked me to write a profile of a new coloratura soprano named Luciana Serra, a young Italian woman who was performing in Bellini's *La Sonnambula* at Covent Garden. Sally Soames came along to take the pictures; so enchanted was I with Señorita Serra that I arrived late for a party thrown by the *Observer* to celebrate our return. That dismal fact got into public prints, too: the diarist on the *Guardian* thought I was rather rude, and chastised me in rather intemperate terms. Once again – ah, well.

Ian and Tony and their respective families then took off for holidays, courtesy the *Observer*, and a grateful Donald Trelford. Ian and Margaret went off to Sri Lanka, and eventually Hong Kong;

Tony and Hilary took off for Mauritius. The *Sunday Times* had other plans for me. I took an RAF VC-10 to Ascension Island, and a Hercules – with two mid-air refuelling sessions – back to Port Stanley to write another piece. Symmetry, I said to myself, is all.

It had been nearly four months since the little LADE Electra had dipped down through the autumn rains onto the runway. Then, Stanley had looked like a remote western Scottish village, green and windswept and rain-washed. Now, as the great transport plane bumped down through the afternoon mist, my dominant impression was that I was being dumped into some infernal scrapyard, an urban nightmare splattered, all oil and twisted black metal, in the middle of some muddy field. The feeling of revulsion you occasionally get when, after rounding a bend in the lane deep in the Cotswolds, you are confronted with a dump for used cars – that was what I first thought upon seeing the 'liberated' Stanley, with smashed glass and bent and rusting iron rearing starkly up against the softer outlines of the peat bogs and low moors of grass and moss.

True, the peat smoke still hung heavy and sweet in the breeze, and the gentle splash of the waves in Stanley harbour and the soaring gulls everywhere were a powerful reminder that this was an island capital. But fighter aircraft roared up into the sky, leaving the sweeter, sickly smell of aviation fuel; a pair of enormous yellow stone crushers clanged and shook without pause, bent on turning Falklands boulders into MoD specification hard core; mud-spattered jeeps, armoured cars and three-ton Bedfords roared their way through the deep puddles of *eau-de-nil* porridge, and smoke from dozens of cookhouse fires mixed with the smell of frying, and boiling clothes.

This, I felt sure five minutes after I stepped from the plane, was not what those who had come to the Falkland Islands had wanted. Of course, they had their Britishness, their 'unique way of life' preserved, and all to whom I spoke over the three days the Ministry of Defence permitted me to stay (for a cost of considerably more than three thousand pounds a flight) were grateful for that. But behind the relief I encountered, I felt distinct signs of unease and disappointment: that the new, 'Fortress Falklands' that had been created in place of the forgettable – and forgotten – island haven of four months before was not what was wanted. Many people, I wrote, would leave; the islanders would not accept the militarization of their island that was the inevitable corollary of their having been so expensively rescued by the Task Force, and by the heroism and professionalism of Three and Five Brigades.

The article I wrote upon my return from Stanley said as much; it painted a portrait of a disillusioned, disheartened people, for whom all hope of normal life had now vanished. A lot of readers wrote to me expressing their dismay at my conclusions. If they were true, the war would seem to have been a wasted one; and I could only agree with them. The Falklands war had been a terrible, irresponsible and ghastly mistake, and one that left a legacy in the South Atlantic that was every bit as tragic as the legacy of more than two hundred bereavements in England and a thousand or more in Argentina. This other legacy was the newly created armed camp of a colony which the Falklands has now become; an armed camp the very existence of which is a blow to our self-esteem, a blot upon our hopes for international respect, an embarrassment to our Exchequer, an irritation to those who expect our responsibilities to extend to Europe and the North Atlantic, not old colonies eight thousand miles to the south.

It was not a popular message, and it was challenged. A reporter for the *Observer* – not Ian Mather, I hasten to say; he returned to his last, as the paper's Defence Correspondent – visited the islands five months later, and reported a wholly different scene. A content population, well disposed to the resident British garrison, confident that the British would stick by them in the event of any future challenges from the giant neighbour to the west, eager to knuckle down to making the Falklands a prosperous member of our tiny Empire. Frank Giles remarked on the difference between the articles; I asked him to wait and see what would happen. I was sure there would be signs of growing dissatisfaction from Stanley, and, sooner or later, it would be reported.

Gradually, it was. Robert Fox, the BBC radio reporter whose wartime despatches – and whose subsequent book – were among the best and most vivid to spring from the events of that summer, returned at Christmas, and painted a portrait of a people less than wholly happy with their lot. Members of Parliament who visited found problems and uncertainty among the islanders. And in

March it was noted with some sadness that Don and Margaret Davidson, the proprietors of the little guest house known as the Malvinas House – its name was changed subsequently to Harrier House, in honour of the remarkable aircraft that performed so valiantly during the war – were leaving the islands, and going back to Britain.

I had eaten the Davidsons' splendid food on my second day on the Falklands, before the invasion – we had goose, and lamb, and fresh vegetables from the garden they had so carefully tended in the hope of one day making a business of it. I had stayed at Malvinas House on my return visit. I was impressed by the thoughtful tolerance Don, an old Antarctic hand from Inverness, had displayed towards the islands' extraordinary year. Yes, he had hated having the Argentines in possession – but he and his family had managed. Yes, the British authorities were perfidious, but who can blame them wanting to be rid of their long distance responsibilities. Yes, the newly resident troops were spoiling the atmosphere they, the Davidsons, had come to the islands to find, but on the other hand soldiers had to be there now, didn't they, in order to guarantee the islanders' freedom and to protect their way of life?

He said all this – and yet I knew at the time he didn't believe it, and in March the truth came tumbling out. The way of life had been ruined, he said – not protected at all. And even if it had been protected, it wasn't worth having done so with all the lives that had been lost. It wasn't worth even one of those lives.

And so the Davidsons were selling up and coming home – one of the sadder and more poignant footnotes to what some had seen as a glorious reminder of our imperial past, but which others – myself included – regarded as a most wicked act of folly. Wicked because, as a few British journals were to point out, the principal reason for the prosecution of the South Atlantic War was politics – on both sides of the conflict. That politicians, for their own self-serving reasons, can still send young men off to die and to be wounded because of their inability to solve their differences at the conference table, displays a departure from civilised behaviour that is, in the literal sense of the word, quite wicked. That it could still happen to a supposedly civilised and tolerant nation like our own astonished me while I was in prison, astonishes and dismays me still.

Of course I could understand those who felt – and still feel – we should 'stand up for what we believe in' and that a whole raft of important principles was at stake in the great waters of the South. But the situation has its realities, too; what we believe in, and what is important, are not necessarily the same thing. We believe in preserving the British way of life for those who want it preserved – but the Falklanders weren't living any more than an ersatz copy of the British way of life – they weren't even properly British, in terms of nationality, until well after the war was over and Parliament decided to correct an administrative oversight that had condemned them to a decidedly inferior status. We believe in retaining imagined oases of power and responsibility across the globe, from Pitcairn to Tristan da Cunha to Diego Garcia, and remain wholly unaware that by doing so we have become the butt of a thousand little jokes – not said unkindly, but with pity. Why cannot Britain drag herself out from under her old Imperial baggage, and take note that the world outside has changed, and Empire – reality and concept – have faded away, for good.

And matters of important principle at stake? The principle that says 'aggression shall not pay', and 'the strong shall not bully the weak', and 'questions of national sovereignty shall not be settled by force of arms'? When, in our Imperial progress, did we eschew aggression as a means of expanding our power and influence? Did we, as the Strong, deal fairly with, let us say, the Ilois of British Indian Ocean Territory when, ten years ago, it was decided that their presence there was inconvenient, and we should boot them out of their homes and send them elsewhere for the sake of our American friends? Did we not bully the weak, for expedient reasons? And as for using force: did we not issue a clear invitation to the Argentines to settle their longstanding claim to the Falklands by force by announcing the withdrawal of our only naval vessel in the area – and then, adducing nobler reasons, use force against the invaders to settle the question of sovereignty our two decades of intransigence had failed to address?

Suggestions that anything grander than party politics was at stake that summer seem to me to be wholly specious; whether history will judge the perpetrators of the Falklands war as well as did those who responded in the opinion polls taken once the great ships of the

Task Force were back home, victorious, is, in my view, open to very great doubt.

Once home from the islands, I took some holiday: I went with my wife to North Wales, and then to Shetland – and how similar Britain's most northerly island of Unst was to her most southerly possessions. I was reminded of a curious, and delightful quality of island people there; while we were waiting for the ferryboat between Yell and Unst the local postman's wife was telling me of her neighbour, a man who was currently on the island of St. Helena. He had spent much of his career working on far-flung rocks and skerries of the Empire – Mauritius, Zanzibar, Socotra, Fiji, Pitcairn, Anguilla, St Vincent. 'Island people are a different breed,' she said. 'The people here knew just how the Falklanders felt. Many of them had been to Stanley, and had friends there. There's great solidarity among islanders.'

Slowly, routine came back. The brief distinction I had enjoyed faded slowly – and I wasn't at all sad to see it go. Temporary fame is a heady business; but it is a distorting mirror, and too many fall for its charms, too many suffer from its delusions. I was happy to merge back into the woodwork, from which vantage point all reporters do their best work. When a National Front newspaper condemned me – for some error perpetrated months before – and said that I was a person 'whose only distinction was being locked up in Argentina . . .' I felt the proper degree of anonymity had been restored (though at the time the remark stung, I must admit).

And how had the experience changed us? Well, I have not seen Tony Prime since our paths diverged at Gatwick. Ian Mather came to tea once. But reporters being what they are I have no doubt we will all stumble into one another in some godforsaken bar in some forgotten little country as it shakes itself into a frenzy over some unimagined argument. For the moment though I have no way of knowing how my two cellmates have weathered a year that, as Ian remarked, was unique in being possessed of three winters.

And as for me? I believe – and my family seems to agree – that I have become more tolerant, more patient, more philosophically disposed to the setbacks that customarily afflict us all. When the three of us began to irritate each other, when a remark was made that might have caused an explosion, I would always turn away, count to ten – and then find that the problem had receded into a more manageable perspective. If prison left that single legacy, it would have been worthwhile.

I learned enough Spanish to hold my own at table. I saw the 'Uttermost Part of the Earth'. I came to understand something of Argentina's curious attitudes to the world beyond her borders and her shores. I came to appreciate my family. And, perhaps more than anything else, I came to realise the strength of friendship and the kindness of strangers. The letters – simple and unaffected though they may be – which I have included in this brief account, are testament to the unadorned kindness of civilised humanity: to have learned of that, and of the powers of faith, prayer, companionship and love, is a lesson for which I owe a debt, ironic though it may seem, to those in Argentina who, that Tuesday morning in the Rio Grande airport, said 'You must go with these men. The Admiral wants to see you.'